MONK'S
TALE

At home in Sorin Hall

MONK'S TALE

Way Stations on the Journey

Edward A. Malloy, C.S.C.

University of Notre Dame Press

Notre Dame, Indiana

Manufactured in the United States of America

Library of Congress Cataloging-in-Publication Data

Malloy, Edward A.
 Monk's tale / Edward A. Malloy.
 p. cm.
 Includes index.
 Contents: v. 1. The pilgrimage begins, 1941–1975.
 ISBN-13: 978-0-268-03522-8 (v. 2 : cloth : alk. paper)
 ISBN-10: 0-268-03522-9 (v. 2 : cloth : alk. paper)
 1. Malloy, Edward A. 2. Malloy, Edward A.—Childhood and youth.
3. University of Notre Dame—Presidents—Biography. 4. College
presidents—Indiana—Biography. 5. University of Notre Dame—Faculty—
Biography. 6. Catholic universities and colleges—United States—Case
studies. 7. Priests—United States—Biography. 8. Catholic Church—
Clergy—Biography. 9. Catholic Church—United States—History—
20th century. I. Title.
 LD4112.7.M35A3 2009
 378.772'89—dc22
 [B]

 2009022894

∞ The paper in this book meets the guidelines for permanence and durability
of the Committee on Production Guidelines for Book Longevity of
the Council on Library Resources.

CONTENTS

ACKNOWLEDGMENTS

My heartfelt thanks go:

To my colleagues in the Notre Dame theology department and Provost office, especially Provost Tim O'Meara, who welcomed me and provided encouragement and support during my term of service;

To Bill Beauchamp and Dave Tyson, who shared the time of preparation and evaluation as candidates to succeed Ted Hesburgh as president of Notre Dame, who remained friends throughout, and who have gone on to lead with distinction at Notre Dame, at Portland, and in leadership of the Indiana Province;

To the rectors, hall staff, and students in Sorin Hall, who continually welcomed me into their company even as my outside responsibilities shifted dramatically;

To the board members, directors, and staff of the various not-for-profit organizations that I have had the privilege to serve as we attempted to enhance the quality and broaden the range of their respective activities;

To Joan Bradley, Walt Collins, Carole Roos, and Sue Barnett, and my student interns Joe Shaheen, Greg Rustico, Mike Ryan, and Andrew Owens, who assisted in bringing this project to completion.

From the beginning, my memoir, *Monk's Tale,* was intended to be comprised of three volumes. Volume One, *Monk's Tale: The Pilgrimage Begins, 1941–1975,* appeared in 2009. It describes my family roots and early Catholic education in Washington, D.C., including my athletic successes at Archbishop John Carroll High School. Then it turns to my time as an undergraduate student at the University of Notre Dame, to my experience of a call to become a priest while on a summer service project in Mexico, to my seminary years and ordination, and to my doctoral studies in Christian ethics at Vanderbilt University in Nashville, Tennessee. Throughout this depiction I attempted to weave my personal story into the broader narrative of fundamental changes going on in American society, in the Roman Catholic Church, and in the world.

Volume Two, *Monk's Tale: Way Stations on the Journey,* is intended to prepare the ground for the final volume, which will focus on my presidential years (1987–2005). In *Way Stations,* I provide chronological coverage of my life and responsibilities from 1975 to 1987 as well as detailed discussions of aspects of my priestly ministry that were not directly dependent on my presidential role as such—my years of living in a student dormitory (Sorin Hall), my ministry as a teacher, scholar, liturgical leader, and pastor, and my range of extracurricular involvement in the academy, on government committees and entities, and on a number of not-for-profit boards. Special attention is given to my fifteen years of participation in the process that led up to the formulation of Pope John Paul II's document on Catholic higher education, *Ex Corde Ecclesia,* and its implementation in the American context. Finally I describe the process that led to my selection as

Notre Dame's sixteenth president in November 1986 as well as how I used the interim before I formally assumed the responsibilities of president on July 1, 1987.

Like the first volume, this second account is full of stories about people, places, and events. I describe in some detail sub-cultures, such as seminary life or sabbatical times or Vatican processes, that some may find rather far removed from their every-day experience. Nonetheless, I hope that much of what I share about my life as teacher, dorm staff person, international traveler, major administrator, and board member will touch a responsive cord with many.

The image of "Way Stations" is intended to convey that who I am as a person and the way my life has unfolded is not reducible to any one role that I have played or any particular set of experiences that I have enjoyed. While my eighteen years as Notre Dame's president has surely been my most prominent and publicly visible role, as with all human beings, there is much more to my story. What I did after joining the Notre Dame faculty, how I prepared for the post to which I was elected, and what else I did during these years is the subject of this second volume.

Back to the Seminary

After completing doctoral studies at Vanderbilt University in 1973, I moved back to Notre Dame full of energy and enthusiasm to function as a priest in full-time ministry for the first time since ordination. Even though I was still writing my dissertation, I was aware that an initial period of preparation in my life was at an end. My three years in residence at Vanderbilt had gone quickly. The Divinity School was a friendly, supportive environment for study and for broadening my base as a practicing theologian, and I was confident that I had something to offer as a teacher and a scholar. I also looked forward to serving as a liturgical leader, a counselor, and a pastoral presence in some more permanent setting.

I was a bit surprised when I was assigned to be the director of the College Seminary program at Moreau Seminary. Part of the surprise was related to my concern, sometimes expressed publicly, that the college years, especially the first two, are not the best time for entering the seminary. My own experience in the Holy Cross Order's seminary system, admittedly at a time of great transition within the Church, indicated that the progress-to-ordination rate was rather low for those entering at the beginning of college. On the other hand, the recent liberalization of seminary life offered more leeway for seminarians who were not yet

under vows to participate in regular college life. I hoped the new model would work more successfully.

My new home was a staff room on the northeast corner of the fourth floor of Moreau Seminary, facing Saint Joseph Lake. It had a work/lounge area, a bedroom, and a bathroom and was spacious enough for my books, other accouterments, and a couple of chairs where I could meet with students. Located at an end of the building, it was generally quiet except for the birds and bats that enjoyed strafing runs after sunset along the length of the long, curving structure. From my room I could see the Golden Dome. Little did I suspect that someday that building would become my base of operations.

In 1973–74 there were approximately fifty seminarians at Moreau, of whom twenty were in the college program. Father Jim Kelly, C.S.C., was the superior to whom I reported; however, the college program contained the largest single group in the house so I had a fair degree of autonomy in putting together its internal workings, including team meetings, counseling and evaluation sessions, liturgies, and apostolic projects. For the rest — community worship, meals, soirees, and the internal work schedule that served the common life — we were part of the larger house.

Moreau Seminary was no longer the place apart it had once been. Guests were now welcome, including family members, friends from campus, and, occasionally, people from some of the seminarians' apostolates. Thursday was the big community day, with mass, a social, and dinner for the whole house followed by *lucenarium* (a version of evening prayer with the lighting of candles) and then a long social event. Thursday was also a dress-up day, which meant coat and tie for the seminarians, although the dress code through the week was generally relaxed and informal within the house. Monday was another community day but with no special evening gathering. The team meetings were fitted into the remaining days of the week, allowing for a more personal level of interaction between the staff and the seminarians.

As someone who was ordained only three years earlier, I was relatively young to have a central role in the formation process. I was assisted by Brother Chet Ziemba, C.S.C., a coadjutor brother of the Indiana Province of Holy Cross, whose main duties included tending to the grounds of the seminary and adjoining properties. He had come to religious life in his thirties and was blessed with street smarts and an "in" with the underground gambling syndicate in Chicago. Another assistant was André Leveille, C.S.C., who had been a teaching brother for many years and was now preparing to be ordained a Holy Cross priest. In my second year we were joined on the staff by Dick Rutherford, C.S.C., a theologian who was working on a research project.

The young men in the college program were bright, hardworking, and quite sincere in their process of vocational discernment. Some had enjoyed a loving, supportive family background while others had had to deal with family dysfunction and/or divorce. Some had good ego strength and self-confidence; others were still in search of their best selves. While celibacy is always an issue in seminary life, the collegians were not prohibited from social involvements with women; most such interactions were within group activities anyway. For most, the debates about the vows were more theoretical than urgent. A more pertinent dilemma for some, and part of what the staff had to be alert to, was the related issue of sexual identity in an all-male living environment.

As with most young people, good times were often identified with the consumption of alcohol. All the Moreau residents had access to alcohol, and most of the time it did not pose a problem. However, a few in the college program, as well as some post-Novitiate seminarians, manifested unhealthy behavior in this regard, so the staff had to wrestle with appropriate responses. This was a time when religious communities in general, along with the broader society, were starting to come to grips with the disease model of chronic alcoholism and the need for firm, supportive intervention.

The most important responsibility for the staff was to evaluate on a regular basis the seminarians entrusted to our care. At the college level we were primarily preparing young men to lead good Christian lives, whether or not they persevered in their initial decision to give the seminary a try. Some candidates took only a few months to decide that religious life and priesthood were not for them; they parted at the end of the semester or the end of the year with some appreciation for what they had learned and the friends they had made. The rest of the college group would eventually move on to the Novitiate, where the process of discernment was more concentrated. The hardest cases for all of us were those who enjoyed the security of seminary life but lacked the requisite personal skills and/or maturity to fully invest themselves in the program.

Since directing the college program was my first regular responsibility after graduate school, I invested much time and energy in it, but also focused on finishing my dissertation and reading widely in preparation for what I hoped would be my first teaching assignment. That moment arrived when Professor Stanley Hauerwas, a Protestant ethicist and a dominant figure in the Notre Dame theology department, was asked by Father David Burrell, C.S.C., chair of the department, to husband my candidacy through the various stages of the hiring process. Stanley and I hit it off despite our theological differences, and he invited me to co-teach an undergraduate class with him in the spring semester of 1974. It was my first teaching opportunity at Notre Dame since the seminars that I oversaw during my deacon year of 1969–70. I did not have to do much to prepare for the course except read the assignments and interact with Stan in front of the class. He was, and is, a controversialist by disposition, so he enjoyed the intellectual combat. The students seemed satisfied that they had signed up for a course where professors actually disagreed with each other in public.

My teaching appointment carried the rank of instructor until such time as my dissertation was completed, when I would auto-

matically become an assistant professor. That meant that for the remaining three years of my directorship of the college program, I would also be engaged as a new, enthusiastic, excited faculty member.

In the summer of 1973, the Indiana Province Chapter elected Father Bill Lewers, C.S.C., as the new provincial. This was a moment of decisive change for the Province and for its apostolates. Bill had come to religious life after years as a law faculty member. He was worldly wise, yet full of high ideals. He had spent time in Chile after ordination and this had a profound effect on his hopes for the Church and his commitment to social justice. These values would remain with him the rest of his professional life, as a faculty member in the Notre Dame Law School and as the director of the Justice and Peace office of the U.S. Catholic Bishops Conference.

I was an active delegate at the Chapter at which Bill was elected, and he invited me to become a member of the Provincial Council, a group that met monthly to discuss the works, issues, and problems of the Province. I was honored by the invitation and went on to serve on the council for the next fifteen years, under two different provincials. Our most difficult decisions were not about finances or policies or apostolates but about personnel. Membership on the council and participation in its deliberations taught me early in my priestly life that there are limitations of power and office for those overseeing the well-being of a group of male religious, all of whom had personal histories and memories and could not be simply ordered to proceed in lockstep according to some Provincial decree. As councilors we had to take into account the strengths and weaknesses of each religious, the needs of our various apostolic commitments, and the rather explosive realities of a Church going through dramatic change.

Because of the Holy Cross Community's heavy involvement in higher education, many of the positions that became open had specific requirements attached, such as a doctorate or its equivalent, and many of the administrative tasks presumed years of

experience as a prerequisite. Some religious desired to work in new settings, and some of these in the absence of a community support system. There were also tasks that were necessary for the well-being of the Province, such as local superiors and heads of the various stages of formation. These jobs usually demanded personal sacrifice of those asked to assume them. In the end, there always turned out to be positions that went unfilled and individuals who (because of their own unsettledness) were unassignable. The meetings of the Provincial Council during my years on it were a constant reminder that the Indiana Province was like any large family—we had our high performers, our generous souls who would do anything they were asked to do, and our members whose mental, physical, or spiritual health meant that the rest of us would have to provide for their needs rather than have them involved in the active apostolate.

Learning such lessons while I was responsible for nurturing potential religious vocations was good for me. We had much to be proud of as members of Holy Cross, but there were no guarantees that early enthusiasm and manifest piety would necessarily lead to a healthy and successful life in ministry under vows. The old wisdom of Aristotle and Thomas Aquinas remained true: grace builds on nature and character, and self-integration and a loving heart are the work of a lifetime. The collective job of the seminary staff was to use our best skills of observation and counsel to enhance the chances that our seminarians would make good choices about what God was calling them to.

The seminarians' year always began with a retreat at a Holy Cross camp in Deep Creek Lake in far western Maryland. In my own days as a seminarian, the social order of camp life was much more hierarchical and regimented than it was by the 1970s. The staff now lived in one of two locations—a well-constructed stone house in the center of the facility or an old farm house on the periphery, but except for the special living status for staff, interaction between seminarians and staff was non-stop. There was mass and prayer and meals in common every day. The rest of the time

was spent in team meetings, athletic competition (on land or water), reading, touring, and relaxed moments. For the new members of the Moreau community it was a great opportunity to become acclimated and get to know names. Playing pitch-and-putt golf or going canoeing or playing volleyball after dinner were all excellent ways of getting a feel for the group and its style of interrelating. There were always chores to be done, from outdoor work to meal preparation to keeping the facilities clean and serviceable, and these too provided unpressed physical proximity.

One of the staff's responsibilities was to introduce the men in a preliminary way to the history of Holy Cross, to the vowed life, to the expectations for the common life at Moreau, and to the practices of prayer, including the Divine Office. The staff wanted all the college men to make a smooth transition, and we were always observing, somewhat clandestinely, the social dynamics, alert for signs of homesickness or social unease. As in any comparable group, likes were attracted to like, and soon recognizable affiliations developed. No one ever left the program from Deer Park, so the experience must have been reasonably pleasant, even to the shy and questioning.

Part of my challenge as director was to achieve rapport with each of the collegians. In addition to participating in their athletic competitions and lingering at meals, I got in the habit of going on long walks with each college seminarian to guarantee a more private context for conversation. It had become fashionable by that time for seminary staff to be addressed by their first names, although some of the younger members never got to that point with the senior citizens among us. Since I was never much for titles, it was second nature for me to go by Monk, the nickname I had carried since grade school. I was Monk not only in the seminary but also with my students after I started teaching and with my dorm-mates later on in Sorin Hall.

Living in close quarters with college-age students meant that they inevitably discovered everyone's strengths, weaknesses, and idiosyncrasies, and seminary life always develops a few mimics

and humorists who ease the tension and keep everyone amused. Father Jim Kelly, C.S.C., the superior and rector, was a big man in every way—tall, stocky, and very much of a physical presence. His voice and mannerisms were relatively easy to imitate, so he became the most common focus of mimicry. Father Charles Sheedy, C.S.C., one of the oldest members of the staff and arguably the most popular, had so many memorable sayings and quirks that any seminarian of that era, even decades later, could tell stories about him. The coadjutor brothers who resided with us were universally loved and considered great models of committed religious life.

During these years I regularized the tradition of Monk Hoops on Monday and Wednesday nights in the Moreau gym. I was still close enough to my prime that I was a prolific scorer, and the rest of the seminary team was good enough for us to win most of the games. I always figured that such contests disabused the ND students of some stereotypes about seminarians and seminary life.

One side result of spending time with seminarians in basketball contests was the insights the sport helped me gain into their character. I could observe how selfish or team-oriented they were, how they handled success and adversity, and how persistent they were in developing their God-given talent. Such perspectives were only available to me for those seminarians who were reasonably coordinated and knew the basic elements of the game, of course, but as time went on I came to discover that the intuitions I gained about people on the court were usually reinforced by my fuller involvement with them in the rest of the common life.

One of the traditions of Moreau was a spring entertainment that the seminarians put on for the residents of the house, including the coadjutor brothers and the sisters who worked in the kitchen. From year to year this extravaganza could vary widely in content and quality. Since we always had a fair number of seminarians who could play musical instruments or sing, it was safe to have them perform the popular folk tunes of the day as well as

more classical pieces. Non-musicians might read some poetry or a short creative piece they had written. The real challenge came when some group moved toward satire or local humor. For me, the operative standard of bad taste had to be what the eldest residents would both understand and find offensive. More importantly, we had to worry about the ego strength of any candidates who might find themselves imitated or mocked. There was always a temptation for seminarians to get even with peers who had offended them or to pick on the most vulnerable. They were more reluctant to spoof the staff directly, although in my eyes that would have been a healthier alternative.

One year when the college team was supposed to contribute a humorous act, I had to censor several items I saw in the rehearsal. I did so reluctantly, yet I knew that one or two of the seminarian targets (who had real problems) would have a tough time bouncing back from unsubtle attacks on their dignity. Generally, though, the entertainment ended with smiles all around. I was always happy when we survived another evening fraught with the potential for young creativity run amuck.

Because the seminarians had no required time for retiring and because I was by disposition a late-night person, I often ended up engaged in late bull sessions. We would touch upon every type of topic under the sun, from ND football to married priests to presidential politics, from welfare reform to the morality of contraception to our hopes and dreams for the future of the Catholic Church. Most of us saw ourselves as progressive Catholics, truly committed to the reforms of the Second Vatican Council. The more conservative among us would speak their minds as well, but their point of view was often muted both by the pace of change and the absence of a rallying point of generalized concern. Despite the continued controversies in American society and in the Church at large, our group was a hopeful lot, not deterred by disagreements or instances of the persistence of human malevolence. As a staff member, I had the extra advantage of my doctoral work and my level of experience, yet I never sensed that I inhibited

the nature of those late-night conversations or unfairly steered their outcome.

Role reversal is an integral part of the passage to adulthood. Children become parents, students become teachers, athletes become coaches, low-level workers become bosses, and seminarians become priests and seminary directors. In my case, I always had a strong inclination to become a full-time academic and a priest/pastor/counselor, but it had never occurred to me that I might someday serve as director of the College Seminary program. Yet I had plenty of opinions about religious formation and vocational discernment in my years of preparation, and I was in favor of the vast majority of the changes in seminary life and culture that came in the wake of the Second Vatican Council. In some cases I was myself an active agent of progressive restructuring, either as a public critic of the traditional way or as a representative of my peer group in various deliberative bodies.

In the end, I feel that I received an excellent theological education, if at least partially at my own initiative, and that my apostolic experiences (on service projects in Latin America, in inner-city Detroit, teaching seminars at Notre Dame, at a mental hospital, and serving as a resident assistant in a dorm) were eye opening and consciousness raising. I began my priestly ministry with self-confidence, zeal, and a strong sense of being part of a collective ministry based on community living and mutual support. Despite what I considered the limitations of the pre-1960s Holy Cross seminary system, it nonetheless provided me with the tools for effective priestly ministry and an ever-emerging ecclesiology in terms of which I could imagine my future role in service of the Church and the Congregation. Now that I was assigned a full-time responsibility for a subsection of the Moreau Seminary program I had to figure out how to exercise constructive leadership, how to model in a personal way the ideals of Christian living, and how to competently instruct and fairly evaluate the young men entrusted to my care.

My problem with the highly rigid, rather autocratic seminary system of the past was that it was too easy for young men in formation to hide behind formal adherence to the rule and enforced separation from the world. Now that college seminarians had more freedom and a more typical college lifestyle, the challenge for staff was to encourage them toward a greater maturity of decision making and a recognition that they would be evaluated not only on the minutiae of their observance but on the overall pattern of their involvement in the program. For some this was welcome news. Others were frightened by the responsibility and the seeming ambiguity of expectations.

One example: We expected the men to be faithful to common prayer, to perform their internal housekeeping tasks consistently, to be successful in their studies, and to be apostolically engaged. When there was failure in any of these regards, the evaluation process (especially the self-evaluation component) was the fitting place either for an explanation of what went wrong and/or for some commitment to amelioration. All of us on the staff knew that we were dealing with nineteen to twenty-two year olds—a time when resistance to rules, expressions of independence, periodical bouts of moodiness, or seeming lack of fervor were to be expected, at least on occasion. The art of our oversight function came in establishing expectations and in putting in place workable accountability processes.

We knew that some of the college seminarians had special burdens, from family dysfunction and personal health problems to learning disorders and poor religious preparation. Not only were our college men younger and presumably less mature than the other seminarians in the house, but individually they represented a cross section of native ability, overt religious motivation, and comfort in large group settings. We expected more of seniors than of first-year students. We looked for generosity, initiative taking, leadership skills, resiliency in the face of disappointment, and capacity for friendship. While none of these qualities is

unique to religious life, they are good indicators of potential effectiveness and happiness in a celibate male community with diverse ministerial opportunities.

The combination of being director of the College Seminary program while in transition from graduate school to the Notre Dame faculty and still finishing my dissertation did not seem out of the ordinary at the time, nor has it seemed so since. I have always been engaged in multiple, simultaneous tasks.

My apostolic path was not unusual in the Indiana Province. A composite picture of our average priest would be someone who was educated in the best schools or programs after ordination, given high levels of responsibility rather early in his ministerial career, and sometimes asked to serve the Province in internal roles or as a member of Province-wide elective or coordinating bodies. Few of us ever concentrated on doing one thing well (in this regard we were much different from the Jesuits, the religious community that we mostly closely resemble otherwise). The old French boarding school model that our founders brought with them established early on the basis of our prevailing spirituality. In an academic apostolate we generally lived with the students and played multiple roles in teaching, administration, pastoring, and liturgical leadership. In fact, that interesting mix of roles was one of the characteristics that attracted me to Holy Cross. My experience has convinced me that this style best suits my personal talents and predisposition. I have always been an activist by nature and I have enjoyed trying to balance multiple worlds and diverse works with as much enthusiasm as I could muster.

After the Nashville years where our Holy Cross group was tiny, I enjoyed being immersed in the broader context of Moreau Seminary where the prayer life was excellent, the meals were fitting social occasions, the availability of the in-house gym meant that opportunity for exercise was convenient, and the prevailing spirit of hospitality sustained the presence of family members and visitors through the course of the year. The Sunday mass

at 11:00 a.m. attracted friends from around the area who were looking for good liturgical music and well-prepared homilies.

The sheer size of the building, however, was sometimes a deterrent to community life. The distance from the faculty recreation room at the south end to the dining area at the north was substantial, especially for the older members. The seminarians' rooms were far from soundproof and activity in the hallways could be somewhat disruptive, but if one wanted to hide out or otherwise be inconspicuous, the physical layout was conducive to that. It was almost impossible to know who was in the library or the gym or the lower rec room or on the various residential floors without going there.

The brothers and priests who were not directly involved in the formation program were quite popular with the seminarians. They were seen as sustainers of the common life by their presence at prayer and meals, and their interactions with the seminarians were non-threatening since they had no formal role in the evaluation process. On the other hand, the older religious tended to have a rather idealized picture of the seminarians since they were not as directly exposed to the vocational struggles or the group dynamics or the hijinks. As a result, the staff members had to interpret off-handed comments about individual seminarians by the non-staff religious, to decide whether they grew out of some special insight not available to the rest of us.

The 1970s were a time of profound change in Catholic life in America. Just about every dimension of the structure of church life came under discussion. There were debates about the role of the pope and bishops and about lay participants in the community of faith. In the liturgy, parish life was full of efforts to implement the changes that came in the wake of Vatican II, from the use of English in the mass and the other sacraments to communion in the hand to the appropriate roles of readers, acolytes, and communion ministers. Altars were pulled away from the wall and the priest began to face the people. There was also a great deal

of experimentation with contemporary forms of church music. As in all periods of rapid change, some of the efforts were crude, theologically uninformed, or just plain dumb. Nevertheless, for the most part the average Catholic quickly grew accustomed to the new forms and the spirit behind them.

The variety of influences underlying the evolution of seminary life complicated the roles of everyone involved in the recruitment and formation process. First there was the debate about the nature of priesthood and who should be eligible. The number of advocates for the ordination of married people was growing, and a smaller but vociferous group wanted to extend this openness to women candidates as well. Second, a real hemorrhage had begun of priests leaving active ministry; they left for a variety of reasons, but many to marry. Speculation was rampant that the institutional Church could only sustain the level and quality of an ordained ministry by lifting the prohibition against married priests, and some predicted that it would come sooner rather than later. Theologians who entered the debate reminded everyone that married priests had prevailed in the Church up until the twelfth century, and that it was really a disciplinary rather than a theological matter.

A third influence was the rediscovery of notions of the Church that emphasized its role in the transformation of the world. The parish community (and those who led it) could no longer see itself as a sacred enclave separate from the evil world. Prayer without service to the poor or efforts to reform unjust social structures was said to be a misunderstanding of the holistic Gospel mandate. A fourth issue was related to the newly felt mandate to educate candidates for lay ministry on a par with candidates for ordained ministry. This meant designing new academic courses and support structures as well as providing opportunities for first-class spiritual and pastoral formation.

Finally, there was a growing consensus that seminary formation should not begin in high school and perhaps not even in college, or at least not in the first two years. There was a sense

that undergraduate candidates needed more time to mature and more experience of the world before they undertook formalized training for religious life and the priesthood.

As I began my four-year term as director of the College Seminary program, I was of course aware of all of these trends and discussions. The Indiana Province and the broader Holy Cross Congregation had pondered how to proceed, and in Provincial Chapters and meetings of the provincial with his council, some decisions had been reached. We closed our high school seminary. We moved our Novitiate to Bennington, Vermont, where candidates for both the Indiana and Eastern provinces were prepared together. We kept open Saint Joseph Hall on the campus as an entry point for undergraduate students, but we welcomed post-college candidates to a specially designed new program at Moreau Seminary. We sent undergraduate candidates who had finished one year at Saint Joseph Hall to the college program at Moreau. We did not consider young men as candidates for the Novitiate until they had graduated from college.

We began to develop the possibility of inserting a regency year into the program for post-Novitiate theologians; this would extend their time of formation but also enrich their pastoral experiential options. For some, the regency year was a necessary and welcomed time of discernment before taking final vows. For others, it helped refine the forms of future ministry that they might find especially attractive. We also made the fourth year (mostly composed of deacons) a time for nearly full-time ministry in an academic, parish, or missionary setting, but with supervision from the Moreau staff and structured sessions of peer sharing.

Even given all these adjustments to the traditional formation regimen, there were other lingering issues that were more local in impact. As the total seminarian population began to decline, there was a sense that the physical facility could be seen by some candidates as too overwhelming and impersonal. Some voices began to advocate a smaller facility, or at least more opportunities for small-group living during formation. Another issue

was the absence of alternative sites away from Moreau during the course of a long period of preparation. Back when most seminarians did their theology in Washington (or Rome or Chile) after the college years and the Novitiate, the geographical separation from Notre Dame was seen as enriching. Now a candidate could theoretically spend all his formation years except for the Novitiate year in one place, and some considered this too stifling. As a consequence, more theologians began to take regency years elsewhere, and new theology options were later developed in Berkeley, California, at the Graduate Theological Union.

By the time I joined the staff at Moreau, the separate but related responsibilities of the Notre Dame theology department and Moreau Seminary were rather clearly defined. The theology department and the University were expected to attend to all matters related to academics and the awarding of the degree. Moreau Seminary had prime oversight for everything to do with seminarians' spiritual and religious-life formation, and the evaluation of candidates for final vows and ordination. The director of the Master of Divinity (M. Div.) program was expected to work out any points of disagreement or disappointment.

Periodically, issues would flare up on one side or the other, such as academic preparation, courses taught without sufficient attention to the pastoral dimension, and inequities between clerical and lay candidates. Since I eventually became M. Div. director after my years on the staff at Moreau, I can say in retrospect that generally things functioned smoothly in the dynamic between the two institutional components.

Memories of my time at Moreau tend to be amusing. For example, one of the college seminarians who was quite witty cultivated the persona of an Italian chef. Periodically, he would set up shop on the seminary roof where, decked out in white chef's hat, apron, and accompanying garb, he would serve a meal to a small circle of friends. They would look out over the lake toward the Golden Dome and the heart of the campus and act as though they were Roman nobility surveying their property.

Father Charlie Sheedy was in his late seventies or early eighties when he joined the staff, and he was a much-loved presence. He weighed hardly a hundred pounds but he was always carrying around some tome he was reading that resembled *War and Peace* in bulk. Charlie was famous for his pithy way of summing things up. In a homily one time he complained about self-serving reminiscences, which he defined as the practice of some speakers and preachers to put themselves in the center of the stories they told, usually with heroic overtones. Once, in a staff meeting to evaluate seminarians at the end of the year, the discussion was focusing on an individual with a reputation as an insincere suck-up who seemed to be play-acting his way through the system. After a few staff members who knew the person only peripherally had spoken of him favorably, Charlie intervened and described the individual in a blunt, somewhat profane way that the rest of us thought got to the essence of the matter.

Charlie experienced health problems throughout his life and was open to any method of medical intervention that promised some relief. One day he decided to try acupuncture, and he agreed to undergo his treatment publicly so that anyone interested in the procedure could observe. At the assigned time he showed up in the rec room, stripped down to his underwear—looking like a survivor from Dachau—and let the doctor insert needles into various parts of his body. This event was the talk of the seminary for weeks.

Most of the social dynamics at Moreau were healthy, but occasionally something would take place that reminded us of our collective humanity. One evening at dinner, a priest in residence who was known as very smart but also emotionally sensitive, was badgered and teased by a seminarian who delighted in pushing the limits. After a particularly vociferous exchange, the priest stood up, picked up a pitcher of water, and poured it over the seminarian's head. Then he stomped out. No one knew what to do at first, and while most of us thought justice had been done, no one was disposed to warrant such behavior. So we just snickered,

helped clean up the mess, and retired to more intimate settings where the incident could be rehashed.

In the 1970s long hair was in, as were mustaches and sometimes beards. This was true not just of the college seminarians but also of the older members of the house. While such freedom of self-expression would have been unheard of a little over a decade earlier, the operative standard was that seminarians needed to be neat and presentable. But loose as that standard was, a few individuals tried to push the system farther. I was fairly tolerant of such propensities since I saw them as simply a function of youth. The closer people got to ordination, the more concerned the staff became about professional appearance.

There was an art studio in the seminary where individuals could pursue their God-given talents and/or fulfill requirements for certain classes. The room was stocked with easels, canvases, oils, and clay. One time in the midst of winter, I decided to promote the arts by advertising a competition for the best work by a seminarian or staff member. In order to encourage wide participation, I announced that I would do a painting myself. To provoke curiosity I kept my developing work under cover and warned my housemates not to peek. Most of them were not sure whether I was serious or not. What I actually did in the moments when I was in the studio by myself was throw or daub paint on the canvas with nothing particular in mind, kind of like a trained monkey. On the evening when the contest entries were to be judged, I held off unveiling mine to the end.

Several of the pieces were reasonably accomplished and worthy of consideration for honors. As my turn approached, I was asked what my painting was called. Privately, I had given it a scatological title, but publicly I called it Monk #1. When Monk #1 was at last unveiled, no one knew how to react. They wanted to laugh, but they were not sure how serious I was or whether I would be hurt by derision. In the end, I received polite applause. Overall, the contest was a great success. It broke up the cold, drab

days of winter and it promoted the arts, at least for most of the participants.

Moreau Seminary developed the tradition of having a low-level football pool each week of the college football season. It cost a quarter to enter, but it was run professionally, with the expert advice of Brother Chet Ziemba who had run numbers in Chicago in his earlier life. We used up to the minute data from oddsmakers, which meant not only that we had to pick who would win or lose, but we had to beat the point spread as well. For me the big problem was that it was the Era of Ara, and there was no way I could bet against Notre Dame even when the Irish were a twenty-plus point favorite. The pool was a frivolous way to have fun and to test out our knowledge of the collegiate football landscape. It was also a good preparation for the future, since just about every Holy Cross priest and brother, anywhere in the world, might be asked about Notre Dame football, and all of us by force of final vows were expected to have something to say, whether we could distinguish a touchdown or field goal from a triple play or a slam dunk.

A retrospective analysis of the Moreau college program during my years would have to take into account many factors. What was the quality of the admissions process which purportedly filtered out immature or improperly motivated candidates or those who carried heavy baggage from their personal and family backgrounds? How long did they stay in the program, and were they highly regarded by their peers and the staff? What were the conditions under which they left the seminary (if they did), and was their time there full of intellectual, personal, and spiritual growth? Did they have any bad experiences with the staff or other seminarians? Did they remain engaged later in life as practicing Catholic Christians? Finally, did the percentage of those who proceeded on to final vows and ordination warrant the financial and human investment of resources?

These questions are difficult to answer because a sophisticated study of the college seminary participants from 1973 to 1977

has never been attempted. At best, we can say that we have positive anecdotal evidence from those who remained in the community or have kept in touch. From the latter group I have never heard any sustained critique. Statistics, however, can at least raise the question of whether the resources expended were worth the results in terms of first vows and ordination.

In my four years as director, about 65 percent of the men who took the first step in the College Seminary program moved on to Moreau. During that period we had a cumulative twenty seniors—fourteen of these were approved for the Novitiate and five eventually were ordained. From the total senior class during those four years, twenty-five were ordained in the end. If I focus on the fifteen underclass candidates who were still in the program in 1976–77, two would go on to eventual ordination, one for a diocese and the other for Holy Cross.

Those numbers may not suggest an impressive cost/benefit ratio, but numbers are not the whole story. Those who participated in the college program in that era and went on to ordination included a future provincial, a religious superior, a high school principal, a Notre Dame faculty member and artist, an African missionary, a parish priest and chaplain, and a scripture scholar. In other words, the dropout rate from the college program was high but among those who stayed the course were some important contributors to the life and apostolic success of the Indiana Province.

Many of the others went on to marry, have children, and to live good Catholic Christian lives in the world. Even those who chose a different path, therefore, became productive citizens.

From Corby to Berkeley

Life in Corby Hall

Corby Hall, located just west of Sacred Heart Basilica, is named after Father William Corby, C.S.C., who served twice as president of the University (1866–72 and 1877–81) and was an army chaplain throughout the Civil War. In 1863 he accompanied the Northern Army to Gettysburg where he blessed the members of General Meade's Irish Brigade prior to the battle called Pickett's Charge. The scene is captured in a memorable statue on the fields of Gettysburg that is replicated on the lawn in front of Corby Hall.

For many years, Corby served as an undergraduate dormitory, but in 1937 it became the main base on campus for Holy Cross priests and brothers. It is the residence of the local Holy Cross superior and a cross section of priests and brothers, most of whom are retired or semi-retired. Occasionally priests or brothers from other religious communities or dioceses reside in Corby while they pursue graduate studies or work on some sabbatical project. Corby's several guest rooms (including a bishop's suite) are available for short-term occupancy, especially on busy weekends like home football games and commencement.

The Holy Cross Community at Notre Dame is quite diverse in age, temperament, interests, levels of education, and ministerial

responsibilities. A good percentage of the Community's members live in undergraduate dormitories, which means that when school is in session they have responsibilities where they reside. Others serve in the faculty ranks and need to interact on a regular basis with their colleagues as well as the students entrusted to their care. For those who serve in the administration, schedules are erratic and involve campus functions, often in the evening, and a fair amount of travel.

All this means that on a given day or week, some percentage of the Holy Cross group will be involved outside of Corby. Yet having a central location for common prayer, common table, and common life is critical to the well-being of the local Community. Thus it is incumbent on the rest of the membership to sustain the schedule of prayer, meals, and general morale, and Corby Hall makes that possible. As a counterweight to the centrifugal pressures that lead Holy Cross priests and brothers to be active elsewhere, a Corby tradition has developed that puts special emphasis on Wednesday night mass, social time, and dinner, as well as social time and dinner on Sunday nights. There is also an annual community retreat and times during the year when other groups are asked to join the Corby contingent for dinner—for example, trustees, alumni representatives, rectors, seminarians, or diocesan clergy. Corby is, in fact, a center of hospitality for the Indiana Province, and all of us take seriously our responsibilities in this regard.

When I moved into Corby for the 1977–78 academic year, I knew that it would only be for one year since I was scheduled to be on sabbatical in Berkeley the following year. I moved out of Moreau Seminary because my term of service there had ended and I was beginning my administrative duties as director of the Master of Divinity program. In that role I would still be involved with seminarians, but now primarily through their academic courses and their degree requirements. I chose Corby because it provided me with sufficient independence from the daily life of Moreau to make a break from the past.

Until I moved in, my outsider's impression of Corby Hall had been primarily negative. I stereotyped it as a concentration of older men, mainly conservative, who looked askance at many of the post–Vatican II changes in religious life in general and in seminary formation in particular. In my occasional visits to the Corby dining room, the tenor had seemed excessively formal and tradition-bound. I detected none of the spontaneity or relaxed interaction across generations that I so enjoyed at Moreau. The parlors seemed uninviting, and the corridors were hung with pictures of long-dead colleagues who, in the fashion of their time, were rather grim in visage.

Corby Hall also had the reputation within the Holy Cross Community, and on the campus at large, as a center of power and influence. Many of the major University officers lived there, and rumors were always circulating about decisions being made behind closed doors or around the evening dinner table. Corby in the popular imagination exuded a sense of wonder and mystery, much as the Wizard of Oz did before the true reality was revealed.

As I moved onto the third floor, I brought many of these prejudices with me. What I found over the course of the year was much different. In general, the residents were friendly and welcoming, hardworking, devoted to prayer and the apostolate, and intensely interested in the world around them. The prevailing expectation at table, for example, was to avoid conversation about business in order to protect those with administrative roles from being hounded or feeling on the spot. Sports, the weather, material from the student newspaper, faculty scuttlebutt, local news, Church matters, and national and world events were always fair game. The secret to a good mealtime was to have everyone involved while avoiding topics that exposed raw nerves. By custom, some tables attracted the same diners day after day, but generally people moved around throughout the dining area as time and circumstance allowed.

One of the hardest adjustments for me stemmed from the fact that Corby residents tended to be early-to-bed, early-to-rise

types, while I was just the opposite. Instead of having to deal with unwelcome dorm or seminary noise late at night, I had to get used to early morning conversations between neighbors or among some of the staff who cleaned the rooms. I kept my traditional hours, which had me going to bed around 2 or 3:00 a.m., and I am sure that the woman who served the third floor as a maid wondered all year why I slept in every morning. Hopefully she gave me the benefit of the doubt.

I was accustomed to the regular, scheduled prayer life of Moreau so that feature of Corby living was a positive one. Yet the style of liturgy (both for mass and for the common house recitation of the Divine Office) seemed subdued and impersonal. In order to provide some balance in this regard, I volunteered during the course of the year to celebrate mass in Sacred Heart and in some of the dorms. Most of my time that year was devoted to academic responsibilities. I prepared classes and taught a full schedule, though with a one-course reduction each semester, and I engaged in administrative tasks as M. Div. director. I also met with seminarians and focused on preparing materials for publication.

One of the other third-floor residents that year was Father Claude Pomerleau, C.S.C., who was on sabbatical from Notre Dame's government department in order to prepare some research publications. Claude and I kept the same hours and shared many of the same opinions about the Church, the Congregation, and the world, so we enjoyed each other's company late at night over a bite at the snack bar. Among the residents of Corby at that time was Brother Cosmos Guttley, a holy and dedicated religious who used to get up some time after 4:00 a.m. I used to kid him that we should have a formal ceremony each night when we would pass along the keys to the house, kind of like the military guards who keep twenty-four-hour watch at Arlington National Cemetery.

Since I did not feel comfortable having my students come to my personal room for counseling sessions or oral exams, on occasions when I did not want to use my M. Div. office in O'Shaugh-

nessy Hall I would reserve one of the parlors in Corby. I think the students enjoyed getting into the inner sanctum that they had heard so much about. One afternoon I was giving an end-of-the-semester exam to one of my women students when, seemingly on the spur of the moment, she opened up what appeared to be a picnic basket and took out a couple of glasses and a plate, and then a bottle of wine and some cheese and crackers. A few minutes later, she invited me to look out the window, where I spotted one of her classmates walking by with a sign encouraging me to pass her on the exam. In fact, she was an excellent student and there never was any doubt about her passing. Toward the end of the exam I got into the spirit of the moment, and we shared together a light snack and a little wine. I suspect it was a first for a Corby Hall parlor.

Evening meals at Corby were sit-down affairs served by girls from local high schools. We had our own kitchen, so the girls mainly had to prepare the dining room, serve the meal, and clean up afterward. Over the years it became a plum assignment, and some girls worked for several years before moving on to college or the workforce. The main reason Notre Dame students were not chosen as servers was that the young ladies would stand by the walls during the meal, awaiting the next course or any special requests. This allowed them, if they were interested, to listen to some of the conversations. The general wisdom was that we did not want University students sharing snatches of the table talk with their peers. As far as I know, the employment of local teens worked well and we never had any untoward disclosures.

Sometime in the 1960s, the Holy Cross Community purchased a property on Lake Michigan north of New Buffalo, Michigan. It was called Creevy House and contained five or six bedrooms, a kitchen, a dining room, a common area, and a large basement. It stood forty or fifty feet above Lake Michigan with access to the beachfront by way of a wooden stairway. For many years Creevy House was the location for the Province-wide Fourth of July

celebration, which drew community members from all over the Northern Indiana and Chicago areas. I was a regular attendee, and I would head up to the lake with friends at other times as well.

When I was on the staff at Moreau Seminary, we took turns covering two mission parishes in the vicinity of Creevy House. A couple of times I ended up staying overnight at Creevy, and when this happened outside of the prime outdoor season, I often was there by myself. This was okay except for two things. First, it was a big house, and when the winds whistled off the water it often sounded like someone was trying to break in. I had viewed too many slasher films not to have some fearful moments. Second, the main fire retardant on the first floor (where I slept) was a series of glass containers hanging from the ceiling which were designed to suck all of the oxygen out of the air to stifle any fire. In other words, if a fire broke out when I was asleep, I would be dead before I even heard the alarm. Otherwise I enjoyed my trips to Creevy.

The permanent residents of Corby Hall tended to be seventy, eighty, or ninety year olds. Many had been faculty members, rectors, or administrators, although a few had spent most of their ministerial service in parishes, missions, or high schools. Most were exemplary religious who were highly regarded by the rest of us, although there were a few curmudgeons as is true in any large family and the challenge of the common life was to keep them from being unduly disruptive. As they grew older, some residents began to experience the first stages of dementia. Others may have struggled with addictive behaviors at various times in their lives. For the local superior and the provincial, one of the hardest duties was to make decisions (in consultation with experts) about how best to attend to the short- and long-term health needs of the individual religious.

For those suffering from addictions this usually meant a sustained period of time at Guest House in Michigan. For those no longer able to attend to their own physical and mental health needs, it meant assignment to Holy Cross House, our health and

retirement facility on campus. During my year at Corby, I saw the wisdom of such active involvement in the lives of those older religious who needed help in returning to health and relative well-being. It was not only important for them individually, but it also at times dramatically improved the overall morale of the largest house in the Province.

Because I was usually the last one to go to bed in Corby, I would often pay a visit to the snack bar at 1 or 2:00 a.m. I never ate breakfast, so this was effectively my third meal of the day. Just off of the snack area was a television lounge used primarily by the older residents who did not want a personal television in their rooms. My lingering fear was that I would go down one night, find the lights in the lounge still on, and discover someone dead in a chair. Fortunately, it never happened, either on my watch or during my time in residence.

Sometime in the 1930s or 1940s access to cigarettes became a big reward for seminarians, and many religious saw cigarette, pipe, or cigar smoking as a morally licit vice or even a manly prerogative. In the 1970s that was still the case, which meant that at Community gatherings it was common for people to smoke and take it for granted that no one else had a right to call smoking into question. In my year at Corby most residents refrained from smoking at meals, but they more than made up for it by lighting up in their rooms, at social events, on the front porch, and in the enclosed back porch. It also meant that the cars that were available to the Community sometimes reeked of smoke. Fortunately, today the few who still smoke generally keep their habit to themselves in a relatively clandestine way.

The winter of 1977–78 brought the greatest amount of snow in the recorded history of South Bend, 172 inches. A big part of the total—72 inches—came in one long blizzard in January. School was cancelled for five days, driving was prohibited in Saint Joseph County, and many of the service crews, such as police, fire, dining hall, and snow-removal workers, had to be put up on campus. For the first few days the students kept busy with snowball

fights, wrestling matches in the snow, and even a party or two. I took it upon myself to help keep the walkway in front of Corby Hall as free of snow and ice as I could manage. I was amazed when the snow piles on the side became higher than my six-foot-plus height.

The first break in the siege came when the University of Maryland men's basketball team under coach Lefty Dreisell managed to fly into the South Bend airport. (Ted Hesburgh, who had been stranded in Maryland, arranged to come with them.) Anybody who could make it to the basketball arena in the Joyce Center was allowed to get in free. The result was a packed arena full of pent-up fan energy. A very good Maryland team did not have a chance that day.

Little by little, the cleanup crews got the campus functioning again, though one problem was where to dump all the snow. At the time there was a large, empty lot in downtown South Bend which received a good portion of the snow scooped up off area roads. Someone developed a betting pool to predict when the last bit of snow would melt. It turned out to be sometime in the middle of July.

My year at Corby Hall was designed to be a transition time, and it was. I was productive in my research agenda, I got off to a reasonably good start as M. Div. director, I continued to enjoy my teaching and liturgical involvements, and I came to discover that I was misguided in most of my misgivings about Corby Hall. I knew that when I returned from sabbatical I would live in a dorm, but I now more fully appreciated the necessary role that Corby Hall plays in our common life as a Congregation.

Sabbatical at Berkeley

In the mid-1970s the Indiana Province of Holy Cross bought a property in Berkeley, just north of the University of California's main Berkeley campus. It was intended to be a center for semi-

narians who would study theology at the Graduate Theological Union (GTU), primarily as an alternative site for those who had already spent many years of study at Notre Dame. Other users were faculty members on sabbatical and priests and brothers interested in opportunities for renewal and continuing education. The house was large enough for a core community of eight persons, with individual bedrooms, a small chapel, a kitchen and dining room, and a large common room.

I chose to go to Berkeley that year for multiple reasons. It provided an amenable community-living situation for a year I wanted to devote to researching and writing a book. It was far enough away from Notre Dame that I would not be easily tempted to visit the campus (although I did fly back and forth about once a month for Provincial Council meetings). Between them, the GTU and the university offered excellent library resources. Perhaps most of all, I was intrigued by the possibility of living for a full year in proximity to my favorite American city, San Francisco, and in the midst of the countercultural craziness that characterized the city of Berkeley and the Cal campus. ("Why is Berkeley most like a popular cereal?" went the gag in those days. "It's full of fruits and nuts.")

Because the Berkeley house had several cars available to residents, I did not need to drive cross-country to get there, which made the logistics of moving from Corby Hall to Berkeley simple: I shipped most of my clothes and books by U.S. mail and flew to San Francisco.

Our house was on the corner of Virginia and Leroy Streets, in a neighborhood interesting in its own right. One could hardly go from point A to point B without going either uphill or downhill. I liked to walk as much as possible, so I got in pretty good shape simply by navigating the Berkeley Hills. A block away from us was the Jesuit house of studies for the seminarians and faculty who were part of the GTU. Nearby were other centers, including those of the Franciscans and the Dominicans, and since the GTU was ecumenical by structure and orientation, there were

also Protestant centers as well. The main GTU library was only six or seven blocks away.

Although our neighborhood was home to a concentration of religiously oriented groups, I suspect that a lot of the other residents in our vicinity had never in their lives been inside a church, or any other religious gathering place for that matter. The prevailing spirit of the late 1970s was "whatever turns you on," and it was not unusual to see someone walking down the street only partially clothed or decked out in a red Afro or looking like Salvador Dali. The shopping area closest to us included a small local theater that featured *avant garde* films, several student-oriented bars, and the usual array of small retail stores such as a laundry, a drug store, a clothing store, and an all-purpose store. My two favorites were a local Chinese restaurant that served great food at a cheap price and a hamburger place that was open all night and served double and triple burgers that defied every principle of a healthy lifestyle.

Berkeley was generally thought of as a bastion of liberalism. Ronald Reagan, when he was governor of California, reaped a lot of national attention when he took a proactive role in squelching the free speech and anti–Vietnam War protesters in Berkeley. I discovered, however, that the community had a much more diverse social order than its public image suggested. Interstate 580, running north and south parallel to San Francisco Bay, constituted Berkeley's western boundary. Along the waterfront were trendy seafood restaurants, bars, and boat docks. From that point west up into the hills, the city evolved from poor to middle class to upper middle class. In the lowlands lived mainly Blacks, Hispanics, and a few Asians and Whites. Just west of the Cal campus were middle-class neighborhoods, embracing some students and many employees of the university. Ringing the campus itself were comfortably nice neighborhoods to the north (where we lived) and to the south as far as the border of Oakland. Downtown was south and east of the campus, and its heart consisted of office buildings, department stores, upscale restaurants, the largest BART station

of the local subway system, and the range of retail establishments and service facilities found in any small- to medium-size city. I went downtown when I needed to or when guests came to visit, or to watch a movie or do a little shopping, but Berkeley for me was a combination of the neighborhood we lived in, the Cal campus, and the area south of the campus along Telegraph Avenue and near People's Park.

The sprawling Cal Berkeley campus has grown in spurts and is rather eclectic in architectural style. The oldest parts near Sather Tower, the Doe Memorial Library, Faculty Glade, and Sproul Plaza are quite attractive, but many of the science laboratories and classroom buildings seem massive and impersonal. With its 23,000 undergraduate students and large professional and graduate school populations, the university is generally regarded as one of the great institutions of higher education in the world. It serves a very diverse student body, which today is 53 percent Asian, 32 percent White, 11 percent Hispanic, and 7 percent African American. Thirty years ago the numbers were not that dramatic but they were still noteworthy in terms of diversity.

The number one place of interest on the campus for me, and for most visitors, was Sproul Plaza, the large gathering area just north of Telegraph Avenue. It was there that the Free Speech movement had its birth in the 1960s. By the late 1970s, Sproul had become the symbolic center of undergraduate student life and student activism. At any given moment, there would be long rows of students sitting behind small tables draped with multicolored posters and banners that encouraged passersby to pick up a brochure or sign up as a volunteer for one cause or another, from gay rights to Asian identity to women for the environment to the Marxist-Leninist party. In my year there, I never saw any attempt at coercion or in-your-face advocacy. It was more like a smorgasbord of possibilities for each passerby to mull over and decide for him- or herself.

My favorite experience in Sproul Plaza took place one Saturday afternoon in spring when the weather was perfect and

everyone wanted to be outdoors. In the upper part of the park, Jane Fonda was giving a talk to a couple of hundred true believers. Down below two nude adults, one male, one female, were standing in a fountain, letting the spray cool their bodies. Off to the side were picnickers, people reading books, street people, and a few shocked tourists. What was noteworthy about the afternoon is that no one seemed to think anything unusual was going on.

Telegraph Avenue runs a little over four miles from the border of the campus to Oakland, yet for most people it was the four or five blocks south of the campus that were synonymous with the counterculture movement, rampant public drug use, alternative lifestyles, and the People's Park. On a typical day in good weather, street vendors (many in tie-dye shirts, with leather straps around their wrists and colorful bead necklaces around their necks, with or without sandals) were selling everything from jewelry to drug bongs to t-shirts with obscene messages to postcards with pictures of the big rallies of the 1960s.

On my first visit to the Bay area in the summer of 1969, People's Park had become a symbol of the Berkeley protest movement and the California counterculture. Everyone who visited us in the late 1970s wanted to see the park, but they were all disappointed by the gap between rhetoric and reality by then. When Governor Reagan sent the National Guard to the park in May 1969, violence ensued, and from that time on the park evolved from a visual manifestation of flower power and the ideal of open access to public land to almost a counter-symbol. It was unoccupied except for a few addicted street people and was better known as a place for easy drug transactions than as a center for the promotion of high ideals.

I loved wandering along Telegraph Avenue, partly because I am an inveterate people-watcher and city freak, but also because no conceivable social interaction could be ruled out. I saw drug deals go down. I saw encounters between freaked-out street people and adamant Middle Americans. I saw former radicals whose

brains had been fried by persistent hard drug use trying to eke out a living on the street while their young children sat by their side, seemingly oblivious to their condition in life.

One of the hallmarks of Telegraph Avenue in the 1970s was its first-class bookstores. There was one for every taste, from university press publications to best sellers to obscure foreign works to comic books. Long before the megabookstores came on the scene, Telegraph Avenue booksellers were intent on establishing a relaxed, informal setting where people could dawdle, drink a cup of cappuccino, and have a snack. I was a regular habitué on those evenings when I wanted a break after a long day of research and writing.

The scariest episode I experienced in Berkeley was on a cold, blustery night when I was walking home around 10:00 p.m. Telegraph Avenue was pretty deserted, and just as I was passing a closed storefront, a liquor bottle went sailing past my head at eye level. It was thrown with great force and missed me only by a few inches. Over on a darkened stoop I saw a drunken man completely oblivious to his surroundings. He had not targeted me; he had merely gotten rid of an empty. As I continued my walk home after settling down a bit, I pondered what a meaningless way to die it would have been. God's protection kept me from harm on that potentially disastrous evening.

The Berkeley police force had a reputation as one of the more progressive departments in the country. Part of their style was simply a function of the neighborhoods they had to patrol and the social climate of the city. One weekend around 9:00 p.m., I watched them deal with a SWAT team–style problem in one of the housing units about a block off Telegraph Avenue. They went through all the procedures, blocking off the neighboring streets and establishing a communications link. Then an hour or two passed and I could see that they were in no rush to invade the premises. Their strategy was to avoid confrontation and let time be their friend. Eventually I left since I was not prepared to spend all night observing a relatively passive interaction.

A better illustration of the police approach took place more than once about a block away from our house. A severely mentally ill man in his thirties would periodically flip out. On two occasions he picked up a chain saw from his garage and used it as a threatening weapon. When the police arrived, they would create a perimeter around the man with classic yellow police tape. Then they would chat casually with the man until he grew tired. After he surrendered the chain saw, they would arrest him and take him away for psychological evaluation. A couple of weeks later he would be in his yard as though nothing had happened.

At the beginning of the academic year in Berkeley we had eight residents in our house. Father Glenn Boarman, C.S.C., was the local superior, which meant that he was responsible for organizing the common life and paying the bills. Glenn had been head of campus ministry for many years at Notre Dame, and in the 1960s he worked for a number of years on the staff of the Democratic Party in California. During our time in Berkeley, he was semi-retired and helping out as a chaplain in various religious houses in the area. Beside myself three other priests resided in the house that year: Fathers Jim Kelly, C.S.C., the former superior at Moreau Seminary, and Rollie Stair, C.S.C., and Steve Sedlock, C.S.C., two parish priests who were participating in a renewal program. Jim had a doctorate in sociology and was sitting in on classes at the GTU and catching up on reading in his field so he could begin to teach again.

My sole responsibility in Berkeley was to oversee the formation of three seminarians who began the year there. One was Phil Krill, who was staying at the house after completing his M. Div. degree at the GTU and before starting a regency year with our community in Bangladesh. The other seminarians were Austin Collins and Brad Trenary. Austin was in his first year in an M. Div. program in the Franciscan part of the GTU. He would eventually complete the program there, go to graduate school in art, and later join the faculty in the Notre Dame art department. Brad had vocational problems and left the community in the fall semester.

Since all of us were involved with projects of one kind or another, we decided to advertise in the newspaper for someone to cook our evening meals. The woman we hired was married to an inventor. Whenever one of his patented ideas hit it big, the two of them would travel the world and live the high life until they ran out of money. Then they would return to Berkeley and start the cycle over again. Because she had literally seen the world, our cook prided herself on never repeating a menu. As a result, during the course of the year we sampled just about every cuisine that there was, even though I would have been more than happy with a cycle of a week or two of our favorite items.

One of our good friends that year was U.S. Court of Appeals Judge John Noonan, who had once been a faculty member in the Notre Dame Law School and whose work as a scholar and writer I deeply admired. John would sometimes join us for 5:15 p.m. weekday mass in our chapel, and then stay for our social time before walking home to have dinner with his wife. John is one of the brightest and most humble intellectuals I have ever met. After one of my house-mass homilies when I waxed eloquent about the essential role in Christian history played by the martyrs, he said to me, "You know, if everyone were a martyr, there would be no Christian community left." His insight seemed so self-evident that I did not know what to say.

On Sundays we usually spread out to celebrate mass at different locations. The Newman Club at Cal Berkeley, which was staffed by Paulists, had excellent, well-prepared liturgies and an enthusiastic mix of students, faculty, staff, and area residents. Sometimes we went to the Cathedral in Oakland, which had an integrated congregation and an excellent Gospel choir. The Cathedral was attractive to liberal Catholics for a variety of reasons, including the makeup of its worship community, the quality of its preaching, the roles that women played, and its support for an extensive social-action menu.

I also got involved one or two days a week celebrating mass for the sisters at Holy Name College in Oakland. It was a relatively

easy drive there, and the sisters were appreciative. In Holy Week they asked me to be the celebrant for the Good Friday services. Everything at the rehearsal went well, but at the part of the service when the priest walks up from the back of the church and sings three times (in a progressively higher pitch) "Behold the wood of the Cross!" while stripping the cloth cover from the crucifix, I lost my voice (or perhaps my courage). Literally nothing came out of my mouth. We went on with the rest of the service and afterward no one complained, but I knew they wondered what happened.

In addition to the Catholic worship connections, I made sure to visit Glide Memorial Church in downtown San Francisco where Cecil Williams was minister. Glide was well known for reaching out to the poorest of the poor, to drug addicts, and to gays and lesbians. The typical service was full of hymn singing, fervent testimony, and great enthusiasm. Everyone who visited the Bay Area wanted at least one exposure to Glide Memorial and Cecil Williams.

Not too far from his church was a Franciscan-run homeless shelter in the Tenderloin area of San Francisco. I volunteered to serve food there one evening so that I could get a better feel for how they had structured the operation. The demand for their services was so heavy that the center had hardly moved its agenda beyond providing housing and food. They offered few remedial services.

By my time in Berkeley I was thirty-seven years old but still intent on keeping in shape as best I could. Walking the hills of Berkeley and San Francisco was one good way, but what I needed in addition was a place where I could play basketball a couple of times a week, preferably around the noon hour. After checking, I found that there was an open session in a physical education building for any students or employees who were interested. The first day I showed up I had a sense that my relative age and graying hair were liabilities. I knew that I had to establish myself as more than some old guy trying to keep past glories alive. In any

case, after a couple of weeks I found my groove, and for the rest of the year I enjoyed this outlet.

My main objective in Berkeley was to write the book that ultimately was titled *Homosexuality and the Christian Way of Life.* A word may be in order to explain how I arrived at the topic and to convey some of the experiences I had in gathering materials. When I went on sabbatical I wanted to pursue a research project that could both sustain my interest and make a distinctive contribution. During my years at Notre Dame and in the seminary setting I had confronted a number of individuals—in the classroom context, in counseling, and in confession—for whom issues of sexual identity and practice were major concerns. Given my upbringing and my social circles, the world of the homosexual subculture was almost a complete unknown to me. Once in high school I had to deal as student body president with an unfortunate incident between two students, and occasionally, like most teenage boys, I had seen evidence of restroom habitués who seemed to be on the prowl for potential liaisons. However, when I had my eyes opened about the prevalence of homosexual identity struggles and what the Christian Catholic tradition had to say about the matter, I decided that I had much to learn. I wanted to be sure, before I wrote a book about the topic, that I was as well informed as possible—theologically, medically, legally, and social-scientifically.

San Francisco in the 1970s was (as still is) one of the most liberal cities in the country when it comes to lifestyle questions, including sexual identity. Compared to many cities, a fairly high percentage of the citizenry was openly gay or lesbian. Of all the neighborhoods where such individuals concentrated, none was better known than the Castro district. For many visitors to San Francisco, a walking or riding tour through the Castro was *au courant,* especially on weekends. In this era before the AIDs epidemic became well known, the prevailing ethos in the Castro was that any form of sexual behavior was acceptable as long as consent was given. This included gay bath houses (where anonymous,

multi-partner, unprotected sexual activity was commonplace), sadomasochistic subgroups, and the use of drugs to enhance and/or prolong pleasure. The Castro was in-your-face flamboyant, defiant of accepted cultural mores, and unconcerned with what the future might bring.

But the homosexual world of the Bay Area was much more diverse than I expected. There were male partners and female partners who had lived mutually faithful, committed lives for a couple of decades or more and who avoided the public eye altogether. And there were gathering places for just about every sub-subculture. As time passed, it became progressively more difficult for me to generalize about the phenomenon. What I tried to do was to read widely, be a keen observer of the public social dynamics, and try to achieve a kind of empathy so that I could capture multiple points of view in my final analysis.

In my reading, I gradually exhausted the best-known material and began to look for less mainstream appraisals, from theological treatises to social science literature to advocacy texts to portrayals in fiction and film. In order to expand my horizons, I would visit small bookstores that specialized in gay/lesbian literature and large standard bookstores that had sections with that focus. As a result, I encountered some people at the checkout counters who raised their eyebrows with a look of scorn and some who invited me to support groups or even recommended other works.

I never realized when I began doing research on the topic of homosexuality that I would be on hand when San Francisco went through a series of traumatic events with deep resonance for the city's gay-lesbian community. On Monday, November 27, 1978, Mayor George Moscone and an openly gay member of the San Francisco Board of Supervisors, Harvey Milk, were shot and killed in San Francisco City Hall by a former supervisor, Dan White. An ex–San Francisco police officer and firefighter, White was elected to the Board of Supervisors in 1977. In order to keep that job, he had to resign from his higher paying job with the fire

department. During his time as supervisor, White had engaged in sometimes acrimonious disagreement with both Moscone, over growth issues, and Milk, over a landmark gay rights ordinance that the board had adopted over White's negative vote. Unhappy with the way city politics worked and suffering financially, White resigned his seat on the supervisors board. Because his resignation would allow Moscone to appoint a successor and break the existing vote deadlock, White tried to get his seat back. Moscone hesitated and then was distracted by news of the November 18th massacre of the members of the People's Temple in Jonestown, Guyana. This group had previously been based in San Francisco.

When I heard about the murder of White and Moscone on the news, I drove to City Hall and actually walked through that building a couple of hours after the event. I saw the site of the shootings and listened to the news reporters as they broadcast from the scene. All of my ambulance-chaser instincts came to the fore on that occasion, and I had the freedom to go where the action was.

The following May, Dan White was found guilty of manslaughter and given a seven-year sentence, of which he served five years before being paroled and subsequently committing suicide. White's defense lawyers gained some renown during his trial when they attempted to argue the so-called "Twinky Defense," which suggested that White was "high" from the elevated sugar levels of the well-known snack, and that this should mitigate his guilt.

After the verdict was read, a crowd gathered at Castro and Market, made up mainly of gays and lesbians from the Castro district. Gradually the crowd swelled and decided to march to City Hall in protest of the light sentence. As the march got bigger, it attracted young men who were gang members looking for trouble. When I heard about the demonstration on local television, I asked if anyone at our house wanted to accompany me into the city to observe the protest. Austin Collins was the only one who seemed eager to join me. As we drove toward the scene, we heard on the

radio that the crowd was moving toward City Hall. I decided to park about three blocks away on a side street.

The sun had gone down and the scene at City Hall was pretty chaotic. The police had lined up about fifteen squad cars in a row on one side of the park in front of City Hall, presumably to block off that section. The mood of the crowd got angrier and no one seemed to be in charge. A few among the mass of people started breaking windows and lighting small fires in the trash receptacles outside City Hall, but the real problems started when some of the street toughs broke the windows of squad cars and set them on fire. Soon all the police cars were burning and the police in riot gear began to retaliate.

Somewhat earlier than that, Austin had wanted to join the protesters in the center of the park but, battle-tested that I was, I sensed that the temper of the crowd was getting out of control so I demurred. Pretty soon, my advice looked prescient. Once the violence began with some intensity, I suggested to Austin that we make our way back to Berkeley where we would have an interesting story to tell and where the smell of smoke and tear gas on our clothes would give us instant credibility.

Right from my first prolonged visit to the Bay area back in the summer of 1969, I was taken by the beauty and cultural diversity of San Francisco. Back then I rode the cable cars, walked the streets of downtown, ate at Pier 39, visited Twin Peaks and the Sunset district, and generally had a quick look at the tourist-oriented sites recommended in the guide books. So when I returned in 1978, I felt I had had my basic orientation and I was eager to explore all that I might have missed.

To dispel any impression that I spent most of my time in non-academic pursuits, let me say that I did manage to complete my book manuscript through the course of the year. I also read widely and prepared other materials for submission to academic journals. The big difference was that I was not teaching, I did not have many formal responsibilities, and I was accustomed to shouldering an array of activities. After a full day of work I was

usually ready for something else before it was time for sleep. Sometimes I focused that energy on Berkeley, sometimes on San Francisco, and sometimes on the broader Bay Area.

As is my wont, I walked from neighborhood to neighborhood, taking in the street scene and trying to observe the little things that distinguish one area from another. Over time, I worked my way from the Embarcadero to North Beach to the Marina district to the Presidio. I wandered the length of Golden Gate Park, explored the beach areas of the Sunset district, and even paid a couple of visits to the zoo. I spent time in Haight-Ashbury and the Castro district, drove down crooked Lombard Street, walked the campus of the University of San Francisco, and sought to discover the best overlooks and the steepest streets. In addition to riding BART trains and the cable cars, I also sampled streetcars and buses and took elevators to the top of the tallest buildings. By the end of the year I felt I knew San Francisco relatively well.

I also discovered that the city was often best appreciated at a distance—from the Berkeley and Oakland hills, from Sausalito or Mount Tamalpais, from a plane preparing to land at San Francisco airport or a boat in the harbor. I loved the tour of Alcatraz prison and the redwood forests in Muir Park. One of the mysteries of the city is how the fog completely transforms a given view from one moment to the next. When the interior regions adjacent to the Bay are the hottest in the middle of summer, the city itself can be unusually cool until the fog lifts later in the day. Mark Twain's claim that the coldest he had ever been was in July in San Francisco has a ring of truth to it, not only because of the fog effect but also because visitors often come unprepared in dress for the climate's quick changeability.

Our group at Berkeley used to eat out on the weekends when our cook was not available. We sampled the restaurants in Sausalito and Tiburon, the waterfront places in Oakland and Berkeley, the neighborhood establishments in the city, and even interior locations in Concord and Walnut Creek. It was the company more than the food that we savored, but I also knew that

we were lucky to have so many options in a year away from our normal routines.

In the summer of 1979 the three priests in the renewal programs left and we were joined by Fathers Mark Poorman, C.S.C., and Bill Beauchamp, C.S.C. Our cook had finished her term of service by then, and Mark took responsibility for choosing someone new. He put an ad in the local newspaper, basically saying that six men were seeking a person to prepare their evening meal five days a week. That drew some interesting responses from applicants who had strange ideas of what we were looking for. He eventually chose an African-American woman who was a meat and potatoes type of person, a major contrast to our previous cook who favored exotic meals of varying provenance.

I felt my year in Berkeley was productive, interesting, full of adventures of one kind or another, and an excellent time of transition in my ministerial and professional career. I was supported by a compatible community that provided some regularity in my life, but I also had sufficient freedom to explore the wonders of the San Francisco area. I was stimulated mentally and culturally.

In subsequent years I returned to Berkeley for short visits and to San Francisco for conventions, meetings, speech making, and Notre Dame events. I always looked forward to having the chance to walk the streets, study the terrain, and learn even more about an ever-changing urban environment. In between visits I read books about the great earthquake and fire of 1906, the development of San Francisco from its earliest days, and the history of the University of California. Due to the rich experience I had in 1978–79, I have never grown tired of either Baghdad by the Bay or Berkeley.

A Special Memory

Remembering San Francisco always brings to mind my father's visit. He spent ten days living with our Community in Berkeley

that year. He came to common prayer, ate with us, and very much enjoyed spending time with the local contingent of Holy Cross people. I took him on tours of Berkeley, San Francisco, and the Bay Area. I think he was most fascinated by Chinatown, Golden Gate Park, the cable cars, Golden Gate Bridge, Twin Peaks, and Sausalito.

It was a privileged period for me. Dad and I talked about many things, family and otherwise, on our rides and walks. I sensed that he was proud of what I was doing and pleased to have more than a short-term exposure to my life as a priest. Given our atypical circumstances in Berkeley, we had more freedom and variety in our daily life, which meant Dad never felt his presence was an imposition. Our days together were relaxed and warm-hearted and a real gift. When he finally had to go back to D.C. to be with my mother, I took him to the airport and we shared a long embrace and expressed words of our mutual love. It would be my last prolonged time with him before he died of a heart attack at home at the age of seventy-seven. When I received news of his death, I felt a real sense of consolation that this time together in Berkeley had given both of us an opportunity to share those emotions between a father and son that are too often deferred until too late.

The Sorin Years

When I prepared to return to Notre Dame from my sabbatical year in Berkeley in the spring of 1979, I wanted to live in one of the undergraduate residences. I learned two would have openings—Morrissey Hall and Sorin Hall. In either place I could add assistant rector to my responsibilities as assistant professor of theology and director of the Master of Divinity program.

I would gladly have gone to Morrissey if it were the only hall available, but I was much more attracted to Sorin for a variety of reasons. First, it was a dorm with a great sense of tradition. Second, in size and layout it resembled Badin Hall where I lived during my junior and senior undergraduate years. Like Badin, Sorin had a porch, high ceilings, a variety of room configurations, and a relatively small number of residents (around 175 during my first year). A final attraction was its location in the historic center of the campus, next to Sacred Heart Basilica and Corby Hall and not far from the library and the classroom buildings.

Dave Porterfield, the newly assigned rector of Sorin, was a deacon that year prior to his ordination and eager to have a Holy Cross priest on the hall staff. Once my assignment to Sorin was confirmed, I shipped my books and other gear to the dorm so I might get settled into my room before the students arrived for orientation. My own experience of dorm living had been so positive

that I was confident the arrangement would bring a nice balance to my life: teaching, administration, and a pastoral role in the dorm.

Sorin Hall dates back to 1889. It was part of an experiment in Notre Dame's undergraduate living, boasting fifty individual rooms. Until it opened, the University had been modeled on a French boarding school with academic space, library, chapel, dining area, faculty offices, classrooms, and residence accommodations all concentrated in the Main Building. Tradition back then called for open dormitories and open study halls — *in loco parentis* to the nth degree — but in the middle 1880s, Father Matthew Walsh, C.S.C., decided to make a few rooms in the Main Building available as private rooms, and this proved both popular and academically successful.

In the spring of 1888 ground was broken for a more expansive version of this experiment. Initially called Collegiate Hall, the new building's cornerstone was blessed by Father Sorin during the celebration of his Golden Jubilee, and from then on it was known as Sorin Hall. When it opened in January 1889, the rooms were said to be "large enough to encourage study and at the same time small enough to discourage visiting." This was, of course, long before the invention of the myriad electronic devices that now take up significant portions of each room.

The hall's first floor originally had a chapel on the north side and the Notre Dame law department on the south. Colonel William Hoynes (the title was honorary, if not imagined) had come to Notre Dame as a one-man law faculty in 1883. He moved into Sorin when it opened and is said to have been a man completely dedicated to his duties yet prone to inflated oratory and an idiosyncratic lifestyle. He was, in other words, a "character" in every sense of the term.

Colonel Hoynes was indirectly responsible for the construction of the famous Sorin porch. As the story goes, one day a group of students on the third floor was taking delight, as students sometimes are wont to do, in clandestinely dousing unsuspecting passersby with buckets of water. By accident (or so they claimed),

they soaked the Colonel as he was making his way in the front door. Not long afterward, construction began on the porch, which, among other things, made it more difficult to catch the unwary by surprise with water ablutions.

During my time in Sorin we had a reenactment of this famous incident. A student stand-in for Colonel Hoynes—garbed in sartorial splendor and carrying a briefcase—walked south from Sacred Heart, and just as he turned into Sorin, some students stationed on the roof of the porch hit him squarely with an abundance of liquid. The Hoynes stand-in, true to character, huffed and puffed and then made his way inside, accompanied by cheers from all sides.

Sorin Hall grew by stages. In 1897, the president of the day, Father Andrew Morrissey, C.S.C., was facing an uptick in enrollment and decided to add two wings, providing room for a hundred additional students. Since then Sorin has undergone two major renovations. The first was driven by the concern about fire safety. With its wood construction and open stairwells, it was estimated Sorin would take about twenty minutes to burn to the ground, so in the summer of 1980 a sprinkler system was installed, the outside fire escapes were torn down, and two interior staircases were added. A jarring reminder of the risks posed by fire was provided that same year when Saint Edward's Hall burned down, caused by an acetylene torch being used to disentangle the exterior fire escape.

In the summer of 1982 Sorin was extensively renovated, and in 1996 the entire basement was gutted out and rebuilt, new study and social space was created, and the staff rooms were modernized. To facilitate that renovation process, I moved temporarily to Fischer Graduate Housing, but when I moved back to Sorin, I felt I was truly coming home.

At first I lived in the second-floor turret room in the northeast corner of the dorm, directly above Professor Paul Fenlon, the last of the University's "bachelor don" professors. Paul had moved into Sorin Hall in 1917 at the age of twenty and lived there

for the next sixty-three years. It boggles the mind to think how much the nature of dorm life changed over those six decades. Gradually the disciplinary rules were eased, the role of the rector became less discipline oriented, and, most of all, electric amplification of music became more pronounced. Dave Porterfield told me that Professor Fenlon had requested that I be assigned the room above his because the student residents who occupied that room were constantly disturbing him with their music and their jumping up and down for dancing and horseplay.

I quickly came to know and respect Paul. He was polite, cultured, patrician, and deeply Catholic. He loved the students and was proud that he had taught multiple generations of the same family. On home football weekends his room would be full of a constant stream of visitors from all over the country who considered him a hallmark of the best of Notre Dame's residential tradition. Paul invariably called me Father even though everyone else called me Monk. In the latter stages of his life he began to suffer from Alzheimer's, and I knew he was slipping when he started hailing me as "Big Fellow." Paul was a smoker and a great reader, and his room resembled a Victorian-era drawing room with books everywhere and trays full of smoked cigarettes in front of his desk chair and his favorite leisure chair.

In his later years he grew accustomed to the way his room was arranged, and he resisted any attempt by the maintenance department to renovate it. One time a group of seniors who were good friends of his, in collusion with the hall staff, photographed his room from just about every angle. Then, during one of the break periods when Paul was away visiting relatives, the students removed every bit of furniture, the maintenance people plastered and painted the walls and performed a thorough cleaning, and the students moved everything back exactly as it was before. When Paul returned he made no comment and presumably had no idea what had occurred

As his dementia grew, Paul gradually started being cared for in the Student Health Center, even though the Sorin room was

still technically his. He died at eighty-three, having served Notre Dame faithfully all his adult life. His passing marked the end of the tradition of the bachelor don professor who lived with undergraduate students and mentored them in academic, personal, and even religious matters.

During my first five years in Sorin I lived in room 241, a turret room that looked out on Sacred Heart and the Main Building. It had a bedroom, a small bathroom, and an inner room that functioned as my work area and social/meeting space. Most of the time I liked being surrounded by student rooms; when my main door was open I could see directly along the north-south corridor and to the right I could look west along a shorter corridor. Since I was blessed with good hearing, even when my door was closed I could keep a handle on what was happening on most of my floor.

Good hearing was not an unmixed blessing, however. Given the porosity of my walls, ceiling, and door, I was often able to hear more than I wanted to from the adjacent rooms and the corridors. I was also concerned about others overhearing privileged conversations in my room, including confessions and counseling sessions. Even though I went to bed between 2 and 3:00 a.m., later than most of the students, I was desirous of having greater control over the sound flow into and out from my private space.

At some point I heard one of the rectors talking about a noise-muffling device called Sleep Sound, which produces a steady, constant tone like a purring motor. I invested in one and found it quite effective up to a point. (I still have my original device and use it every night, whether or not anyone else is in the dorm.) But I also had the maintenance department close off the door from the corridor into my bedroom and fill in the space with soundproofing material. Eventually, I had them do the same in my turret walls, with the result being a major improvement in my noise quotient.

When Sorin Hall was constructed it did not enjoy universal acclaim for its architectural style. For example, a contemporary professor, Austin O'Malley, was quoted as saying, "You have

here such a lovely church. And right next to it that monstrosity, Sorin Hall. It looks like an old-fashioned ice box, turned upside down!" Like all the buildings in the oldest part of the campus, successive generations of graduates have embraced Sorin as distinguished, stately, distinctive, and a perfect fit for its location. All of which is to prove that tastes change, and memory has a big influence on our relationship to physical structures.

The Sorin attic is a dwelling place for bats and other such creatures, but is also rich in graffiti, including many that go back to its earliest days. Although the attic is usually shut off from student access, somehow or other students seem to find ways to get in and leave their marks. When the dorm opens at the beginning of the school year, the commotion of students moving in often frightens the bats, and a few of them make their way into the occupied areas. A common occurrence is for upperclass returnees to teach freshmen how to knock bats out of their flights with a tennis racket. It is not that the students are bloodthirsty or anti-bat, but once a bat gets inside a building it is extremely difficult to get rid of it without killing it. Twice I have awakened in my room to discover I had a bat for a roommate. In both cases I was able to dispatch the creature eventually, although with some effort since I have nineteen-foot ceilings. During my time in the hall, at least one freshman was bitten by a bat that had been captured in a sheet when he reached in to take its wings. Although the student had to undergo rabies shots for a while, he was not infected.

Bats were not the only hall pests. For a number of years, the students ran a food sales operation out of the Sorin basement. The menu revolved around pizza, sandwiches, chips, soft drinks, and a few desserts. As might be expected, sanitary conditions were not always ideal and at one point we discovered a rat had set up shop nearby. For months it lived in a symbiotic relationship with the food-sales proprietors, neither side seeming too upset so long as they did not encounter one another. Finally, the maids and janitor found out about the rat and an exterminating

crew was summoned. After the rat's demise, I had the sense that the food crew felt they had lost a friend.

Two of the rectors of Sorin during the period before World War II exhibited lighthearted, avuncular spirits. Fathers Eugene Burke and John 'Pop' Farley, C.S.C., both personified the best of the Holy Cross presence in dorms. Father Burke would sometimes assemble his charges in the rec room and ply them with hot dogs, sandwiches, and ice cream. Then he would move to the piano and play a number of favorite ditties to the delight of the students. Sometimes he was joined in these festivities by then-president Father John Cavanaugh, C.S.C., who had a reputation for Irish charm and wit.

Father Farley, in a later generation, was noted for his practice of hand-delivering the hall mail. Gathering the men around him, he would sniff suspicious letters for that hint of perfume and then josh the recipients about their hometown honeys. He knew everyone by name and tried to keep up with the most important events in everyone's lives.

Fathers Burke and Farley set an admirable example for later rectors. They considered the young men entrusted to their care a sacred responsibility. They functioned in a time in the University's history when the rules were much stricter than they are today, yet they were person-centered and self-confident enough to know that students sometimes misbehaved and challenged authority. The important thing, they felt, was to focus on the development of the students as individuals and the quality of the common life. For them, youthful missteps never obscured what it meant for them to be educators in the faith according to the Holy Cross model.

During WWII, when Notre Dame suffered a hemorrhage of students to the draft, the financial health of the institution was sustained by training large numbers of U.S. naval officers, who went through a shortened course of undergraduate education. The South Quad in those years was used by military detachments marching in formation. Civilian undergraduates were relatively

few in number, and approximately 250 of them were assigned to Sorin and Saint Edward's Halls. In the campus pecking order, the civilian students had low status. For probably the only time in its history, to live in Sorin was not considered a special privilege.

In 1969, a group of Sorin residents decided to change the name of the hall to Sorin College. A wooden sign with that name was hung on the crossbeam over the front porch. It was all tongue in cheek, since no approval for the name change was sought or conferred, and it provided no real independence or exemption from campus rules. Nevertheless, the fact that the sign remained in place in such a public location suggested that the University administration was not prepared to challenge the naming.

By the time I moved in, the residents were still alternating between Sorin College and Sorin Hall in describing were they lived. I found myself doing the same. Sometime in the 1980s, we discovered one morning that the Sorin College sign was gone. No one knew what had happened to it, though all my instincts told me that some other male dorm had conspired to steal it as a prank. I suggested to the rector that rather than make a new sign we leave the space where the sign had been nailed empty for a while. I thought we should lie low because it was very likely that whoever perpetrated the raid would be unable to keep quiet about it. Lo and behold, about two weeks later the sign reappeared one morning. Just as I had predicted, a rector at another dorm was able to identify a team of thieves. After he alerted them to the potential penalties from the Student Affairs office, they saw the wisdom of repeating their operation in reverse.

The first Sorin Talent Show took place in 1974 during a home football game weekend and was dedicated to parents. Except when prevented by severe weather, it has been repeated every year since. Unlike the Keenan Review, another long-standing campus tradition, Sorin's show is characterized by an absence of rehearsals. The custom is to recruit individual and group performers and take it for granted that they will figure out what to do, perhaps by osmosis. That is fine when it comes to experienced musicians

and entertainers, but even in the best years those sorts of acts have constituted only a small portion of the ninety-minute show.

The most memorable performances, at least in the students' eyes, are usually the ones that push the limits of civility, à la *Animal House* or teenage male "road" movies. Eating large quantities of unsavory foods in a short amount of time (for example, goldfish, Buffalo wings, pizza, French fries) has always been considered the pinnacle of humor. Chugging gallons of milk or soda is another. Lip syncing and karaoke allow the shyest of residents to stand before a crowd with confidence. Another perennial favorite is dressing in female attire with balloons for breasts, and either blasting out some Motown favorite or imitating the ND cheerleaders in some routine.

Most of the time the evening passes uneventfully (which means no four-letter words, no nudity, no crass sexism or racial references, and no belittlement of a least favorite resident). In my time as assistant rector, when I had official responsibility for the good order of the dorm, my goal was to get by without incurring an angry letter from any of the spectators at the event. The Talent Show (which I took to calling privately the Untalent Show) always took place on an outdoor stage that jutted from the hall porch. A microphone system was set up and usually one of the more gregarious residents served as emcee. Early in the week, publicity blurbs were hung on the hall bulletin boards and in the dining halls and LaFortune Center. The size of the crowd depended on temperature and meteorological conditions. In a good year the show drew one or two hundred, at least for part of the performance. Most of the attendees were either related to someone in the dorm, or had a friend in the show, or were simply curious about contemporary student life.

After I became a University administrator I almost always had to miss the Talent Show due to obligations elsewhere. When I would return to the hall later in the evening, all I had to do was ask the rector or the resident assistants (RAs) or one of the students and I would get a full account of the event, including a

critical evaluation of the acts. The students operated on standards different from mine, even though most of them did not want anything they did to threaten the tradition.

One of Sorin Hall's great claims to fame is that in 1908 two of its residents composed the "Notre Dame Victory March." John and Michael Shea were brothers—Michael, who had musical training, composed the melody, and John, who had a way with words, wrote the lyrics. It is reported that the brothers first performed the song using the organ in Sacred Heart Church. A few months later, the song's public debut took place in the Main Building rotunda. From that point on, the "Victory March" became a favorite of Notre Dame people and eventually the whole nation. For me, the official beginning of the academic year is the moment when I hear the "Victory March" as the Notre Dame band makes its way across campus during orientation week. Sitting in my room in Sorin, it is as though the Shea brothers are just down the corridor, sounding out their new musical composition.

For much of its history, Sorin Hall was restricted to senior undergraduates, and for that reason, and also because it had a reputation as a small, elite place to live, an unusual percentage of well-known athletes tended to be Sorinites. Both Knute Rockne and Gus Dorais lived in the Sorin basement. So did two of the Four Horsemen—Harry Stuldreher and Dan Miller. Three Heisman Trophy winners also resided there—Johnny Lujack, John Lattner, and Paul Hornung. Future football coach Hunk Anderson and future athletic director Ed "Moose" Krause also spent their formative years there. Closer to the present, athletic residents of note have included Pete Demerle, Ken McAfee, Dave Casper, and Steve Beuerlein.

Father John O'Hara, C.S.C., who later became president of Notre Dame, archbishop of Philadelphia, and a cardinal of the Church, lived for many years in the room I now occupy. After serving as dean of the College of Commerce, Father O'Hara was made Prefect of Religion in 1924, with responsibility for the spiritual well-being of all ND students. He quickly became an advo-

cate of frequent and even daily reception of communion (generally during mass, but not always). This form of religious practice was a significant change from what had prevailed in the decades before when even the most devout Catholics did not receive communion frequently.

O'Hara believed that communion, often accompanied by a fervent confession, was an effective means of engaging young men in the life of the Church community at a pivotal time in their lives. He began publishing a daily *Religious Bulletin* and he made periodic surveys of campus religious practices. Rather prudish by today's standards, O'Hara seemed far more interested in the success of the football team than in the flourishing of intellectual life. Still, a great many students of that era have testified to the profound influence he had on them.

Father O'Hara made his room in Sorin the center of his pastoral work. Students visited him for counseling and spiritual advice. A door in the chapel connected with his room, and students could summon him for confession or communion by ringing a chapel bell. Even though the configuration of my room has changed, I still consider myself fortunate to be immersed physically in a part of the hall where two giants in Notre Dame history—Father O'Hara and Professor Fenlon—dwelt before me. With a little imagination I can hear echoes of those privileged conversations that took place in this space across the decades. I hope and pray that I can be as faithful to my tasks as were my two distinguished predecessors to theirs.

The Case of the Traveling Statue

The full-size statue of Father Edward Sorin standing south of the Main Building and looking down Notre Dame Avenue has an honored place in the iconography of the campus. A half-size version of the same statue in Sorin Hall claims a speckled and intriguing history. When I was an undergraduate student, I remember the

smaller statue going on travels and sending back postcards from around the world. The statue was said to have a will of its own, although everyone knew it was an ongoing student prank.

I vividly recall two instances when the statue reappeared dramatically on campus. One took place on the banks of Saint Mary's Lake, near the Grotto. Word had gone out the day before that the statue would arrive at a certain time and place, and a fairly large crowd had gathered. Near the appointed hour, we could see in the distance a rowboat with a figure perched astride the middle. As the boat got closer, it became evident that the statue had been lashed to the vessel. No one else was visible— the pranksters had rigged a small motor in the rear of the boat and guided it by an electrical device. As the boat nudged the shore, everyone cheered. Edward Sorin had returned home once again! The second instance in my era took place during a football game. At halftime a helicopter circled the stadium, accompanied by music from the Notre Dame marching band, and Sorin was let down in a supporting net to the delight of all present.

Then the Sorin statue disappeared once again, spawning rumors about who might have purloined it and where it might be. Word seeped out that it was being kept in the basement of a Notre Dame graduate's home. It turned out that he was one of my undergraduate classmates and friends. Under dire threats about revoking his degree or some such penalty, he returned the statue to campus where it was secured in the room of one of the Holy Cross priests. It remained there in relative seclusion for several years until an extensive renovation of Sorin Hall began. The statue's hollow interior was filled with concrete and a steel rod that was connected to the floor in a location immediately outside the rector's room. After some testing, word got around that the statue was now impregnable.

Meanwhile, another tradition involving the statue developed. Any student who touched the toes and the nose of the statue daily, it was said, was guaranteed to be graduated in four years. Despite the fact that our students are more religious than is true

on most college campuses and seem oblivious to the appeal of superstition, this became a well-established bit of campus lore. One could sit outside the rector's office any day and see a good percentage of the dorm residents participating in this ritual of assurance, similar to rubbing Saint Peter's toe in the Vatican for good luck.

With the passage of time, one of the sons of the classmate of mine who had hidden the statue in his basement became a student in Sorin Hall. He informed me on his first day in the dorm that his call in life was to emulate his father's behavior and find a way of regaining control of the statue. On several occasions I noticed him hovering around the statue, looking for a point of vulnerability, but he reached graduation with nary a sign of having followed in his father's footsteps. The weekend of commencement I had a brief conversation with father and son, telling them I was hopeful that they would let memories of the temporary possession of the statue suffice for family history.

There are no guarantees that the half-size version of Edward Sorin's statue will never take another journey, but since he serves such an important and critical function in the lives of contemporary students, it would be contrary to the common good if he ever left home again.

The Annual Pigsty Award

One of the conclusions I have drawn from living in a student dormitory, especially a male dorm, is that some percentage of the student body, once they are away from family standards of cleanliness and orderliness, revert to an almost pre-civilized form of life. They apparently never make the connection between dirt, grime, and sickness. They rely on knowing that if their parents are coming to visit for a weekend, they can make a quick cleanup. Not all male students fall into this category, but enough of them did when I was assistant rector that I began handing out an annual

Pigsty Award to the room that exemplified the poorest standards of cleanliness.

I never had any defined criteria for the award other than a quick judgment at the end of the school year to determine which room contained the most pieces of old pizza, fast-food wrappers, dirty jockstraps, smashed crackers, uneaten bread, discarded socks, half-eaten candy bars, moldy popcorn, crumpled papers, empty soft-drink and beer bottles, and a messy array of old clothes and tossed-out paraphernalia. One way of narrowing down the leading contenders was an aroma test. If the odor was strong enough, it was a sure sign of a winner. Another test was clutter: if one could walk into a room in a straight line, that room was eliminated.

Usually, the award was easy to make. No announcement was made outside the hall, and the winners' parents, of course, never found out. Their pride in their sons being students at Notre Dame and growing in every possible way remained unshaken. They need not have feared anyway, because the same male students who were contenders for the Pigsty Award usually turned into quite respectable husbands and fathers who presumably ordered their children to clean up their rooms.

Monk Hoops

"Monk Hoops" began during my years in the seminary and on the seminary staff. When I moved into Sorin I wanted to revive the tradition. In part, my intention was to provide an option for the students to play among themselves. Another part was to help me get to know them better by interacting in an informal setting. I liked the idea of combining regular exercise for myself with a low-key pastoral outreach, and I had access to the Moreau gym in off hours when no one else was using it. Our assigned times were Mondays and Wednesdays from 10:30 p.m. to midnight. Those were perfect hours for the students, since hardly any of

them went to bed before midnight, and they were compatible with early evening study and various activities. The hours were also a good fit with my lifestyle.

When I announced Monk Hoops in Sorin, the students had no idea what to expect. Most of them knew I had played on the Notre Dame varsity team, but they did not know whether I was over the hill (I was thirty-eight) or whether the Moreau facility was as good as the Rock, the side gyms in the Joyce Center, or the courts in the Stepan Center. Right from the start I developed a routine that we faithfully adhered to through the years. The players and I would gather on the first floor of Sorin, next to the bulletin board, a little after 10:00 p.m. and walk *en masse* over to Moreau, entering the main entrance that led directly to the gym. I would turn on the lights and pull out the basketballs from the white laundry bag I carried them in. After a few warm-ups, we would choose up teams and start playing. The games were usually to 21 baskets, changing ends at 11. If your team won, you kept playing.

Monk Hoops had both egalitarian and elitist aspects. On the one hand, no one was ever turned away. Especially in the first weeks of the semester, we might have twenty or thirty extras waiting to play—this out of hall census of 170. As the semester moved on and academic responsibilities picked up, attendance became more manageable. The really committed included a good percentage of the best athletes in the dorm and a few others who were less talented but still savored the competition and camaraderie. Without a lot of fanfare, I would begin to put the best players on one court and all the rest on the other. From that point on the games became more intense and more fun.

Participating in Monk Hoops twice a week was a great way for me to get everyone's name down. Not only did I establish some rapport with a good cross section of the dorm, I also began to have a feel for their personalities and their styles of relating to each other. Sometimes the shy and laconic turned out to have a passionate side. Other times I observed the emergence of leadership skills that would eventually lead to roles in hall government or as RAs.

I have an implicit theory that team-oriented, competitive athletics are a window on the inner self, at least for those individuals who possess sufficient talent and experience to master the fundamentals of a sport. I am sure that the same might be true for other group endeavors, such as symphony orchestras, marching bands, theater troupes, and newspaper staffs. In any case, the old mantra, "the thrill of victory, the agony of defeat," suggests that a wide range of human emotions eventually surface in sports — the only questions are when and to what degree. Over the years I saw Sorin men display their aggressiveness, their resiliency, their kindness, their self-centeredness, their inconsistency, their quick-wittedness, and their capacity for growth. The contests were only one among many sources of insight, yet I am convinced that they were a privileged forum for learning the dimensions of people's personalities that were not so readily apparent in normal dorm interaction.

One of my favorite hoops memories is of Mike, a fine and extremely competitive athlete who was a regular on the Moreau court. In his senior year he served as an RA, and he did an excellent job of learning the freshmen's names and welcoming them to the hall. In the second week of Monk Hoops, a short, wiry freshman stole the ball and was moving down the court for an open layup when all of a sudden he was hit from behind, took a couple of somersaults, and crashed into the wall. He was unhurt, so he brushed himself off and apparently missed hearing the low-voiced warning from Mike that "there are no unmolested layups in Monk Hoops." About ten minutes later, the same thing happened. The freshman stole the ball and was taken out from behind by Mike. This time he got the message and lost his naiveté about the difference between high school and college. Mike went on to finish a doctorate in economics and is now a highly regarded university professor. The younger student eventually became a career officer in the Army and has been promoted numerous times.

We operated without referees. This meant the player on the offensive team had to call the foul if he thought his rights had

been violated. Usually a consensus prevailed, though there were a few prolonged disputes about such matters. Some players were rougher than others, especially those who played close to the basket. Most of the time I shot from long distances (the older I got, the longer the distance) so that foul calls were not a big deal for me. However, one year Chris (a walk-on with the Notre Dame basketball team and an excellent athlete) was guarding me at the conclusion of the third of three games between the best players in the hall. We had each won one game, and the final contest was tied. What happened next was a matter of some controversy. Chris stripped the ball and raced to the other end for a layup. Meanwhile, I called a foul. Players on both sides defended the interpretation of their respective teammates. In the end I prevailed, both because the offensive player has the prerogative and because I was older and deserved a break. And also because I was right. To this day, this story is retold with all its nuances of interpretation.

The most unpopular players were the minimally talented ball hogs. Some of them had played varsity ball in small high schools, others had excelled in another sport and just took it for granted that basketball would be a snap. No one ever wanted to throw the ball to the hogs since their teammates would never see it again. That took all the fun out of the game and totally destroyed any notion of team. Once individuals developed a reputation as ball hogs, they found themselves denied access to the ball, either from out of bounds or from a cross-court pass. Eventually, most stopped coming and found other ways to get exercise. In fact, the lessons we learned on all sides in these gatherings were not unlike the social dynamics of the so-called real world.

While Monk Hoops could be rough, most of the physical harm incurred was minor. I personally suffered two dislocated fingers and a couple of mild ankle sprains. Through the years, ankle and knee injuries were the most common complaints. There were also cuts, black eyes, and shoulder trauma. Once or twice a semester I would have to fetch my car and take a player to the hospital emergency room, but fortunately no one was ever injured

so severely that it affected them for life. There were always a few players who had such a kamikaze style of play that they were prone to injuries that kept them out of action for weeks at a time. Sometimes I found out that they lived the rest of their lives that way as well.

In my early years in Sorin, the rector, Dave Porterfield, worked in the Admissions office. One bonus of his job was that Sorin managed to get more than its share of non-varsity basketball and football players, many of them students who had turned down athletic scholarships in Division II schools to come to Notre Dame. The prime outlet they had for basketball was the combination of Monk Hoops and interhall competition. In those years Sorin won the interhall league a couple of times and was usually in the running otherwise. Thus Monk Hoops served as a form of pre-season practice without the hassles of scheduling and coaching.

In my later years, during the winter months when interhall leagues were going strong, I would occasionally invite students from other halls, along with seminarians and even coeds, to participate in Monk Hoops. This was partially to fill out the teams, but also to give non-Sorinites some exposure to what had become a well-publicized Sorin tradition. The women players were all proficient, and after some initial hesitation on the guys' part to be too physical, they were soon pushing and establishing position under the boards like everyone else.

Once I was named president, the media were always looking for a handle to describe my background and my potential style of administration. Many of their early reports were preoccupied with the fact that I had been a varsity basketball player (since not very many university presidents had that kind of pedigree). In my first year, the television show *60 Minutes* spent several days on campus taping what was billed as a typical week of activities. One of the component parts of the twelve-minute or so segment that finally aired on the network was related to Monk Hoops.

The camera crew arranged to accompany us to the Moreau gym and film some of the action. The students, of course, all knew that they might end up on national television, so they were eager to be in the game. The evening was a bit out of sync, since the director would ask us to pause periodically for a better camera angle or to do interviews.

On the date of the broadcast, which came right before the end of the academic year, I watched in my room surrounded by various Sorin residents and my first cousin once-removed, Jimmy Malloy, who lived in the hall then and had participated in Monk Hoops during the filming. Jimmy's father and sister were also in the room. Once the show began, I was preoccupied with the overall image of me that emerged (in the end I was pleased with the outcome), but the students were all focused on whether they appeared in any of the scenes, some of which had been shot in Sorin.

The relatively small exposure the show gave to Monk Hoops had me shooting in one clip and the ball going in the basket in the next. Though it looked seamless, there was no guarantee that I had really made the shot. In the next scene, cousin Jimmy Malloy took a shot and clearly missed. It was his only appearance in the show. Jimmy's sister told him, in a semi-joshing way, that he was a disgrace to the family, and a little later his other sister called from Scranton to say she had taped the show and would be replaying his performance all summer long.

The intensity level of Monk Hoops varied depending not only on the quality of the players but also on the time of year. Near mid-semester and final exams, most students were looking for a way to relieve stress and prepare mentally for their tests, so games at those times tended to be hyper-intense. Another peak time for non-stop action was during tryouts for the two Sorin interhall basketball teams. The hardest times to get good attendance were nights in late January and early February when the wind was howling, the snow was falling heavily, and the temperature was bitter cold. It took real commitment then to make the passage around Saint Joseph Lake.

In addition to the twice-a-week Sorin nights, I would sometimes gather a group of top-notch players from around the campus on a Friday night or Saturday morning. These games included students and some faculty or administrators. Two of my all-time favorites were Joe Sweeney and Bubba Cunningham. They were both point guards and, since I had a reputation as someone who liked to shoot, they both seemed to find a way to get me the ball when I had a chance to score. The spirit in those contests was intense but lighthearted. Usually the talent levels were quite close, and in the end it really did not matter who won. We just enjoyed the company and the action.

I continued to play in Monk Hoops until I reached the age of fifty-seven in 1998. Even as my athletic skills declined, I persisted and was lucky enough to avoid major injuries. I constantly adapted my type of play to what I could get away with, which meant I played less defense, I shot farther from the basket (I knew that driving down the lane put me in greatest peril), and I paced myself. Despite all this, I still worked up a sweat and scored consistently enough to avoid utter frustration.

What brought me to choose retirement was a medical examination that revealed tendinitis in both shoulders. This meant I could no longer shoot the ball with reliable control over arc and distance. Around the same time, Chicago Bulls superstar Michael Jordan was going through one of his multiple retirements, and I decided to tell my friends that, like Jordan, I wanted to go out on top. So without fanfare I quit Monk Hoops in 1998 after more than thirty years of participation.

Even today, however, the men of Sorin gather for Monk Hoops once a week in the Moreau gym. A couple of years ago I went over for their first fall session to give moral support and provide some sense of continuity. It was not the same. Now when I see the note on the bulletin board reminding the men about the scheduled departure time, it is like an event from the past to which I have only a marginal connection.

As far as I can tell, the present generation of students thinks that the "Monk" in Monk Hoops is an honorary designation, like dedicating the new swings on the front porch to me when I stepped down as president. And of course that is how it should be in the oldest hall on campus, as each Sorin cohort accepts practices and traditions from the past and reshapes them to suit the interests and the needs of the moment.

Bookstore Basketball

In the spring of 1972, before Notre Dame became coed, two student leaders—Fritz Hoefer and Vince Meconi—had a bright idea for livening up the time prior to and during *An Tóstal* weekend, the University's version of Spring Fest. They decided to create a basketball tournament that would be open to any five-man team on campus willing to play by the rules used in the Rockne Memorial gym (call your own fouls, games go to 21 points, with each basket counting one). No substitutions are allowed, and the games are played outdoors no matter what the weather conditions. When the teams are whittled down to sixteen refs are provided. By the end of the first sign-up period, 256 teams had been formed.

In the early years, the semis and finals were played on the two courts behind what was then the Notre Dame Bookstore (now replaced by Coleman-Morse Hall), in the area between Corby Hall, Bond Hall, and Walsh Hall—hence the name Bookstore Basketball. Soon the Bookstore courts could not accommodate the crowds of spectators, however, so the last two rounds were moved to a temporary court set up behind Joyce Center. Until the Bookstore courts were torn up for new construction, early round games continued to be played there, and the name of the tournament was retained.

Each year more and more teams took part, some just to be able to say they had been in one game during their undergraduate

career. With the advent of coeducation, a second, all-female schedule and championship were added, although women were also eligible to compete in the open tournament. In the early years, only one varsity basketball player was allowed per team, though up to three varsity football players could play on a team—or two if there was a varsity basketball player on the team. Closer to the present, when the NCAA began to tighten regulations for varsity athletes, only senior varsity basketball players were eligible and some of them chose not to participate for fear of injury before they began their professional careers.

Bookstore games quickly became major campus events. *Sports Illustrated* and ESPN both covered the tournament at various times. Most of the teams that made it to the Final Four through the years contained a good number of varsity athletes, and the professional schools contributed players with NCAA experience at some divisional level. For example, one two-time winning player was a former starting point guard for Princeton who was studying at Notre Dame's Law School.

I was a regular participant, and by sheer force of longevity I must be among those who have played in the most games. My strategy was to form a team of people I knew and enjoyed being with, and that generally meant seminarians and priests when I was at Moreau and Corby, and Sorinites during my years in the central administration. Later on I favored teams that were older and included a mix of faculty and administrators. This meant, of course, that the predominantly undergraduate crowds rooted against us.

One year, after I became president, I was invited to be part of the symbolic opening game, which matched a team of campus celebrities with a student team containing no members taller than 5 feet 7 inches. On my team were Dick Rosenthal (then ND's athletic director and a former professional player), Lou Holtz (football coach), Tony Rice (star quarterback), and Karen Robinson (a women's basketball star). We got a pretty good crowd for the

game on the Bookstore courts. The other team arrived with a script that predetermined every play. We went along with the frivolity for awhile, but eventually decided we needed more action because the fans were growing bored. The elders among us deferred to the two undergraduate athletes, so we set up Tony Rice for dunks and Karen Robinson for outside shots.

Through the years, the most controversial part of the tournament was the team names, some of which were in less than elegant taste. The Student Affairs office tried to put pressure on *The Observer* not to print the offensive names and use the teams' registration numbers instead. Eventually, of course, the real names got around.

The names of some of the teams I played on were "Four Sinners and a Monk," "Wounded Baby Ducks," and (after I was elected president) "All the President's Men." When my three nieces, Susan, Maureen, and Maggie, were enrolled as students and living in Walsh Hall, they each played in the tournament with their roommates and friends under the title "All the President's Women." One year the bookstore commissioner arranged for "All the President's Men" to play against "All the President's Women." The *Observer* sent a photographer to the game who caught me tugging at Maggie's sweatshirt after I let her steal the ball. The problem was that the blurb under the front page photo said nothing about her being my relative; it made me look like a dirty player.

During most of my years in the tournament, I had a relatively low profile. But one year my team had a game on one of the Lyons Hall Courts. We were the better team and won rather easily. However, the guy I was guarding (who seemed not to have absorbed the expectation for a physical style of play) kept calling fouls against me and shouting four-letter epithets at me. The next day I received in the campus mail a letter of apology. He said he had not known I was a priest and he was sorry if he offended me by his swearing. I wrote back telling him it was no big

deal. I did not tell him that what I really cared about was whether we won, and that if I had felt so inclined, I could have upped the ante when it came to offensive language.

In 1993 Mary Beth Sterling published a book titled *Look Out for the Manhole Cover: A History of Notre Dame's Bookstore Basketball Tournament*. It was full of data about the tournament, including interviews with some of the best-known participants, photographs of the action, and, most notably, a complete list of the teams' names. I am quoted a number of times in the book. Here is a sample:

> I've often thought that there were certain basketball players who were designed to be Bookstore champs. Adrian Dantley was that kind of player. Bill Hanzlik, Kelly Tripucka—they were the perfect fit for the kind of game that you need to go all the way in Bookstore. Also, some of the better Notre Dame quarterbacks were excellent Bookstore players. I just think it's because they're great athletes.

Toward the end of my Bookstore career, when I was well into my fifties, one of my teammates had played Division I-A basketball (as I had), but he was in his late thirties. Thus on paper, our team had two former varsity players, which was illegal. I heard rumors that someone was going to accuse us of being ineligible, so I went to the tournament commissioner and had a philosophical argument about imposing a statute of limitations for the rule against more than one former varsity player being on the same team. He was either convinced by my logic or intimidated by my title and ruled that I would not count against the quota. He never said explicitly what the cutoff age was, but I was clearly beyond it. In fact, I was pleased that I could still make it up and down the court. I was hardly a great threat to the in-shape, youthful teams we were competing against.

Bookstore teams through the years have stretched from comically inept to passably competitive to fiercely committed peren-

nial powerhouses. The most creative team concept I ever saw was that of the "Esophagus Constrictors," who fancied themselves the ultimate all-academic team. They dressed like nerds, with pocket protectors and calculators on their belts. Once they called a halt in the middle of a game and set up a device to measure the speed of the wind and the distance to the basket, after which they sat around calculating all the variables and developing a formula to guide the shot. One of the players got up, stuck his finger up, and proceeded to swish the ball from behind the foul circle. No one could believe he had pulled it off.

The team with the most connection to Sorin Hall was called "Tequila White Lightning." It made its first appearance in 1981, and although it won the championship only once, it was in the running every year but one up through the early 1990s. It was really the connection among sets of brothers that shouldered the team's success from year to year. Lou and Chris Nanni, Tom and Mike Conlin, and Matt, Sean, and Shannon Cullinan set the tone for the whole team.

In addition to Monk Hoops and Bookstore Basketball, I also participated one year in the Graduate School basketball league. I played on the theology department team along with Father Don McNeill, C.S.C., who had also played for Notre Dame when he was an undergraduate. In one of our games against the psychology department, I ended up guarding a faculty member whom I knew well and who was a committed behaviorist. In the heat of play I accidently hit him in the nose and a little blood spurted. I held out my hand in a kind of apology, but all he could say was, "Let me punch your nose and then I'll shake your hand." I, of course, was not interested in the offer.

In the championship game that year, our basic strategy was for Don McNeill to set picks and rebound and for me to take the majority of the shots. The plan worked and we were victorious. The only problem was, Don suffered a broken nose and a dislocated finger in the game. Afterward, I suggested to him that it was a small price to pay for victory. He did not seem convinced.

Sorin Liturgies

The Sorin Hall Chapel has a long and impressive history as a center of prayer and devotion. Since 1979 when I moved into the dorm, it has been completely renovated. Stained glass windows designed by Notre Dame art professor Robert Leader were installed, the pews were refinished, new Stations of the Cross designed by Father Jim Flanigan were placed on the walls, the altar and tabernacle area was reconfigured, and new lighting and ceiling fans were added. The result is a comfortable, adaptable worship space.

In my first year I was usually the main celebrant for the Sunday masses, with Dave Porterfield, the rector and a deacon, preaching some of the time. In those days Sunday mass was at 4:15 p.m., which distinguished us from most of the halls where mass was at 10, 10:30, or 11:00 p.m. I never liked the 4:15 p.m. slot since so many possible conflicts existed, but it took years to change it to the present 10:00 p.m. schedule. Through the years, Sunday mass has been an integral part of the life of the dorm. The music is furnished by student instrumentalists and singers (with occasional coed participation), and all the ministries — lectors, communion distributors, petition readers, and sacristans — are exercised by Sorin residents. Unlike some of the newer dorms, Sorin never got rid of its pews, but the area around the altar is open enough that the celebrant can invite the worshipers to gather around the altar for the canon of the mass, depending on the size of the congregation. This is always the custom at weekday masses.

In the first years after the Vatican II liturgical changes, dorm liturgies tended to be more diverse than today. Some halls have reputations for the quality or style of their music, or for the mix of male and female students attracted by the preaching, but Sorin masses have tended toward the center of the liturgical spectrum, probably reflecting my own predisposition. The spirit is relaxed yet sufficiently formal to preserve the integrity of the sacrament. The hymns are theological in content but contemporary in style.

Those who take an active part in the ministries tend to be drawn from a healthy cross section of the dorm, so that no subculture alienates the average student.

The great challenge for the hall staff in every dorm is how to encourage liturgical participation when it is not mandatory. This is especially a challenge with first-year students, since young men and women living on their own for the first time have many choices to make. They may or may not have been active church-goers in their teens, and it is up to the rector to assist the process by which they begin to fashion their lives at Notre Dame. The convenience and student orientation of dorm-based worship is one of the University's great strengths as a Catholic institution. I have always been edified by the level of participation that prevails among Sorin students, even among the non-Catholic residents.

I get to most of the halls for Sunday mass through the course of the year, and one thing I have remarked is the consistent quality of the liturgical music. In the past, this aspect of worship was excessively dependent on a few individuals who eventually graduated and left the cupboard bare. Now more effort is devoted to preparing successors so that the annual transitions go more smoothly. Just as important is an exponential improvement in the willingness of the hall congregations to participate in the singing, especially in the male dorms.

Another noteworthy change is the form that the exchange of peace has assumed in pretty much all dorms. Beginning first in the female halls but now common in the male ones as well, students are accustomed to giving each other, and a good percentage of those present, a warm embrace as a sign of acceptance and mutual support. I sometimes kid that I am going to give an end of the year award to the dorm with the longest and most enthusiastic sign of peace. In places like Sorin, that interaction takes a distinctively male form (like teammates after a big victory), yet it reveals a lot about the evolving nature of our culture and the needs of young adults within it.

In addition to regular liturgies, a Sorin mass is celebrated on home football weekends a half hour after the game ends. On most weekends the chapel overflows, although the late game starts in recent seasons have had some downward effect on attendance. The rector usually takes a collection during the offertory for some worthy cause (in most years for a Catholic school in one of the Holy Cross parishes in East Africa), and while the outcome of the game has influence on the size of the collection, I claim that what really counts is how the celebrant interprets the theological significance of losses.

In recent years, American Church leaders have debated the notion of holy days of obligation. Christmas is universally accepted when it does not fall on Sunday. The list of the other holy days was reduced for a variety of reasons, including the level of emotional connection to the feast and the problems that occur when it takes place too close to the weekend. On the other hand Ash Wednesday, although not designated as a holy day, is one of the most participated-in celebrations of all, both at Notre Dame and elsewhere. There is something inherently profound about the reception of ashes and the recitation of the traditional formula, "Remember that you are dust and into dust you shall return," in the context of the mass.

An adjustment that some priests may not like is the practice of celebrating the end of the fall semester with a Christmas mass while the liturgical calendar is still in Advent. Sorin usually schedules this mass on the Saturday or Sunday of the study days just before final exams commence. The students are in the mood and will soon be gone for the holidays, so pragmatism prevails. The student musicians and choir sing a selection of carols before the Christmas mass formally begins, but the readings are those of the assigned Sunday of Advent. The homily inevitably combines themes about Advent, Christmas, and the end of the semester. Sad to say, when the students return home for the holidays and go to Christmas mass with their families, they may feel less personally engaged in the spirit of the season than they do in the Sorin celebration.

Different dorms tend to develop a preference for a closing hymn that becomes a signature part of the celebration. It is not sung every week, but when it is scheduled in a given week, there is real enthusiasm in the air. The choice seems to have little to do with the eloquence of the lyrics or the lasting value of the music. By some unexplainable process of group dynamics, it just happens, and for a period of time (often several years) everyone is in sync. Then the mood shifts and another hymn replaces it. At the end of mass, when the last hymn has been sung, the majority of dorms have adopted the practice of all the worshipers slamming shut their hymn books in unison. At first I thought this was a little hokey. Now, I see it as an affirmation of what has been concluded, a kind of dramatic Great Amen.

After I became an administrator, I would usually stay on campus through Christmas Eve. For a number of years, I celebrated mass at the home of Chris and Carmie Murphy, who hosted somewhere between eighty and a hundred people for mass and dinner. After I became president, I began to be the main celebrant at the Christmas Eve mass at 5:00 p.m. in the Basilica. In more recent years, I have been using the Sorin Chapel on Christmas Eve for a blend of Notre Dame faculty and administrators and their children. This has gradually morphed into a mass that engages the talents and energies of as many of the children (of all ages) as possible. A Christmas pageant after the Gospel and homily includes having the younger generation play the parts of the Christmas story, with props and costumes included. Afterward, there is a celebration at Lula's Café on the southeast edge of the campus

Welcoming the New School Year

From feedback I have received through the years, both parents and students rate the experience of orientation for first-year students quite highly. While much of that event is carried by staff

in the First Year of Studies and the Student Affairs offices, the rector, the hall staffs, and the hall government play roles as well.

Because Sorin is a relatively small dorm, the incoming class usually consists of between thirty-five and fifty-five students. Once the new undergraduates are assigned to a dorm, communication between the rector and the student/family commences. The rector usually asks students to send pictures in advance, a practice that is useful for recognizing them when they arrive. All the rectors during my time in Sorin have made a real effort to master names and faces, and incoming students are flabbergasted when the rector identifies them at first sight. It establishes a sense of community and belonging that very much fits the Notre Dame model of residentiality.

Another surprising detail is the presence during hall orientation of the so-called "Frosh-O" team, which is made up of sophomores and sometimes juniors who return to campus early from summer break to facilitate the newcomers' move-in. These volunteers wear distinctive t-shirts and are expected to carry as much of the frosh students' gear as possible so that the student, parents, and other family members have less to cope with. This display of hospitality is an impressive introduction to life in Sorin.

During my three years as assistant rector, one of my functions was to sit outside the rector's office and greet each family. The big challenge for the rector and assistant rector in the first day or two is convincing the parents, particularly the mothers, that they are not spending good money to have their son live in a slum. It is fair to say that Sorin rooms, before they are occupied, have a certain drabness to them (this was even more marked before the various renovations were undertaken). Frosh live in doubles, triples, and quads in Sorin, and the whole room or combined rooms usually contains less area than the student's own room did back home.

One of my ploys in the face of maternal panic was to quickly bring the parent down to my room and assure her that all the rooms would look more like mine. This claim lacked any credibility,

but most of the time it was sufficient to diminish the emotional level. One year I was showing a family to their son's triple in the basement. The first two students had already arrived and staked their claims to two of the desks and beds, but at the moment they were gone from the room. When I entered, I found that the third bed was missing, all except the springs which were sitting on the floor. I glanced at the mother and could sense that she was about to lose it, so I suggested that the cleaning crew must have moved the bed next door by mistake, although I privately believed it had been purloined by a returning upperclassman. I proposed that we leave the luggage and other goods on the floor and go upstairs. Meanwhile, I grabbed an RA and told him to take one of the beds out of an upperclass room, figuring we could handle that problem when we came to it. When I returned to the triple a bit later, everything was in order and parental tension had dissipated.

For many years, move-in time for freshmen included building lofts to maximize the space in an old building with high ceilings. For returning students this task stretched over several days, but for new students, the pressure of constructing a loft often fell upon the fathers, most of whom had no carpentry skills and little inclination to learn. These parents desperately went in search of expertise and tried to throw money at the problem. When a manually skilled father or upperclass student was tracked down, the negotiations moved briskly lest a rival father move in with a competitive offer. My brother-in-law, John Long, who had three daughters go through Notre Dame, was one of the rare fathers who loved to build lofts. If he had had enough time and energy, he could have become independently wealthy just on the income from first-year orientation in Walsh and Sorin Halls.

One of my favorite orientation moments was the time three sets of Sorin parents came to my room and demanded that their sons be moved out of their assigned quad. The problem, it turned out, was that the fourth student in the quad had diabetes, and they had seen his insulin kit with needles. The parents knew intellectually that there was no risk at all that diabetes could be passed

from one student to the other. Nevertheless, the sight of the needles evoked deep-seated fears about drug use, danger, and lack of control. Meanwhile, the four students were bonding well and had no idea that this conversation was going on. Gradually I was able to convince the parents that their concerns were irrational (although I never used that word) and that I would monitor the situation in the quad and inform them if there were any grounds for alarm.

As it turned out, the four students were roommates for four years and became lifelong friends, and the student with diabetes became a successful physician. At the time of their graduation, I gently brought up the matter when I saw all four sets of parents sharing the joy of the occasion. The ones who had come to my room were somewhat embarrassed, yet I reminded them that they acted out of love and concern, and that was what we were celebrating together over commencement weekend.

One of the strangest things that happened at the beginning of the school year involved the father of an entering freshman whose son was in a special program in Europe and could not make it back for the first couple of days of classes. The father decided to take his son's place, literally. He moved in with the son's roommate, went to all the student-oriented events, registered for the boy's courses, and attended the first class meetings. The University had given permission for the son to come late, but no one had any idea what the father had in mind. By the time we figured out what was going on it was almost over, so we decided to monitor the situation until the son arrived. I have always wondered what the roommate thought when he found himself living for a few days with his soon-to-be compatriot's father.

Homesickness is the greatest concern for the hall staff during the time of transition to college. Until we learn more about the students' families, their medical needs, their academic aspirations, and their capacity for friendship, it is hard to predict who among the newcomers will adjust to college life easily and who will not. Some have never shared a room with anyone and this

can be a real issue of communication and compromise. Sometimes when there are three or four frosh in a room, two or three hit it off and the other feels left out. Matters can get even more complicated if roommates come from different religious, racial, ethnic, or socioeconomic backgrounds.

For students whose first language is not English or who have never before lived in the United States, the very practices of American young adult culture may be at the heart of the problem. Whatever form the challenge of adjustment takes, it is the responsibility of the rector and his staff, including the priest-in-residence, to be alert for difficulties, to plan strategies of response, and to ensure that the student is given every opportunity to be happy at Notre Dame.

When I think of homesickness as an issue, I recall two students in particular. The first was a star athlete, student government leader, and peer model in his high school in the western United States. I expected him to make the transition smoothly, since the other first-year students liked and admired him and he was doing well in school. Still, he felt something was missing in his life. He developed the habit of stopping in my room most evenings, and he inevitably said something like, "I think I will go home next week and drop out of school." Each time I would respond, "Just give it another week." This exchange went on for the whole fall semester, and I was worried about the winter break. But he returned for the spring semester and the conversation began all over again. In fact, it took three semesters for him really to feel comfortable. As far as I was aware, his peers knew nothing about his uncertainties. In his sophomore year things began to click at last and he finally found a home here. By the time he graduated, his uncertainty had disappeared and he was a true Domer.

The second student went through the same transition blues, but his threats to pack it in were more frequent and more adamant. Part of it was roommate related, yet I knew there had to be more. When things finally got worked out, he went on to spend

seven years on campus (including three in a professional school) and he served on a hall staff as assistant rector, where he helped other frosh with challenges comparable to his own.

One of the components of the Frosh-O for the staff in Sorin is holding separate meetings with all the parents and all the frosh. These sessions take place in the chapel and are a key to setting the tone for the year. All the staff members introduce themselves and say a few words. The rector covers such matters as his own role, communication with parents and vice-versa, the residential tradition in general, the specific traditions of Sorin as the oldest campus residence, the rules and their interpretation, and information about the deadline for fixing up rooms. On occasion, a question period brings out some deep-seated anxieties. For first-time participants, the old saw surely applies: "The hardest challenge of parents is first to give their children roots and then wings."

Football Weekends

After orientation week, the next hosting opportunity we have for students' family members occurs on home football game weekends. Because of Sorin's central location, it tends to be on just about everyone's campus exploration route. Old grads return to knock on the doors of their former rooms and ask to take a peek. Often, they are accompanied by offspring, who can seem slightly embarrassed by a father's bout of nostalgia (little do the kids realize that these visits are part of a not-so-subtle ploy to get them motivated to attend Notre Dame themselves). Sometimes the knocks on the door come before the occupants of the room are awake and are not ready to be entirely cordial in sharing a bit of hall lore with visitors.

From the Sorin Hall porch on football weekends one can watch the marching band step off from in front of the Main Building promptly at 4:30 on Friday afternoons. Or one can watch the constant stream of visitors stopping in the Basilica or making

their way to the Grotto. All day Saturday a temporary food service stands in front of Sorin, run by one of the student groups. From my room I can hear them hawking their wares, and normally I welcome the sounds. I confess to some aggravation, however, when a student volunteer gets hold of a megaphone and repeats his sales pitch over and over *ad nauseam.*

After the team mass in the Basilica on Saturday, the players and coaches walk from the front of the church to the stadium, passing directly in front of Sorin. On both sides of their path, supportive fans cheer them, and the scene is a little like gladiators walking through the streets of Rome. The players are dressed in coat and tie and remind us visually that Notre Dame wants to operate at a high standard in the world of intercollegiate athletics.

After the game, Sorin is one of many campus dorms offering a special mass for visitors. Notre Dame is the only place I know where the stadium public address announcer lists mass times during games. Those who come to Sorin for the celebration tend to be former Sorinites and their families, present students' families, and those who heard about it and like the ambience. Depending on game time (and perhaps the result of the contest), the chapel is usually overflowing, and the biggest challenge for the celebrant is to cram as many people into the available space as possible, knowing that a few will end up being stuck in the corridor. I am always moved on these occasions by the presence of multigenerational families from all over the country and all over the world, people who think it important to worship with us in Sorin. As I have grown older, I relish seeing former students come back with their own children, some of whom eventually dwell in Sorin as well. It is a sign to me that we must be doing something right in the common enterprise.

In the Notre Dame calendar, the three great moments of the year are orientation, Junior Parent Weekend, and commencement. Most of the events of Junior Parent Weekend take place away from the halls, although on Saturday the dorms host lunches for juniors and their parents. In Sorin this has never been very elaborate

(sandwiches, chips, brownies, and soft drinks), yet it is a prized moment when many of the parents get to interact with their sons' roommates and best friends. In many ways it is a warm-up for commencement, but less pressured and more relaxed. In my presidential years I was formally involved in many JPW receptions, such as the mass and the grand Saturday night dinner in the Joyce Center, but the internal Sorin gatherings have always been favorites because they allowed me to have more of a personal presence for my hallmates.

For a few years when I was still playing Monk Hoops, some of the juniors decided to arrange a basketball game for fathers and sons and me on the Saturday morning of JPW. I had a suspicion that this was not the fathers' idea, but we always had sufficient turnout to enjoy a slow-paced but fun game. I insisted that both teams play a zone defense, since this required less running and forced both teams to pass the ball around. I often wondered if we should have an ambulance standing by. Fortunately the worst injuries ever incurred were a minor ankle sprain and a cut lip.

On commencement weekends, parents and family members can choose to stay in one of the dorms (which are cheaper but much less comfortable than the commercial alternatives). They do not necessarily end up in their graduate's dorm because the newer halls with air conditioning are more attractive. But no matter where their families are staying, students who have remained in Sorin for their senior year inevitably gravitate back and I always enjoy seeing them. It is a tradition for the new graduates, decked out in their robes, to gather on the porch for family pictures. It has always been thrilling to join them, especially when I was wearing my ND gown and had the presidential medal and chain around my neck.

In my early years in Sorin, when I really knew all the graduates and was close to many of them, the question was when the final goodbyes would be said. Often that was the Sunday night or Monday morning following the ceremonies, when tears would flow and warm embraces would be shared. Like all farewells, these

were necessary and desirable and grace-filled, yet still sad. I always felt privileged to share these relationships and hopeful for what these young men and women had to offer the world. For the few students whose parents went home right after graduation, the temptation was to linger and put off the inevitable. The latest goodbye I can remember took place on Wednesday night.

Fortunately, I knew in my heart of hearts that I would stay involved in the lives of at least some former Sorinites, with football weekend visits, phone chats, marriages, baptisms, funerals, and other occasions. And so it has turned out. I have discovered that even after a couple of decades of separations, reunions with former students quickly reestablish the bonds as the old stories get recast and the tales of their youth become embellished with details and variations that begin to approach the mythical.

Noises and Remedies

As the oldest residence hall on campus, Sorin College was not designed for the era of sound amplification. The walls were simply not built to impede the passage of sound from one private space to another. Whenever I lost my patience, I got in the habit of calling down to the offending students' room and, without announcing who I was, saying something like, "My teeth are rattling around in my mouth" or "I feel like I am in the first row of a rock concert." Whoever answered the phone was bright enough to recognize the caller and make the proper adjustment.

But internal noise control was only part of the challenge. In the first years, I shared with the other Sorin residents a distaste for the bells of Sacred Heart Church, which signaled the hour, each quarter hour, and after 10:00 p.m. the playing of the Alma Mater. In addition, before every liturgy in the upstairs church, before and after special feasts, and upon the death of a Holy Cross member (and before and after the funeral), bells were rung for a prolonged period of time. In the warm weather, this cacophony

was more disconcerting because in the absence of air conditioning all the residents kept their windows open. Gradually I adjusted to the rhythms of the hourly sequence and even the Sunday mass call to prayers. It was the continuous ringing on special occasions and the funeral toll that affected my sanity.

When Father Dan Jenky, C.S.C., was rector of the Sacred Heart and I was not yet CEO of the institution, we exchanged letters addressing the matter. I appealed with great eloquence (I thought) on behalf of the men of Sorin Hall, whose study, sleep, and social well-being were negatively affected by the tintinnabulation of the bells a stone's throw from our rooms. I pleaded for a reduction in the frequency and duration of the chiming. In reply, Dan evoked the tradition of Father Moreau and Father Sorin, both of whom had grown up in nineteenth-century France where the freedom of the Church to publicly beckon its flock to prayer with bells was a sacred privilege in the aftermath of the French Revolution. He reminded me that money had been raised for each bell, and that the largest and most resonate of them had been cast in France and shipped across the ocean. It took me little time to conclude that my efforts had been for naught.

After almost thirty years of residence in Sorin, my psyche has learned to block out pretty much all the noise emanating from the spire next door except for the funeral toll. Perhaps that is just as well, since I am getting older and can well use the reminder that my time will eventually come as well.

Sometime after the turn of the millennium, the Notre Dame marching band drum corps established the tradition of playing their game-day routines at midnight Friday night on the steps of the Main Building. At first this drew only a small crowd, and I anticipated that the drummers eventually would move on to some other venue. I could not have been more mistaken. The drum show quickly became an established tradition and now is even announced in *The Observer*. In my early years in Sorin, when I went to bed in the wee hours, I did not care. After I became an administrator I started to retire around midnight, which meant

that for six or seven Friday nights each fall I forced myself to stay awake until the thirty-five-minute show was over.

During my years as president, it became a tradition on the first home game Saturday for one of the women's halls to send a delegation to the Sorin dorms around 6:00 a.m. and chant "Monk wake up. Monk wake up," followed by "Sorin wake up." A little later, various men's dorms would make their presence known with chants of their own concoction. By then I could hardly stay in bed since I was already alert and the adrenalin was flowing with excitement of the day of the game.

Student Paper Help

The hardest balancing act for a hall staff member is how to be student-oriented, friendly, and available without becoming overly involved in the daily life of an individual student or the entire hall. The challenge is to give students sufficient space to be truly on their own and to form peer friendships, make mistakes, and take responsibility for their growth and development. We need to be there for them as a significant adult presence and a potential counselor, confessor, academic advisor, and model of integrative living for a Christian person in the world. In a hall of 170 young men (closer to 150 after several rounds of downsizing) I always knew that time, circumstances, and personalities would lead me to be closer to some students than to others. Early on, I tried to develop certain practices to maximize my opportunities to know a fairly wide cross section of Sorin.

In addition to Monk Hoops, Bookstore Basketball, hall liturgies, and an open door policy, I established a pattern of offering to assist students in the composition of their class papers. In some cases I helped them to clarify their ideas and the nature of their arguments—especially in courses like philosophy, theology, and the social sciences. On other occasions I would point out potential resources, particularly back before computer data bases

were so ubiquitous. It was in the composition and literature classes and the writing seminars that I had my greatest challenges.

I wanted to assure that the final product was theirs, yet some of the poorest writers needed considerable work on spelling, grammar, and style. The worst students to deal with were those who were slightly dyslexic and those whose first language was other than English. There were two brothers in the hall from Puerto Rico whose writing skills in English were atrocious. When they would bring me a paper, I would read it through and not know where to begin. Nevertheless, they both made it through and are successful dentists in Puerto Rico.

The side effect for me of becoming the hall composition guru was that many hall residents got comfortable with visiting my room, and I got to know them better. Any improvement in their academic performance was a bonus. My tutoring was time consuming in the midst of multiple responsibilities, but I gauged that it was worthwhile, primarily because of the relationship building it fostered.

Hall Staff

In my years in Sorin, I have been blessed to work with some excellent rectors, assistant rectors, and RAs. Sorin's group of four RAs is really a cohort best served by a mix of personal qualities and interests. I always thought it advisable to have one RA who was physically impressive (tall, muscular, and a dominating presence), one who was connected to the liturgical life of the dorm (as a musician, song leader, or sacristan), one who was a bit nerdy (a high achiever academically), and one who was a campus activist (preferably with strong social justice concerns). That way just about every new freshman should be able to find one to admire, trust, and feel inclined to share their life's story with.

No matter how involved with students the hall rector is, the RAs often have insights into residents that only a peer can. In

their formal training RAs touch on many topics, from *du Lac* rules to eating disorders to parietal violations to diversity matters to homesickness, but it is impossible to prepare them for all the challenges a given year may bring. Through my years in Sorin, RAs have been involved in student, parental, and family deaths; serious illnesses; suicide attempts; fist fights; racial insensitivity; theft from rooms; unannounced overnight guests; serious alcohol-related incapacitation; roommate disputes; damage to hall property; girlfriend problems; sexual identity issues; academic failure; and other such matters. The RAs have to learn how to accept their identity as part of the administration of the hall while still being part of the peer culture of undergraduate life. This is a skill learned only by living it out from day to day, and most RAs testify at the end of their year that they learned much more than they gave, and that the positive aspects of the job far outweighed the stress points. Being an RA is a great preparation for future parenting and for leadership roles in every walk of life.

The assistant rectors during my time in Sorin have generally been law students, although a few have come from the graduate school, the M. Div. program, or the MBA program. Some were Notre Dame undergrads who knew the system and had a head start when the school year began, yet some of the best did their undergraduate work elsewhere and brought a fresh perspective to the role. The biggest pressure on assistant rectors comes from the responsibilities they carry as full-time students themselves. They tend to be under the same level of anxiety at exam time as those under their care in the hall.

Ideally, both the assistant rectors and the RAs have credibility in the eyes of the students because they are perceived as people of character and quality. Students expect fairness and consistency, especially in the interpretation of the rules and the assignment of proportionate penalties. When they find, in addition, wise counsel and genuine concern, that is a real plus in forming a sense of hall community.

The role of the rector is an honored one in the Notre Dame residential tradition. It demands the ability to live by student hours (far later, on the average, than the hours kept by rest of humanity), to be *au courant* with every fad and trend in American youth culture, to be tolerant of every style of music (no matter what the level of its amplification), to be a guru, a hall manager, a disciplinarian, an inspiring presence, and a potential friend all at the same time. Additionally, it helps to be omnipresent and omniscient about the lives of the students and the affairs of the hall without being intrusive, nosy, or excessively judgmental.

The range of personality types that have been successful as rectors would suggest that above all else, the young men or women entrusted to their care must respect them and believe that their rectors love them and want to help them grow into mature adults. The students will tolerate (and even celebrate) idiosyncrasies in rectors, ranging from health phobias to wooden speaking styles to odd hobbies to refined interests in classical music or medieval literature, so long as the rectors are available to students and manifestly committed to their well-being.

As of the 2007–8 school year, I have resided in Sorin under seven rectors. Dave Porterfield was the first. The second was Brother Tom O'Malley, who had previously been a Holy Cross brother in high school and reform school ministries. Joe McKenna, an Irish-born graduate student, served next as Sorin's first lay rector. He was succeeded by Father Steve Newton, who held the position for eleven years while at the same time being involved externally with activities serving the homeless and the addicted. An African-American doctoral student, Sean Seymore, was Sorin's second lay rector, followed by Father Sam Peters, C.S.C. The current rector, Father Jim King, began his tenure in 2003.

My years working with Dave Porterfield spanned a time of rather significant change in the life of the hall. Sorin had had five rectors in five years before we arrived. Continuity had been lost and the traditions being passed on were often negative ones. The building was dilapidated and certain forms of student misbehavior

contributed to its decline. In some ways, Sorin was out of control. We knew that what we did in our first year would be decisive for how subsequent years would unfold. Both of us were convinced that short-term confrontation might be necessary for long-term gain.

My personal strategy as a first-year assistant rector was to focus a disproportionate amount of time and energy on the entering freshmen while not neglecting the upperclass students. That was the year Sorin's version of Monk Hoops began, and I initiated the practice of taking freshmen out for dinner in groups of five. I wandered the dorm, stopping in student rooms, sitting on the porch, and otherwise signaled my interest and presence. I retired sometime between 2 and 3:00 a.m., which resulted in many late-night visits to my room by students who wanted a break from studies, some quick advice, or a friendly ear.

On weekends Dave and I tended to be around on both Friday and Saturday nights, especially from 9:00 p.m. on when most of the action took place. Whereas the returning students were accustomed to doing what they wanted after they figured the staff had retired for the evening, now they could never be sure. Between Dave and me, we were able to establish sufficient rapport with enough students that when something went wrong, we usually found out who had been involved. By the end of the spring semester we were confident that the hall was on the right track.

Parties and Alcohol

What were the issues that we had to face? The first, not surprisingly, was the widespread abuse of alcohol. In the days before more stringent campus alcohol policies were put in place, it was legal for underage students to drink, and many held happy hours on Friday afternoons and open bars with kegs on the weekends. Not every party got out of hand, yet enough did that we came to dread nights when a certain dynamic was underway. On more

than one occasion we had to deal with female students or visitors from town who had drunk so much on an empty stomach that we had to call an ambulance. (One such female visitor who weighed about 115 pounds consumed eleven vodkas with no food.) Some of the Sorin students would get belligerent and had to be restrained. Others would throw up in the bathroom or in their room.

Our first strategic move was to keep alcohol out of the common areas and hallways. Some of our interventions went smoothly enough, especially early in the evening, but others had a more confrontational air about them. Those were moments when I was happy to be taller than the average human and not easily intimidated. Then we began to deal with the parties in the turret rooms, where wall-to-wall people were simulating having a good time. When the word would go out to the women's dorms and Saint Mary's that there was a party in Sorin, they would come in waves. Our goal with regard to parties was not to curtail them but to limit their scale and disruptiveness.

Hall dances, when the whole common area of Sorin was converted into social space, were popular in those early years. The plan was to decorate the space according to some theme (the Roaring Twenties, Disco, Moulin Rouge) and hire a deejay. The attendees had to dress up and there had to be provision for food and non-alcoholic refreshments. Student Affairs required that in order to qualify as a dance, 70 percent or more of the hall residents had to agree to attend. This standard was hard to meet and often got fudged.

But the dances generally were less problematic than the room parties. The whole hall staff was present, most of the activity was out in the open, and the special nature of the event attracted enough solid citizens that a different tone was established. It was typical, for example, at the end of the evening to find cups here and there around the dorm that were three quarters full, usually because coeds feigned drinking and hid their cups behind the curtain or under a table. The biggest challenge with in-hall

dances came from the pre-dance parties in the rooms, where some tried to get a buzz on. When the night was finished, the women guests were gone, and nothing egregiously untoward had happened, the staff gave a deep sigh of relief. We had made it through another chapter in the rhythm of the school year.

Those who work in the disciplinary side of the Student Affairs office consistently claim that 90 percent of their worst cases are alcohol related. That is true in just about every institution of higher education and I am convinced there is no magic solution. Peer culture, the entertainment industry, huge advertising budgets, inconsistent law enforcement, parental ambiguity, and the loss of *in loco parentis* in most institutions—all these contribute to the issue. From my own undergraduate years when alcohol use and possession were forbidden on campus but still took place off campus, to my early years in Sorin, which had the most liberal set of policies and practices in the history of Notre Dame, to today, when the on-campus realities are much improved, I have seen firsthand how perplexing it is to chart the course that can have the best buy-in from students, parents, faculty, and alumni. There have been two major efforts at Notre Dame in the last two decades to deal openly and straightforwardly with the problem of alcohol. These efforts have sifted through data, listened to all sides, laid out a set of recommendations, and provided impetus to improve the overall health of the campus in this regard. We have made real progress, but each year a new group of seventeen and eighteen year olds join our community and we have to start all over again.

Most of the time, a fair number of our students are a joy to live with and stimulating to interact with. I feel that they have kept me young. The important thing for the staff is to constantly remind ourselves that we cannot allow the misbehavior of a few to sour us on the whole group. The same individuals who sometimes drank too much often were otherwise excellent students, regulars at hall worship, involved in a wide variety of activities, and generally polite and respectful. We had to help them grow up.

Drugs on Campus

Even in the late 1960s and early 1970s, Notre Dame never had a substantial drug culture. Some students experimented with marijuana and some tried mushrooms or LSD, but few ever ventured as far as heroin, cocaine, or crack cocaine. Even today, when various forms of methamphetamine are ravaging the country, very few cases have surfaced here. When any form of drug use is discovered—and more so for drug dealing—we respond vigorously. The most visible incidents of this only appear in the press when student-athletes are involved, yet the student body as a whole knows what the standards are.

In dorm life, marijuana use has been the most prevalent drug issue. In a hall like Sorin it is hard to keep things secret, and if a couple of roommates are smoking pot, the word eventually gets out. Their peers give them nicknames or incorporate them into their humor, and the users try to mask their behavior by burning scented candles (a telltale sign) or smoking blunt cigars with the pot stuffed inside or escaping to an obscure area down by the lakes. Sometimes they are difficult to catch in the act, although first-time users often are so stupid that they almost demand attention.

In my early years in Sorin, a student down the corridor from me, who was called Mad Dog by the other students, had a reputation as a user. Every time he called attention to himself by cranking up his stereo too loud, I would visit his room alert for evidence of drug paraphernalia or suspicious odors but I never found any. One day, I had a knock on my door from a non-student from town who asked if I was Mad Dog and proceeded to offer to sell me drugs. I yelled at him to get out of the hall and told him if he were not gone in five minutes, I would call the cops. That was confirmation that Mad Dog's reputation was probably well earned.

Many years later, following a talk I gave on one of the nationwide reports I had chaired on substance abuse among teenagers, I stayed around to chat with anyone who had a follow-up ques-

tion. Five or six people were in line. At the very end a man asked me if I recognized him. I said he looked vaguely familiar. He informed me that he used to be called Mad Dog and he had been one of my problem cases in Sorin. He went on to say he had met a wonderful woman, gotten married, had a family, and was now working in a Chicago area high school as a substance abuse educator and counselor. His parting words were that we should never give up the fight in the dorms to promote healthy lifestyles and to hold students accountable for their behavior. That encounter was totally unexpected but reinforcing of the day-to-day work that goes on in the student residences.

Life in an Undergraduate Dorm

Just before commencement at the end of my first year in Sorin, I was sitting in my second-floor room with the windows open when I dimly heard what sounded like the voice of an older woman. I did not pay the sound much attention, but gradually I began to pick up bits and pieces of what sounded like a semi-pornographic audio tape, and I decided to investigate. I made my way to the first floor and quietly crept close to the porch. In the study lounge just off the porch, someone had set up a tape deck. Two seniors were sitting outside on the porch rockers, listening to the tape. I considered my options and decided to strip the tape off the machine and walk away without saying a word. I was sure that the two students were going to have some uncomfortable days worrying whether they would be graduating with their class.

The afternoon after the commencement exercises, one of the men who had been on the porch approached me, with the confidence of someone no longer a student, and asked quietly, "Whatever happened to the tape?" With a twinkle in my eye, I responded "What tape?" And that was the end of the incident.

Another time, a group of first-year students put out an invitation to a party for a mock honorary fraternity. I looked out of

my room and saw one of the group dancing down the corridor, facing the other direction, holding a bottle of vodka above his head. I could see right away it was just a student prank and none of them were inebriated, so I made my way silently in their direction, took the bottle from the student's hand, and without saying a word went back to my room and closed the door. Once again I was sure they all would worry about the repercussions. I knew, however, that I had their attention and that was all I wanted. Nothing ever came of the incident, although years later it was still fresh in the participants' memories.

In the year after Paul Fenlon had to move out of the first-floor turret and before I moved down from the second floor, we used Paul's two rooms as study space for the students. One of the really nice guys in the first year came to my room seeking help with a paper, but I was busy and asked him where I could find him a bit later. He said he would be working in the two-room study lounge. About thirty minutes later, I walked downstairs and knocked on the outer door. Hearing no response, I went in and opened the second door. There was the student lying on the bed with his shirt off and with a coed astraddle him, giving him a back massage. (This particular coed had developed a reputation for hanging around the dorm and seeking attention.) I announced my presence, to their shock, by saying I was now ready to read the student's paper up in my room. And I left.

It took only a minute or two before both of them showed up in my room, panicky and worried about what I would think of them. I really had not seen anything that unusual; it was the setting and the element of surprise that grabbed my attention. I decided to pass on helping with the paper, partially to ease the male student's embarrassment. He went on to be a solid citizen in the dorm, a postgraduate volunteer with impoverished people, a leader in social justice ministry, and a loving husband and father. The young woman was never again seen in the dorm.

Not all student pranks were harmless. One Saturday before Sacred Heart Church was air-conditioned, all the church win-

dows were open on a warm spring afternoon. I was in my room reading when I heard an extremely loud stereo blasting from a Sorin window on the side facing the church. It did not take much effort to find the offending room, since its door was partly open. Inside were two seniors who apparently had decided to disrupt one of the weddings going on in the church. Perhaps it was their way of defending their bachelor status, or the devil made them do it, or whatever. I burst into the room and in no uncertain terms ordered them to turn off the machine, then administered a meet-the-Lord type of talk. I am sure they got the point, especially when I said that Father Porterfield would be meeting with them after the staff gathering on Sunday night.

Around that same time we had a problem with someone putting racially insensitive remarks on the bulletin board outside the hall janitor's basement room. We simply were not going to put up with such a thing, but the problem was how to catch whoever was doing it. One evening, almost by accident, I decided to walk downstairs to the basement using a route that took me past the bulletin board. Lo and behold, I saw a student chatting and laughing with one of his friends while actually composing one of the notes. They were so preoccupied that they did not see me come up behind them. Not until the message was completed did the writer turn around . . . and there I was. He knew right away that he had been caught in the act and that the repercussions would be severe. I simply walked away while the two of them stood there befuddled.

Dave Porterfield got the idea in our first year together that we should initiate an annual pig roast for the residents of the hall. I had no idea then that it takes twenty-four hours to properly cook a pig, and the preparation of the pig and the coals is time consuming as well. I was not directly involved in the events leading up to the roast, so I went to the first fest full of anticipation. When the crowd arrived, the meat was not ready and we had to order pizzas delivered. The students did not seem to care one way or another.

The second year's pig roast went smoothly and seemed well on its way to becoming an annual hall event. Unfortunately, the year after Dave stepped down as rector, some students tried to keep the tradition alive and ordered a couple of kegs of beer to liven up the celebration. Campus security raided the event, seized the kegs (which were illegal in public areas of the campus), and shut down the party. That was the end of the pig roast tradition.

Frosh Commandments

In my second Sorin year I developed a presentation I called "The Ten Commandments for Freshmen." It went this way:

(1) *Never eat dinner alone.* The first days and weeks on campus can be a time of anxiety and potential loneliness. Since meals are essentially social occasions, it is important that new students either go to the dining hall with their roommate(s) or hallmates, or gravitate to a table where they are more likely to see a friendly face. If the temperamentally shy eat alone, it may quickly seem that everyone else already has a network of friends. (Years later students told me how important they found this commandment to be.)

(2) *Find a quiet place.* A good percentage of our students never had to share a bedroom growing up, and they can find it a difficult adjustment to share space with one or more roommates. It is necessary for first-year students to look for nooks and crannies around the campus that they can claim as their own. The Grotto, the hall chapel, study carrels, walks around the lakes, a favorite bench, and even an empty classroom can serve in this capacity.

(3) *Don't be afraid to cry.* This is especially important for male undergraduates, who may fear that any display of deep emotion is feminine or will hurt their reputations. In fact, a good cry can be a great release, whether it occurs in private or in the company of a trusted friend. One of the great things about college is that individuals may discover inner resources they never realized that they possessed.

(4) *Be proud of your family.* Notre Dame people constantly talk about the University as a family or a community, and that is exactly what it aspires to be. Yet one must never leave behind one's attachments to, or deep involvement with, one's natural family. At best the University creates a second family away from home. Being proud of one's family (with all of the uniqueness and even idiosyncrasies of its members) means that extraneous differences like wealth, levels of education, or cultural heritage are relatively unimportant.

(5) *Learn all the names.* One of the signals to a first-year student that he or she has found a home in the dorm is that the rector and head staff already recognize them by name and sight when they arrive. It is incumbent on frosh in turn to get to know each other and, eventually, to work hard on learning the names of their upperclass hallmates as well. That is the great value of the ID photographs placed in the glass cabinets on the first floor.

(6) *Don't settle for your present group of friends.* It is important to be reminded that proximity is not destiny. First-year students have no control over who their roommate(s) will be or their next door neighbors or whom they are in class with or are thrown together with in campuswide activities. They need to start somewhere in building a social life and creating a friendship group. However, with the passage of time they will have choices to make — about future roommates, about whom they will date, about who will bring out the best (or worst) in them. By graduation time, each student will have established his or her own world at Notre Dame. From my experience, the choices they make along the way about their central support groups will influence the kind of person they become.

(7) *Don't confuse your GPA with your self-worth.* Notre Dame students are generally bright, industrious, creative, hardworking, and aspirational. Most do well academically, but for those who know failure and disappointment in a class, the blow can be difficult. This commandment can be read both ways. If you have done more poorly in your classes than you hoped to, there are other

dimensions of your life that are equally important. If you have succeeded well from day one and your GPA reflects it, there is no reason for excessive pride or gloating. The real test comes in how this foundation is used to good purposes after graduation.

(8) *Get active early.* Some parents and high school counselors advise first-year students to focus on their classes and avoid extracurricular involvement. I have never accepted the wisdom of this advice. Almost all incoming Notre Dame students have been involved in multiple activities in high school, from sports and cheerleading to student government, band, theater, newspaper, or service clubs. They have learned the skill of multitasking and are adept at shifting gears frequently. I do not think it is appropriate to go from heavy levels of extracurricular involvement to relative inactivity. My observation is that many of those who follow this path end up wasting oodles of time playing video games or in other forms of unproductive labor.

(9) *Listen to alumni stories patiently.* For the residents of Sorin, with its steady stream of visitors, especially on football weekends, it requires a certain learned patience to deal with the plethora of reminiscences evoked by graduates returning to the dorm of their youth. This might apply to parents' reminiscences as well, now that both could be graduates. The best way for the freshman to handle it is to ask oneself: how would I like to be treated in thirty years when I retell the stories and exploits of my undergrad days? Go and do likewise.

(10) *Study, worship, socialize, exercise, serve.* This commandment cheats a bit in its general spirit of admonition, but it does suggest that a true Notre Dame education includes serious academic engagement, time for God, relaxation and fun, a sound body, and committed attention to the needs of others, both on and off the campus. Each of these focal points is important in its own right, but it is the combination that best develops the student's character and prepares him or her for a full and meaningful life.

One of the memorable hall residents of Sorin came from Europe and presented himself as a person of refined tastes and

distinguished bearing. Eventually he revealed that his roots were in Russia and he was descended from the Romanovs and the royal family. I was never quite clear about the degree of propinquity, though. He always struck me as somewhat odd, especially in the Notre Dame setting where little attention is usually given to family wealth or pedigree. In any case, he moved off campus in junior year and invited me to his apartment for dinner. I noticed that his china and silverware all carried the royal seal of the tsars and tsarinas, that his residence was full of books, art objects, and memorabilia from pre-Revolutionary Russia, and that he was seriously awaiting the fall of Communism and the re-establishment of the royal family. He seemed to think that, as a priest and an opponent of godless Communism, I would welcome the return of the old order. The truth was, I did not know what to say. I continue to wonder what he is up to and whether he is playing a role in the new Russia.

Over the summer of 1983, we had to send out a letter to the residents informing them that one of the 1982–83 residents in the dorm had taken his life while on summer vacation. After finishing his first year at Notre Dame, this student had decided to transfer to a school in the Colorado state system to major in electrical engineering. I knew him but not well. He seemed not to want to be at Notre Dame and was somewhat anxious in general, but I had no sense that his problems were anything more than transition stress for the son of a Notre Dame grad. The funeral had already been set up before any of us learned of the boy's death, and none of the staff was able to attend. We did speak with the parents on the phone and sent flowers.

Suicide is rare at Notre Dame, thank God. Still, there are always students who live with psychological problems which may lead them to express suicidal thoughts. We are blessed to have an excellent psychological counseling center on campus where we can send students for evaluation and therapy. For a priest, sometimes there is no clear dividing line between the psychological and the spiritual. In counseling students myself, I usually trust

my instincts to know when I am beyond my personal competence and require the assistance of others with specialized training.

One member of Sorin's freshman class in 1985–86 was Dan Barrett, a positive and upbeat person with a great sense of humor who was legally blind. In his classes he would use note takers, but he was also blessed with a great memory. He read books in Braille and also used student readers. To negotiate the campus, Dan used a cane but not a Seeing Eye dog. He memorized the basic campus routes back and forth to Sorin. It was always inspiring to see him walking around as though he had not a care on his mind. Like most blind people, he relied on his power of hearing to distinguish one person from another by their voices. Dan and I hit it off from the start and we had some great conversations through the year. After graduation he went on to graduate school in the history of science.

In the 1987–88 academic year, a young man from Chicago named Chris Zorich was a member of the freshman class. A soft-spoken football player who struggled with a slight stutter, he seemed to like living in Sorin and we hit it off early on. As a freshman he never played in a game—his claim to fame that year was that he was the only freshman I took to Bruno's Pizza restaurant who came close to finishing all the food. On more than one occasion, I had the chance to meet Chris's mother, who came across as a salt-of-the-earth ethnic white woman. Chris's father was black but he had left the family when Chris was young.

In his sophomore year Chris did not play either. I remember asking Coach Lou Holtz whether he would ever play, and he told me that before Chris graduated he would become an All-American. Not only did Chris fulfill that prophecy, but he went on to great success in the NFL as a member of the Chicago Bears. After Chris's mother died suddenly, he became devoted to charitable ventures in her honor in the city of Chicago. Later he completed Notre Dame Law School. I have subsequently viewed Chris as an example of how, in a student's first year of college, no one really knows what may be in store. Chris struggled against the

odds both academically and athletically at Notre Dame, and his success is a story worth celebrating.

President in Residence

The academic year 1986–87 was a momentous one for me. The trustees were moving forward on the selection of a new president, and the determination would be made in November. The first part of that fall semester was probably the last time in my Sorin years when I could still say I knew most of the residents by name. When it was publicly announced that I had been elected the president of Notre Dame, the residents of Sorin Hall seemed to take a special pride in knowing me and having me as a hall-mate. To my surprise, they hung a congratulatory banner across the top of the Sorin porch. In my new role I needed to devote my-self wholeheartedly to preparing for administrative responsibili-ties, yet insofar as I could, I still celebrated liturgies in the hall, played Monk Hoops, and took freshmen out to dinner. I still wel-comed visitors to my room and I continued to teach, yet I could not pretend that everything was the same.

It was widely predicted that I would not continue living in Sorin as president. No previous Notre Dame leader had ever cho-sen to live in a residence hall, but one reason was that all the ear-lier presidents but one also served as local superior. Only when Ted Hesburgh was coming up on his sixth year as president were the two roles separated out, because the then operative code of canon law limited local superiors to one six-year term. In addi-tion, the prevailing wisdom was that the president needed to live somewhat apart from the demands of undergraduate residence life, with its late hours, weekend noise, and easy accessibility.

Yet I never contemplated leaving the hall. I was comfortable in Sorin, I liked its size, its sense of tradition, and its convenience to Corby Hall and the Main Building. I also wanted to model what I understood to be the fundamental charism of the Holy Cross

apostolate of higher education, namely that we would engage in multiple activities simultaneously. I desired to be a president-teacher-pastor-liturgical leader all at once, although I knew that the proportion of time I spent on each would have to change. I sensed that my continued involvement in the life of the hall would provide a good balance once I geared up to my full presidential responsibilities.

The men of Sorin Hall were invited to the major public events of my inauguration, and many of them came. That was a time when members of my natural family, my Holy Cross family, and my Sorin family had a rare convergence. One interesting dimension of living as president on the first floor of Sorin was that I was theoretically available to anyone who chose to knock on my door. I maintained my custom of hanging a hand-written "welcome" sign at times when I did not have other matters to attend to. At first, a few students delighted in testing out the invitation, but over time most of the Sorinites respected my need for privacy.

My Sorin telephone number was listed, however, and a few times I received late-night calls from individuals with one concern or another. One was a man, usually intoxicated, who wanted to vent about Notre Dame athletics, primarily football. Another was a woman who periodically got upset about matters connected to Notre Dame's religious mission and identity. In these cases, after patiently responding several times I decided that nothing productive was taking place, so I just hung up. Eventually they stopped calling. The most perplexing calls were wrong numbers. I did not usually identify myself until I knew who was on the line, and although I wanted to be helpful, I also wanted to keep the conversation brief. The callers quickly discovered that I was not the power plant or the laundry or campus security. It was only when the same caller rang back a few seconds later that I had to kick the information flow to the next level.

In my years as president, I tried not to make the rector's job more difficult, either by getting in the way or seeming to be judgmental. I never prowled the hall or looked for trouble. Students

who observed my daily patterns knew that I generally used the front door or the back door near Corby Hall, so if I ran into them by accident when they were doing something untoward, it was their fault and not mine. Now that I am president-emeritus with no formal responsibility for residence life, I presume I am even less problematic to my co-residents.

Sometimes I think I am underutilized now, but most days I am sure I have struck the right balance. I am part of what makes Sorin distinctive. I am referred to by the student tour guides when they walk by, regaling visitors with tidbits about the Notre Dame environment. While my level of involvement and my concrete presence are much reduced from my early years, my guts tell me that if it came to a vote of the hall students, I would still receive strong support to keep living in room 141 for the foreseeable future. As long as that remains the case, I am so inclined.

My earliest four years on the Sorin staff were the closest I ever came to realizing my own ideals for residence-hall ministry as a priestly presence, counselor, and friend. Once I became an administrator, I never again had the necessary control over my schedule to be present to a broad cross section of the students entrusted to my care. After the 1982–83 school year, my priorities were directed more to administration and teaching and somewhat less to dorm life. Nevertheless, I still cherished my role as Sorin's priest in residence and I continued some of my traditional practices, such as Monk Hoops, celebrating hall masses, and offering assistance with student papers. Yet to this day I miss the raw, firsthand exposure to the dynamics of hall life and the intimate (sometimes too intimate) exposure to the saga of young adults coming into their own.

In retrospect, my years in Sorin Hall have gone quickly. As far as I know, after Paul Fenlon I am the longest-lived resident of Sorin in its history. In a sense, I have replaced him as a grandfather figure and source of continuity.

As Teacher and Priest

It is difficult to say how the years we spend as students lead eventually to the vocational call that opens the possibility of becoming teachers ourselves. I was blessed with generally fine instructors all the way. In Saint Anthony's Grade School in Washington, I was taught by sisters of the Benedictine Order. Sister Eleanor, my teacher in the fourth, fifth, and sixth grades, had a special influence on my development as a learner. At each step in primary school I experienced the joy of discovery and the importance of self-discipline, though I was not fully aware of these lessons at the time.

At Archbishop John Carroll High School, my teachers were Augustinian priests and brothers. They demanded good deportment and set the bar high in the classroom. No one could get by with a half effort. As time went on, I was encouraged by individual professors and school administrators to aspire to achievement. I began to take it for granted that not only would I be the first in my family to attend college, but I could qualify to attend some of the best schools in the country. When I accepted a scholarship offer from Notre Dame for basketball, I was confident that I was well prepared and that higher education would open up new possibilities for me.

Despite a rocky first year, including being in the wrong area of study, I really blossomed at Notre Dame as someone excited

about learning. I read widely, I kept up on national and world events, I became interested in film, theater, and music, I was exposed to other cultures and ways of life, and I began to refine my personal vocational options. Most of my professors were encouraging, and some were inspirational. I sensed that the mix of responsibilities of a university faculty member was quite attractive. I liked the idea of becoming an expert in a field of study, of testing my insights and opinions with peers and students, and of interacting on a regular basis with bright and talented young people from diverse backgrounds. I enjoyed writing and public speaking, and I had held enough leadership roles by that time to have confidence in my ability to oversee a common project.

As an undergraduate, I knew little about graduate school or GREs or thesis defenses; I was preoccupied simply by the notion of someday becoming a professor in an institution like Notre Dame. When I decided to enter the seminary, one of the roles I saw myself playing after ordination was to combine full-time teaching along with hall ministry and some administrative responsibilities. I felt that my opportunity to become a priest-teacher would be maximized in the Holy Cross community, especially compared to the diocesan clergy.

While I was studying theology in Washington, I taught at a Catholic girls' high school in the Maryland suburbs. The course content was not particularly demanding; most of the challenges had to do with the students' lack of motivation. After one semester I decided to change apostolates and work with the mentally ill at Saint Elizabeth's mental hospital.

The first teaching experience I had that was akin to what I would be doing later took place in my deacon year at Notre Dame when I lived in Flanner Hall and taught six sections of a "Problem of Evil" seminar under the auspices of the theology department, an experience that proved to be a concentrated, challenging, and rewarding test of my capacities as a college teacher. By the end of it, I was certain that this was an extremely attractive form of activity.

My second teaching experience at the college level took place at Aquinas Junior College in Nashville, Tennessee, where I taught a class on "Issues in Christian Ethics." Most of the students were adult learners who had raised families or held full-time jobs. They were not as bright as Notre Dame students, but their life experiences and worldly wisdom led to great discussions. Since I have spent most of my teaching career in relatively elite circumstances, the time at Aquinas is a good reminder that in much of higher education, students are not well prepared and may be balancing full-time jobs and family responsibilities with the pursuit of a degree. They too deserve the very best the American professoriat has to offer.

My last teaching experience before I formally joined the Notre Dame faculty was a course in Christian ethics that I team-taught at Notre Dame with Stan Hauerwas in 1974. Stan was responsible for the course structure, testing, and grades. My function was to share some of the lecturing with him and to challenge him with regard to methodological issues and concrete application.

Stan was then, as he is today, bright, aggressive, strong willed, foulmouthed, and crowd provoking. A Methodist by heritage, he developed into a Christian pacifist with a manifest counterculture critique of American society and of the role of the Christian churches within it. I, on the other hand, was a mainstream, progressively oriented Catholic with an interest in natural law theory and the evolution of Catholic moral tradition. The students in the class had probably never before taken a course in which two professors disagreed so frequently and with such conviction. I was pleased to be able to hold my own in such a context with one of the dominant figures in the theology department.

In the Classroom

When my formal teaching career at Notre Dame began in the 1974–75 academic year, I prepared assiduously for my first round

of classes. Like most new faculty members coming out of graduate school, my head was filled with theories and the names of prominent figures in Christian ethics. I could summarize papal documents and list the major differences among Catholic, Protestant, and Orthodox approaches to divorce and remarriage and other such topics. I was familiar with Freud, Jung, and Adler, Weber and Durkheim, Adam Smith and Milton Friedman. I could distinguish among types of justice and interpret the biblical texts that seemed relevant to discussions about whether or not there is a distinctively Christian ethics. What was uncertain was how I would construct courses that hung together from beginning to end and were geared to reach the students entrusted to my care.

I knew I could be an effective lecturer, yet I also wanted to engage the students in classroom discussions. In my first few semesters, especially at the undergraduate level, I discovered that I needed to set time aside for analysis and debate of concrete cases. Although this ate into my lecture time a bit, it proved to be a good format for maximizing student attentiveness. In my Master of Divinity program courses, I always tried to gear the material for potential use in pastoral settings. That way I sought to bridge the potential separation between theological theory and ecclesial application. My status as a priest-teacher active in various ministries at Notre Dame gave me a certain credibility with the students as well as providing fodder for my own reflection.

When it came to testing, I gravitated to a structure of two tests, one research paper at the undergraduate level, and a long research paper, a written mid-semester exam, and an oral final exam at the M. Div. level. Only later did I begin teaching doctoral courses, which based grades almost exclusively on a long research paper at the end.

When I was assigned introductory courses with undergraduates, I discovered a range of student backgrounds as expected. Some had gone to Catholic primary and secondary schools or had taken several years of catechetical courses. Others either had no formal religious training beyond what their parents taught them,

or they were effectively unchurched. The challenge for me was to find common ground that did not insult the intelligence of the well prepared or overreach the capacities of those starting from scratch. Fortunately, in the middle to late 1970s, students at Notre Dame were hungry to be better informed about the rudiments of their faith. They wanted a religious education comparable in quality to the rest of their academic experience.

The seminarians and lay ministerial students in the 400- and 500-level courses were also a mixed bag. Some had majored in philosophy or theology or had taken additional electives as undergraduates because of their vocational interests. Others had studied in secular universities and had taken no theology since high school, if then. It was complicated at times to sort out vocational questions from academic ones.

Perhaps the biggest temptation afflicting new faculty is to think that, because the students are so bright, they must know more than they actually do. While our students are quite strong academically, they lack a detailed, theoretically sound familiarity with a sub-specialty like Christian ethics. But they do have the inherent capacity to learn quickly, and it is the hope-filled task of the professor to nourish this capacity and even, God willing, to make it enjoyable.

When I began teaching, the standard classload in the College of Arts and Letters was three courses each semester. Years later this was reduced to two courses, an expensive change but one that was necessary to improve the research environment to become more competitive with peer institutions. One way to keep down class preparation time in a three-course system was to allow professors to teach two sections of the same course. Another was to make graduate students available as teaching assistants to grade tests and lead discussion groups. The only time I used teaching assistants, however, was during a semester when I taught an undergraduate course for 273 students. Otherwise I have always corrected all my own tests and papers. Even in that mega-course, I read all the ten-page research papers.

The biggest problem that first year occurred in the fall semester when my two undergraduate sections were made up almost entirely of senior engineers completing their theology requirement. Many of them had low levels of motivation, and writing was not their strong suit. Another handicap was that I was an unknown teacher, and those who signed up were attracted exclusively by the days and the time slot of the course. Only after developing a "reputation" (both in the classroom and later in the dorm) did I begin attracting students who really chose a course because I was the teacher.

During my years as a regular faculty member, I kept refining both the content and the structure of my undergraduate courses. I quickly became convinced that my students should be exposed to some of the most perplexing and interesting areas of contemporary ethical discussion, both within the context of the Catholic Church and in the broader society. As a result, I focused on four problem areas—biomedical ethics, abortion, sexuality, and violence. In lectures, I tried to provide solid theoretical and historical background, including the different approaches among the Christian denominations when there were any. In their research papers students had an opportunity to test out the material presented to them. Among the topics they chose to write about over the years were abortion, euthanasia, nuclear war, premarital sex, women in the Church, homosexuality, behavior control, abolitionism, pacifism, capital punishment, divorce and remarriage, contraception, censorship, organ donation, eugenics, marriage, cloning, papal social encyclicals, sex education, funeral practices, drug addiction, suicide, prostitution, masturbation, military chaplains, pornography, fetal experimentation, labor strikes, prison reform, aging, overpopulation, disarmament, alcoholism, thalidomide babies, torture, mental retardation, priestly celibacy, racism, AID/AIH, and multinational corporations.

Generally, their papers were well done. Sometimes they had strong personal tone, as when their parents had been through a divorce and remarriage, or they had a mentally handicapped rela-

tive, or they were struggling with an uncertain sexual identity. Those who were planning to be doctors might choose a topic in biomedical ethics because it was pertinent to their future, while those in ROTC might want to examine Christian teaching on war and peace.

I always made an effort to lecture about Catholic moral content straightforwardly, distinguishing established Church teaching from contemporary debates among theologians. That was where my historical orientation was helpful. Some of the issues we discussed are never directly referred to in Scripture—like organ transplantation, nuclear war, and cloning. At best, there are texts that suggest the centrality of certain operative values, such as justice or respect for life or marital fidelity. One reason why teaching such a course was so much fun was that the students tended to be inherently interested in the issues we studied. Another was that we know so much more scientifically now about the structure and processes of the human body and the social, political, and economic forces that affect human decision making and behavior.

Of all the teaching devices I used in my undergraduate ethics classes, none was more memorable than the sex quiz I gave on the first day of treating human sexuality as a theme. I would break the class up into small groups, and then establish the operative standard—"acceptable behavior for mature adults acting responsibly." I deliberately asked them to refrain from applying any religiously derived criteria so they could not retreat into "the Bible says"; my objective was for them to take a kind of "natural law" approach. Next I would give them a series of polysyllabic terms with Latin and Greek roots that describe various forms of sexual activity. In mixed male and female groups they had to come to some consensus, and if they did not know the meaning of a term, they had to send up the group leader to ask me what it meant. The purpose of the exercise was serious, but there was always humor, as when the leaders returned to their groups to report that necrophilia meant having sexual relations with a corpse and coprophilia

referred to using excrement for sexual excitation. I would soon be hearing the "ughs" and "ohmygods." Just about every group I taught arrived at a consensus that certain forms of sexual behavior, according to the mature adult standard, were *not* acceptable. Most importantly, that was their conclusion long before I moved on to discuss particular topics in class.

In the spring semester of 1977 I created a new undergraduate course titled "Christian Ethics in America." It allowed me to broaden the range of topics we covered and to tie in some of my life experiences, especially the civil rights movement. The course began with some perspectives from the sociology of religion and then moved to a quick summary of the history of the Protestant churches and the Catholic Church in this country. After this background, I turned to the problem of race, viewing the abolitionist movement with its opposition to slavery as the fount of subsequent reform movements, such as temperance and prohibition, feminism, the labor movement, and the Social Gospel movement. In the last third of the course, I discussed Reinhold Niebuhr and Christian Realism, John Courtney Murray and religious liberty, and civil religion, with a concluding section on nuclear war and crime and punishment.

To be teaching Christian ethics (or Catholic moral theology) in the mid-1970s was exciting for me. In the Catholic world prior to Vatican II, moral theology had been the least reformed area of theology. It was too legalistic, too removed from its biblical roots, and too removed from developments in the human and social sciences. The world of Catholic moral theologians was made up almost entirely of priests (which meant all males), and the widespread use of Latin in seminary courses and in textbooks rendered the field unavailable to the average Catholic lay person. In seminary courses the instructors were preoccupied with the sacrament of penance and discourses about sin, the types of sin, and the role of the confessor in relationship to the penitent. Much attention was focused on sexual morality, and important areas of social ethics were treated only in passing.

When Vatican II called for a concentrated effort to renew moral theology, the burgeoning of the field began as I was preparing to be ordained and going to graduate school at Vanderbilt. I was part of the first generation of Catholic scholars with an interest in ethics to do doctoral work at a historically Protestant divinity school. The general conviction at the time was that Christian ethics (the Protestant terminology) was further developed methodologically than was Catholic moral theology. So it made sense for me, having already been immersed in Catholic theology in my seminary years, to broaden my horizons in a different social and theological context.

When I returned from Vanderbilt, I was even more deeply rooted in the Catholic tradition (an experience not dissimilar from traveling to another country and culture and discovering how American you are), but I was also deeply affected by what I had studied and learned in my doctoral work. For example, Protestant ethicists (except for some evangelicals) had long ago abandoned proof-texting as an acceptable mode of scriptural application to ethical analysis, while Catholic moral literature was rampant with such arguments. In addition, Protestant thinkers were more consistent in their use of findings from psychology, sociology, economics, and medicine. It was no longer going to be fruitful for Catholic moral theologians to draw upon outdated biological theories or to fail to take into account extant debates about the influence of nature and nurture. I felt when I returned to Notre Dame that I was part of a worldwide effort to rethink every dimension of Catholic moral theology, at both the theoretical and practical levels.

I savored the spirit of exploration, hypothesis formation, and rethinking and reformulation that was underway. Inevitably, not all of the reflections would prove valuable, even in the short run. I saw that as simply a part of the process of intellectual debate and of the testing out of approaches in the daily lives of the community of believers. The greatest fear of more conservative elements in the Catholic Church was that the teaching office of the

Church (concentrated for them in the role of the pope and bishops) would be stripped of its ability to function. The debate over contraception and *Humanae Vitae* would become a centerpiece of this concern.

By the mid-1970s some of the ferment had lessened. Yet moral theology (along with ecclesiology) was a branch of theology where discussions could take on an all-or-nothing air, where some liberal elements in the Church were calling for reforms comparable to what took place in the Protestant Reformation, and where some conservative elements wanted to return to what they viewed as the safe and comfortable pre–Vatican II world.

I was not without a personal point of view about the topics I taught in class. I saw myself as a progressive, Vatican II Catholic with deep loyalty to the Church and great respect for its fund of wisdom. I brought a strong ecumenical orientation after my days at Vanderbilt and a conviction that rigorous research, open dialogue, and sensitive attention to feedback from the faithful would lead us to a new era in Catholic moral theology. In my classes and my writings, I wanted to both contribute to the ongoing conversation and prepare my students for the increasingly complicated task of living by the highest moral standards in their daily lives and responsibilities.

Whenever I covered a topic, I always sought to present the most mainstream Catholic position before exposing the students to comparative perspectives from other Christian or non-Christian churches, and before laying out the contemporary debate (often of a reformist nature) among Catholic moral theologians. When asked, I would share my own point of view, but I tried to avoid using the classroom as a forum for fostering my view of the world.

The 1976–77 academic year was the last time I taught a full courseload. In the summer of 1977, I became the M. Div. director, and my administrative responsibilities meant a one-course reduction each semester. This was welcome as I set about learning the nature of my new job. Nevertheless, I was not ready to give

up my teaching opportunities, though I had no idea then that I would never again be a full-time faculty member.

In the spring of 1978 I taught for a second time the doctoral-level course on methodology, this time focusing on contemporary Roman Catholic methodological debates. I also redirected the course away from the usual model for a doctoral class. Instead of a final research paper and no exams, I asked each student to write a one- to two-page critical review of each of the assigned books (ranging from Aquinas to Charles Curran) to be turned in on the day of the discussion. Each student was also to undertake selected bibliographical research, and the concluding activity was an oral final exam. With eight students in the class, each one had to be ready to contribute every time we met.

During the 1979–80 academic year, when I returned to the campus from my Berkeley sabbatical, moved into Sorin Hall, and resumed my duties as M. Div. director, I once again taught one undergrad and one grad course each semester. In the summer of 1981 when I became vice president and associate provost, I needed to shift my daily schedule in order to be more involved in a variety of campus-wide activities, travel more extensively, and (most important of all) prepare myself as one of the candidates to succeed Ted Hesburgh as president. Nevertheless, I desired to teach at least one class. There was no articulated expectation from the board of trustees or from my immediate boss, Tim O'Meara, that I remain active in the classroom. Yet they did not oppose my academic involvement as long as I got my other work done. In fact, it became a point of pride in the provost office that I had regular, firsthand contact with students in the classroom.

In 1982–83 I taught Introduction to Theology both semesters, with 50 students in the fall and 101 in the spring. For the first time I passed out a data sheet in the opening class which inquired about the religious affiliation of the student and both of his or her parents. I also asked about the students' formal religious training, and whether they would classify themselves religiously as

conservative, moderate, or liberal. This data turned out to be a treasure trove in helping to plan my presentations in the course. It was also a reminder that none of us on the faculty could take for granted the religiously relevant circumstances from which our students come to us.

I also gave the students a quick quiz on Christian knowledge, asking them to define, among other things, the Seven Deadly Sins; the Seven Gifts of the Holy Spirit; the Sacraments; the Stations of the Cross; the Ten Commandments; the corporal and spiritual works of mercy; the mysteries of the Rosary; one distinctive teaching of Mormons, Seventh Day Adventists, Greek Orthodox, Pentecostal Church, Quakers, and so on. As might be expected, even those students who had enjoyed twelve years of Catholic education before Notre Dame did not display a broad fund of knowledge about such matters. Part of the reason was the de-emphasis on memorizing formulaic catechetical answers that occurred in the wake of the Vatican II reforms. This test revealed a lack of general knowledge about Christianity in its Catholic and Protestant forms. As it turned out, however, the students were eager to learn and showed a willingness to be schooled in the richness of the tradition.

In the fall of 1986 when I became president-elect, it was a real challenge for me to finish the work of the semester. I had only until July 1, 1987, before assuming my new job, and there was much to do to prepare myself. Everyone on campus wanted my ear, and I was anxious to visit with well-respected sitting presidents at other schools to seek their advice and do some benchmarking. I decided that I should not teach in the spring.

Eventually, much as I wanted to keep alive my classroom contact with students, I determined that I would not teach during my first year as president either. I was resolute about returning to the classroom after that year, however. By the spring of 1988, it was time to construct a new course and get listed by the registrar's office so students could sign up for the next fall.

It seemed best not to go back to any of the undergraduate courses I had offered in the past. I felt I would be hard-pressed to keep up to date in theology and to deal with tests and papers. I wanted to move to a small class and a seminar format and decided to call upon my interest in literature and film. The First-Year Seminar required of all new students seemed a natural fit for my course. It was attractive because first-year students tend to be highly motivated, hardworking, somewhat dewy-eyed, and fun to be with. I chose Sunday evenings from 7:00 to 9:30 because Sunday was the best day of the week for me and the time was compatible with the 10:00 p.m. Sunday dorm liturgies.

One curious dimension of my choice was that the registrar at the time, who was somewhat officious, sent me a letter pointing out that Sunday night classes were not normally allowed, although he would (graciously) make an exception for me. When I told a few other administrators what he said, they laughed. For reasons not connected to this decision, the registrar moved on the following year.

As I took a pause in teaching that first year of my presidency, I could look back at what I had learned about pedagogy, about the makeup of our student body, and about the different skills teaching requires. At the undergraduate level I generally preferred to combine lectures with in-class discussions, usually employing concrete cases. I never lectured from a text or let myself be dependent on a rigid time scheme. I covered the material as well as I could, yet I was constantly looking for ways to relate to the students' interests, experiences, and concerns. I had an advantage over some disciplines since most of my students thought of ethics as practical, applied theology that took up issues they would have to grapple with anyway. I usually assigned seven or eight books and sometimes other readings as well.

The students were bright and generally hardworking, and I was comfortable with them completing the assignments. When it came to evaluating their performance, I found that three tests

spread through the semester was just about right. I always assigned a research paper (minimum ten pages) as well, which gave them the chance to look into the specialized literature, display their familiarity with the nature of the debate, and then argue for one position or another. In the later years, I started asking for a short reflective essay at the beginning of the course to give me an idea of what each student's basic value system looked like. I corrected all my own tests and papers.

At the M. Div. level, I designed my courses with future church ministry (both ordained and lay) in mind. I distributed outlines, passed out bibliographies, and otherwise sought to magnify the resources that I made available. I always gave an oral final, which could be intimidating for some—one time a high-strung diocesan seminarian got so lost in his oral final that he could not even tell me his name. When he ran out of the room and slammed the door, it took about a millisecond for the word to get around the seminary.

My doctoral seminars usually required a lot of reading and revolved around class discussion and a significant research paper. The big problem in the discussions was that some of the best students simply outshone the others. A great temptation for doctoral students was to take incompletes and finish their papers between semesters, a practice I always discouraged. They were better served by identifying a research topic early on and working on it systematically through the semester.

For the doctoral students in ethics, I was the major Catholic presence in those years. Stan Hauerwas (Methodist) and John Howard Yoder (Mennonite) were national and international names in the field and strong voices in the direction of the department; however, everyone on the faculty knew that we owed it to our students to provide a solid foundation in Catholic moral theology. For a while, Enda McDonaugh was on campus and was an additional Catholic voice in the broad field of ethics. Later, other hires brought a better balance in the ethics area.

Back in the classroom after my first presidential year, I began to develop the Sunday night seminar in terms of both content and pedagogical style. I did not want to lecture and I wanted to maximize student participation. I decided to divide the thirteen weeks of the semester in the following way: an introductory class (with strong emphasis on the members getting to know each other in a more than perfunctory fashion), ten content discussions (using eight texts and two films), and a closing session. Once I got into the rhythm of the semester, I went from controlling the conversations by trying to call on all the students in every class, to allowing a greater free flow among the members. I saw my role as eliciting reflections from the shy, a few of whom could go the whole semester without saying anything if I let them, and constraining the gregarious, who would dominate the analysis if given free rein.

I taught the seminar in the President's Conference Room in the Main Building. It was convenient for me and added a certain symbolic prestige to the gathering. In each session I took a fifteen-minute break around 8:30. This meant that we met for ninety minutes, had a fifteen-minute hiatus, and then finished with forty-five minutes of further conversation. To try to go two and a half hours without a break would be foolish. I usually went to my office during the break. I did that deliberately since the lull gave the students a good opportunity to chill out and chitchat among themselves.

Early on I decided to host a final dinner for the class, using a Notre Dame facility and having University Food Services cater so that I could foster a celebratory spirit for our last time together. After dinner I encouraged reflections by the students about what they had learned in their first semester or year of college, followed by game playing. My goal in the recreational part was to tap into their competitive spirit. After testing out various board games, I settled on "Scattergories," which was easy to learn and sufficiently goal oriented to allow the teams to vie for a mythical championship. By a quirk in the scoring basis, I used to push the

rules in favor of my team, making the other teams madder and madder. After a few years, I started bragging at the start of the competition that my team had never lost. This further stimulated the competitive juices.

The formal requirements of the course included writing ten regular papers of three pages and a final synthetic paper of five to seven pages that reviewed the semester's work. Each semester I established a theme that drove the choice of books and films. Some of the themes were "Cultural Diversity and Intercultural Experience," "Gender, Relationships, and Family" (the goal of this course was to "examine the notions of male/female as they influence patterns of human interaction"), and "The Stories of Peoples and Cultures."

Using new material each semester allowed me, over time, to magnify the range of authors and film directors that I drew upon. It also meant that my personal interest in the topics of our discussions was kept fresh. As I searched around for usable material, I became enamored with some authors and began working my way through their oeuvres. Among these were Willa Cather, Chinua Achebe, Carlos Fuentes, Graham Greene, Shusaku Endo, Nadine Gordimer, Walker Percy, Ruth Prawar Jhabvala, Anita Desai, Gail Tsukiyama, and Kazuo Ishiguro.

In the years that I taught seminars as president, I deliberately chose authors and films that emphasized developing a global vision. I also sought diversity in my class makeup. The combination of assigned materials and student heterogeneity led to the kind of interesting (and sometimes jarring) discussions that I was hoping for. I was able through those thirty-four semesters of seminars to focus on all of the inhabited continents and much else beside. In North America we read (or viewed) material set in Canada, Mexico, and the United States and we pursued issues relevant to the constituent American sub-groups—African American, Hispanic, Asian, and Native American. On the global front we examined both the colonist and aboriginal experiences in Australia and New Zealand. In Asia, our coverage included China,

Director of the College Seminary program, 1976–77

Delegate to the Provincial Chapter, 1976

Trip to the Holy Land; five men on a camel

Relaxing in my room in Sorin Hall

Bookstore
Basketball

With Mark Poorman,
good friend
and fellow
Holy Cross priest,
1984

A lively
discussion
with students

With Sorin seniors
Tom Conlin,
Steve Passinault,
and Lou Nanni,
good friends all

With Tim McOsker, Sorin resident,
whose marriage to Connie I celebrated
and whose professional career
eventually brought him back
to Notre Dame

With Maripat Loftus
(Gatter), former
student, who
became a friend of
my mother and
who invited me
to celebrate her
marriage to Rob

With Ann Pequet, future
spouse of Sorin resident
Jeff Rauh, a marriage
I celebrated

From the Press box at
Notre Dame Stadium with family:
(l. to r.) John Rorapaugh,
Maggie Long, Susan Long,
and Mary Long

Moe Ruggiero and
Angela Figliano at
the time of Moe's
graduation from
Notre Dame. Later
I would perform
their wedding in
Cleveland at a
wonderful Italian
celebration.

Sorin Hall provides moral support after my election as president.

A friendly visit to an area Boys & Girls Club

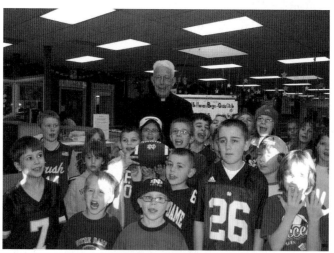

The children of South Haven, Michigan,
welcome me in Notre Dame regalia.

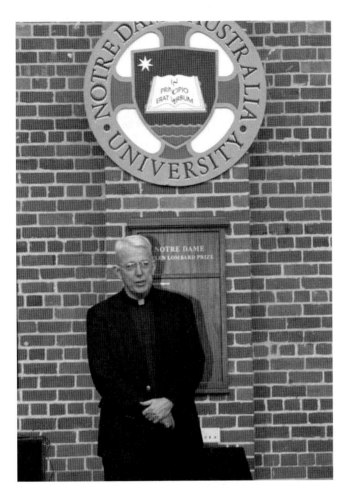

Addressing the
Board of Trustees
and the Governors
at Notre Dame
Australia.
Courtesy of Notre
Dame Archives.

Peter Tannock,
as vice chancellor
of the University of
Notre Dame Australia,
honors my contribution
to its establishment.
Courtesy of
Notre Dame Archives.

CASA's Nineteenth Anniversary Awards Dinner, May 2011.
"A Celebration of American Leadership in Combating Substance Abuse:
A Salute to Joseph Califano." With *(l. to r.)* Joseph A. Califano, Jr.,
Hilary P. Califano, and Anne Davis. Courtesy of the National Center on
Addiction and Substance Abuse at Columbia University.
Photo by Eric Weiss and John Calabrese.

Being welcomed by Pope John Paul II after Mass at the papal chapel
at the Vatican. Courtesy of Notre Dame Archives.

India, Japan, Korea, Indonesia, Vietnam, Burma, Hong Kong, and Bangladesh. In Latin America, we looked at material from Chile, Peru, Brazil, Argentina, Bolivia, Paraguay, El Salvador, and Guatemala. In Africa, the countries we covered included Egypt, Algeria, South Africa, Nigeria, The Congo, Sierra Leone, Kenya, Morocco, and Botswana. In the Middle East, we examined Israel/Palestine, Egypt, Iran, Sudan, and Saudi Arabia.

Next to the United States, Europe was the most common source of course materials. This included England, Scotland, Ireland and Northern Ireland, France, Germany, Poland, Yugoslavia, Italy, Spain, Greece, Russia, Denmark, Norway, and Turkey. Despite the small population in the Caribbean area, the cultural richness of the region led to choosing works focused on Cuba, Jamaica, the Dominican Republic, Puerto Rico, and Haiti. Finally, some of the works I used were chosen from the world of the imagination: *Alice in Wonderland, Animal Farm, The Hobbit, Peter Pan, Lord of the Flies,* and *The Wonderful Wizard of Oz.*

One of the things I particularly enjoyed about the seminars was the combination of small class size and the tradition of meeting for thirty minutes in my room with each class member. This meant I got to know the students better than I was able to when I was teaching courses with thirty-five to a hundred-plus students. In the conversations in my room in Sorin I had a range of topics that I usually covered—the students' family, educational history, extracurricular activities, the roommate situation, health issues, career goals, adjustment problems, and so on. I tried to keep the interaction relaxed, although I was not naive about what it was like for the students to have to spend time one-on-one with the president of the University. I provided some feedback about how they were doing in the course, but that was not the primary reason for meeting. My real goal was both to get to know them better and to establish a personal rapport. Most of the time that was what took place.

Of course, there were a few meetings when we just went through the motions, yet I was sometimes blown away by the

level of sharing we often achieved and by what I discovered about their personal histories. I had students who survived a Cambodian concentration camp; hid out during the Rwandan holocaust and made it to the U.S. safely; was born with one leg and no arms, emigrated to the U.S., and was fitted with three prostheses; had close friends murdered; survived serious auto accidents; had one or both parents die from disease, accidents, or drunk drivers; were high school stars in football, basketball, soccer, swimming, lacrosse, track, baseball or softball, fencing, or golf; formed their own band; wrote music; performed in ballet or opera; acted in major movies; appeared on television; volunteered in high school to work with the poor; were children of heads of state or famous entertainers or financial moguls or leaders in the professions; had parents who served as maids or janitors or factory workers or field hands or drove a cab or were cops or firefighters.

I always taught the seminar in informal clothes, partly because the class was on Sunday night and partly because I wanted to de-emphasize my administrative responsibilities and give the class a life of its own. Overall, I think the strategy worked. The students knew who I was and often saw me around campus and in the media dressed in clerical garb. But Sunday night was a different part of my life, just as my residence in Sorin Hall was intended to be. By the time we shared a semester together, we had a special identity of our own. Some groups clicked better than others, yet they all shared a common status — they were Monk's men and women, a select coterie, who could count on my support for advice, recommendations, and periodic reunions.

In the spring semester of 2002, John Cavadini, the chair of the theology department, talked me into offering a one-credit course titled "Knowing Your Catholic Faith: Morality." It was part of a series of courses intended to provide a richer background for students who felt ill prepared in theology overall or who just wanted to explore theological topics beyond those available in the regular curriculum. I hesitated to agree because it was scheduled for two hours (from 7–9:00 p.m.) on six dates

during the semester. It was a big time commitment for the students and for me, and when thirty students signed up I knew I could not run it as a seminar. I ended up dividing the course into six parts, but by the end of the semester I was frustrated just to be lecturing. They, on the other hand, seemed to think that the course was of value. I was not interested in doing it again so it became a one-shot venture.

During my sabbatical year after stepping down as president in 2005 I pondered what I might teach next. I decided to continue with the seminar format and work with first-year undergraduates, but I wanted to change the theme and content. I chose to teach "Biography/Autobiography: One's Life Story," which I described as "seeking to understand the uniqueness of particular historical persons through an analysis of their stories, as created either by themselves or others." The emphasis was on what can be learned about the person's cultural and historical context.

At the beginning of the course, I informed the students that I was in the process of writing my own memoir. I also assured them that I would be the only one to read their papers, unless they chose to share it themselves. Once I read the first student-produced autobiographies, my concerns about how much nineteen year olds might have to say were dispelled. Through the first few semesters they produced versions of their lives that ranged from six to fifty pages in length. Some were deeply moving to read, while others were less personally revealing.

I was worried about finding books in the genre that were short enough to be usable, since most standard biographies run in the multiple hundreds of pages. Nevertheless, I managed to find good books that I felt could sustain the students' interest but were diverse enough in cultural setting or life situations to meet my goal of reflecting the range of the human condition. The selection of movies was a bit easier, since in the eyes of the students even long films demand less study time than do books.

The only problem I encountered was that gradually the male-female balance in the classes fell out of kilter. I went from eight

to six to four male students out of seventeen or eighteen total. The trouble was not that I did not welcome female students, but I felt a seminar is a great place for first-year students to meet people and hear other points of view in a respectful and supportive context, and I found that a 50–50 gender balance was a good thing in light of the topics and themes that we took up. When I brought the problem to the attention of the First Year of Studies, they agreed to oversee admission to the course with this in mind.

Sacramental Ministry

Through the years of my priesthood I have exercised a variety of roles appropriate to that ministry: I have celebrated mass, preached, conferred the sacrament of the sick, witnessed wedding vows, heard confessions, baptized, made hospital visits, offered counsel and spiritual direction, taught, and administered. I have also presented retreats on occasion and given conferences on spiritual topics. In the years when I was on the staff of Moreau Seminary I frequently gave talks about religious life, the history of the Congregation of Holy Cross, prayer, moral development, formation, and related topics.

I also addressed various groups, on and off campus, in the general area of spirituality. As a theologian with a specialty in Catholic moral theology, I accepted invitations to address ethical issues in a way that could make sense to members of parishes and other groups. Yet my life never led me in the direction of giving a lot of retreats. The main difference between an occasional talk on a spirituality-related topic and leading a retreat is the amount of preparation required for the latter, as well as the need to integrate thematically a series of presentations.

Weddings are another story. As of the summer of 2008, I had witnessed fifty-six of them in thirty-eight years as a priest. That statistic is not very impressive compared to the average diocesan parish priest or those who have served as rectors at Notre

Dame. On the other hand, almost all my weddings involved one or both parties with whom I had a previous relationship. Often I knew their families and peers as well, which made the events surrounding the ceremony almost like old home week. One reason why I did not do more weddings was that I had a limited number of available weekends during my presidential years. Factoring in home football weekends, major feasts like Christmas and Easter, and liturgical seasons like Advent and Lent, as well as the general preference for marrying in the summer months, not too many weekends remain in the year.

The first wedding I performed was in rural Kentucky and involved a fellow graduate student at Vanderbilt and his fiancée. I did not know him (or her) very well, yet I was excited to be doing my first marriage ceremony. What I remember the most was that the father of the bride, a farmer, had never worn a tux before, and after the opening hymn started he kept struggling to get his cummerbund tied. We waited and waited for him as the organist and choir kept singing verse after verse of the hymn, and the congregation kept wondering what was wrong. Finally, the cummerbund problem was corrected and we made our grand entrance.

From the vantage point of the priest, weddings are a fairly major time commitment. At a minimum there are the rehearsal and rehearsal dinner, the marriage ceremony and the post-ceremony reception and dinner. Often there are one or more additional meetings with the couple as part of the pre-Cana instructions (although sometimes this is handled at the parish or diocesan level). Weddings at Sacred Heart Basilica are easier than most because experienced individuals are available to oversee the logistics and planning, and talented musicians and singers are on call for every style of liturgical music.

In Catholic theology, marriage is one of the seven sacraments. The exchange of vows only requires a priest or deacon and two witnesses; everything else is an add-on. But the Catholic marriage takes place best in the context of the Eucharist. This implicitly emphasizes its status as a sacrament and draws upon the

richness of the Roman Catholic liturgy. Even when one partner is not Catholic, it is possible to make him or her feel welcome and fully a part of the celebration. When the marriage takes place outside of the Eucharist, or outside of a Catholic church, it tends to be relatively brief and non-liturgical. It is still valid, but I always feel that something important is missing.

The marriage rite itself, whether in the context of a mass or not, is very straightforward. After some general preparatory comments by the priest (or deacon), the couple is asked a series of questions. Then they exchange vows and rings. Some couples choose to bring the bridal bouquet to the Lady Chapel after communion. Various members of the wedding party may also be involved in bringing up the gifts, reading scriptures or petitions, helping with communion, or ushering. Obviously, the maid of honor and the best man have defined roles as well.

Wedding preparation can be a stressful time for both the couple and their families. Sometimes one or both mothers feel the urge to facilitate the process, which is understandable in human terms but has the potential to bring out the worst in everybody. In my experience, the rehearsal dinner can be a fun event where one can get a better feel for the unique gifts of the couple, or it can be a complete embarrassment. No one really wants to hear toasts in bad taste that feature reminiscences of youthful escapades, previous relationships, or bachelor parties. In addition there may also be tension over members of the family who drink too much or squabble among themselves or resurrect distant feuds. Even worse, the families of the bride and groom can resent each other on socioeconomic, religious, or some other grounds. Some of these same issues may emerge at the post-wedding reception and dinner, especially if the wine is flowing too freely. However, once the dancing begins, an untoward incident is less likely.

My basic theory regarding the role of the priest is that he should let the couple decide about all the variables in the ceremony, although I always recommend repeating the vows after the

priest rather than writing them themselves or, even worse, reciting them from memory. In the rehearsal the priest should give everyone confidence that nothing can really go wrong (and that he will tell them when to play their parts).

In addition to leading the liturgy, preaching, and receiving the vows, the priest's other main role is saying grace at the two dinners. If more than one priest or minister is involved, it is possible to divvy up the responsibilities. One of the hard things to decide for some couples is which priest among several that they invite to the ceremony will formally be the witness for their vows. This is especially an issue in a place like Notre Dame where the couples may have special relationships with multiple clergy. I have never felt offended if the couple preferred to have a relative or someone else be the main celebrant.

The priest's contributions are to make sure that the marriage ceremony is conducted with prayerfulness and class, to congratulate everyone at the post-wedding reception, and then to disappear after the dancing begins. Post-wedding dinner and dancing are all about the couple and the family and the friendship group that has brought them to this great moment in their lives. No one really wants to see what kind of dancer the priest is or worry that he is sitting on the sidelines taking notes.

I would divide the weddings I have done into three categories. First were relatives like my niece or first cousins or their offspring. Second were former students, former hallmates, or people I got to know in the course of my priestly ministry. Last were special requests from University trustees, benefactors, officers, or staff, and those whose connection to me was through the parents rather than through the couple themselves.

Once I started doing the weddings of former Sorin students, I usually knew a lot of those who attended. On a number of occasions we scheduled outdoor basketball games on the morning of the wedding, which turned out to be a replay of Monk Hoops but often led to trepidation on the part of the bride or her parents

that the groom would be disabled before the ceremony. Fortunately, this never happened.

Weddings, in whatever tradition, have many elements in common. Even in Japan, which is about one percent Christian, young people like to get married in a Christian-style ceremony, with white bridal dresses, formal wear for the men, an exchange of rings, and other such features. Jesuit-run Sophia University in Tokyo earns considerable income from making its chapel available for the marriages of its students and graduates.

There is huge cultural pressure in American society, despite its high divorce rate, to spend inordinately on every feature of a wedding, from the quality of the invitations to the number of guests to the elaborateness of the flower arrangements to the cost of the music for the reception. I have done weddings, especially in major cities, where the overall investment was easily into the tens of thousands of dollars. While I am a big believer in the celebratory dimensions of weddings, especially the emphasis on family and mutual interdependence, I consider it foolish for parents and/or the couple to go into considerable debt.

The couple's greatest fear, particularly the bride's, is bad weather. Yet, having done weddings in both ideal and tempestuous meteorological conditions, I never noticed any difference in the turnout or the sense of celebration and pride. Somehow people adjust and focus on the fundamental significance of the rite.

I have many cherished memories of weddings I have participated in and the events surrounding them. Some examples: being the only non-Italian at heavily ethnic weddings and being made to feel like an honorary *paisano;* watching enthralled as the newly married bride danced sensuously before her new husband as part of a culturally assigned script; having the bridal party march across downtown Sacramento from the church to the reception hall, to the delight of passersby; relishing being involved in a wedding when I not only knew the bride and groom and both families but also every member of the wedding party (and having stories I

could tell about all of them). I remember agreeing to do the weddings of identical twins from Saint Mary's in the same ceremony and then confusing which partners belonged together when I began the formal questioning (which elicited howls from the congregation who thought I was just faking it); doing the second marriage of a widow and a widower in the Log Chapel with the two generations of their separate offspring present; watching several teammates of a Notre Dame–grad professional football player devour all the hors d'oeuvres at a pre-dinner reception before any of the other guests had a chance at any; welcoming a good number of post-9/11 police and firefighters to the on-campus wedding of one of their own; and sharing great family moments as my own extended clan gathered for weddings of the next generation.

Other Priestly Roles

While marriage ceremonies and connected events are some of the priest's most enjoyable sacramental moments, the other sacramental rituals are equally important in their own way—baptisms, first communions, confirmations, ordinations, confessions, and administering the sacrament of the sick. Confirmations are normally restricted to bishops and ordinations to the priesthood always are. The typical priest, especially in the parish setting, most likely does many baptisms, confessions, and sacraments of the sick as well as celebrating funeral liturgies and officiating at the graveside services. Those of us who have spent most of our apostolic ministry in a university context, where we live and interact with mainly young people from nineteen into their early thirties, are more likely to be asked to celebrate baptisms and hear confessions than visit the sick or accompany a dying person through the last stages of life.

Most of the children I have baptized have been the offspring of family members or couples I had married or have been related

to the extended Notre Dame family. I like to have baptisms in the context of the Eucharist, but this is not always possible. The baptismal ritual itself is too long, in my judgment, especially when a baby is being welcomed into the community of faith. The behavior of babies is quite unpredictable and everyone's patience is tested if the ceremony is accompanied by endless screams. My goal is always to make everyone comfortable, conduct the sacrament with dignity and efficiency, and pose for pictures at the end. If possible, I have all the little children present come forward so they can see what is happening and even assist with the lighted candle, the white garment, or the wiping off of the oils.

The sacrament of reconciliation (or confession) has changed rather drastically in my lifetime in both its form and its frequency. In my early years in Sorin Hall, most of the confessions I heard were in my room, face to face, with students whom I knew and had an ongoing pastoral relationship with. I have also heard confessions in parishes, at the seminary, on retreats, and occasionally in hotel rooms or other places on the road. During my years as president (on the good advice of Father Hesburgh), I chose not to hear confessions at Notre Dame. This was to avoid any conflict of interest since I was sometimes the court of last resort in disciplinary matters with faculty, staff, and students. Since stepping down from the presidency, I will hear confessions if asked but I do not volunteer otherwise. This is partly as an extension of my previous policy, but also because I do not support the revival of misguided notions of sinfulness that some of the more pious students bring with them to the sacrament.

Visiting the sick is one of the more important corporal works of mercy. I have done a fair amount of it, but other priests and lay people whom I know are more gifted and dedicated in this regard than I am. Very seldom have I administered the sacrament of the sick, which is usually done by parish priests or hospital chaplains.

Most of the funeral liturgies and graveside services I have participated in have been for members of my extended family, students or family members of students, University personnel

or their spouses, or members of the broader Notre Dame family. I have helped celebrate the lives of both of my parents, many uncles and aunts, and even one or two relatives from my own generation. Amidst the tears and the sense of loss, I tried to bring comfort and consolation to those with whom I shared a genetic and familial heritage. Sometimes these funeral liturgies were moments of grace in helping to heal old divisions or to give a renewed sense of togetherness to the next generation. For me, the hardest services are those of the very young or close friends who seemed to die prematurely. I constantly rediscover in these moments the power of ritual and sacrament. When words break down, when no homily or philosophical reflection seems adequate, the beauty and expressiveness of the liturgical acts help to make the mystery and reality of death somewhat more comprehensible.

Through the years, I have frequently celebrated memorial masses in the Basilica for students who died. Often, their parents were in attendance, along with friends and hallmates. For many students, exposure to the death of a peer is quite limited, and these celebrations can be marvelous opportunities for reaffirming the central Christian claim that in Christ's resurrection, sin and death have been overcome; that in the midst of our shock and grief at the loss of someone seemingly in the prime of life, the Gospel can be comprehended in a new way.

For a Holy Cross religious, there is a great sense of happiness and solidarity when one of our younger members takes final vows, receives the diaconate, and then is ordained to the priesthood. We are usually present in large numbers. I especially enjoy the point in the ordination to the priesthood ceremony when all the priests follow the example of the bishop in individually laying hands on the head of the newly ordained. This is a sign of our oneness in the priesthood of Jesus Christ. The same collective manifestation is present in the wake service, funeral liturgy, and burial of deceased priests and brothers. We hear stories about their lives and apostolic endeavors and are reminded that all who are part of the Congregation are equal in death.

The long lines of Holy Cross gravestone crosses in the Community cemetery are an ongoing witness of the charism of Basil Moreau lived out through the generations. I can go to the precise point in the cemetery where the first Community member was buried after I joined, and then walk along the rows from then until now, recalling the company of those who, even for a brief time, have been an integral part of my second family.

Biblical and Other Journeys

In the summer of 1977, after I had joined the theology faculty and was still a member of the Moreau Seminary staff, I had an opportunity to join a five-week exploration of the Holy Land, Greece, and Rome. It was a biblically oriented journey sponsored by Loyola University of Chicago and led by Father Dick Macowski, a Jesuit archaeologist, and Father Jack Kilgallen, a Jesuit New Testament scholar. The priests' roles were to lecture about the significance of what we would be seeing and to provide commentary on our daily riding and walking tours.

Our group had forty-three participants, including six priests in addition to the guides and me, one brother and eight religious sisters, two Holy Cross seminarians studying theology, and two Holy Cross college seminarians. The rest of the party consisted of lay men and women, the oldest of whom was a woman in her eighties who had gone on educational trips every summer for years. She turned out to be one of the most dedicated members of all.

Prior to this journey, all my experiences abroad had been in Latin America. I had been so positively influenced by those journeys that it was just a matter of time and circumstance before I ventured on another international exploration. That summer was ideal for this venture in many ways. I was finished with my dissertation, had received my doctoral degree, and had begun my

teaching career, but I would not come up for a decision about renewal for another year. Since I was accompanied by four Holy Cross seminarians, I had some responsibilities as a seminary staff member for their well-being. Finally, the political and social circumstances in the places we were visiting, particularly the Holy Land, were relatively peaceful, providing us with a calm window in the controversies and violence that have plagued that area through much of its history.

The journey turned out to be profoundly moving in every way—spiritually enriching, theologically stimulating, and personally fulfilling. I was surprised how emotionally responsive I was to being in the land of Abraham, Isaac, and Jacob, of Moses and Aaron, of David and Solomon, of Mary and Elizabeth, of John the Baptist, Jesus, and the Apostles. Even factoring in controversies about true sites, reputed paths of passage, and authentic relics and artifacts, the basic landscape, the central towns and cities, and the special places of devotion were well known and had been pilgrimage sites for centuries. To a lesser extent, those same faith-filled sensitivities were evoked in Greece, where we followed the path of Paul the Apostle, and in Rome, where I was exposed to the many layers of civilization centered there, including the burial places of Saints Peter and Paul and the later center of Catholicism.

In addition to the spiritual benefits of the trip (we had mass every day, often in chapels and churches of ancient provenance), the lectures and accompanying readings were an effective way of filling in the lacunae in my education. It is one thing to study maps and look at slides in order to pass a test in a course on the Bible; it is a matter far different to actually be there and get a firsthand feel for the geographical scale of the land of Israel and its neighboring countries. I relished being able to situate the Sea of Galilee, the Jordan River, and the Dead Sea, to recognize what it meant to go *up* to Jerusalem or to survive a passage across the Negev Desert, and to comprehend how narrow modern Israel is and how vulnerable to being cut in half militarily by its enemies.

I found myself becoming intensely interested in biblical archaeology. We visited digs at Hazor, Beth Shean, and Megiddo as well as the more accessible Capernaum, Caesarea Maritima, and various locations in Jerusalem. We discovered firsthand how tedious it is to kneel all day in the hot sun and scoop out sand in order to preserve some historically significant piece of pottery or a rare coin. We began to comprehend how "tels" or "hills" were really locations of successive layers of civilization that flourished and then were destroyed by marauding armies and eventually buried beneath the constantly shifting sand, waiting to be rediscovered in our own moment of time. The theoretical question was how to learn as much about each civilization that inhabited the spot as the surviving evidence allowed while still preserving undisturbed remnants buried beneath the earth that would allow future generations to probe with more sophisticated techniques.

We were told that Israelis and Arabs possessed a genetic predisposition toward interest in archaeology and found that understandable given the nature of the land and its topography and how the prevailing aridity and the presence of large swaths of desert are perfect conditions for limiting the degradation of ancient potsherds, manuscripts, and ritual vessels. At Hazor, we learned how this isolated fortress town was able to obtain water from a nearby well during times of siege: beneath the settled area they dug a tunnel with enough elevation for local women to carry water jugs on their heads when they sneaked out under cover of darkness, then returned undiscovered, hidden by the trees around the oasis. At Megiddo we were taught the linguistic connection between this central fortress (right in the center of all the ancient routes of travel) and the apocalyptic prediction that it will be the site of the final battle between the forces of good and the forces of evil.

In addition to Father Macowski's constantly enthusiastic presentations on every facet of archaeology, we were equally impressed with Father Kilgallen's manner of having us engage the

New Testament texts with greater sensitivity to the nuances of the respective Gospel authors, to the evolution of the final written material from the earlier oral tradition, and to the role of Paul, the Apostle to the Gentiles, in helping to spread Christianity around the Mediterranean world. As we reached each new location, Father Kilgallen would read from the appropriate texts and ask us to try to imagine ourselves back in that time and in that cultural context (a method cultivated in the Ignatian spiritual tradition). It was easier to create a sense of place in the more isolated settings than in the big cities. (There were no automobiles or neon signs in the time of Jesus.)

Like any relatively large group of tourists/students, we stayed in modest accommodations. The first week we spent in a pilgrimage-oriented hotel in Nazareth. The second and third weeks we were put up at the White Sisters Hospice, right outside the walls of the Old City of Jerusalem. The hospice rooms were okay but the food was horrible. About a week into our time there I got sick (I think from the unpalatable soup they served every day) and had to miss a day of exploration.

In the fourth week we used Athens as a base, staying in a hotel and taking day trips. The fifth and final week we spent in Rome, where our hotel was centrally located and convenient for both vehicular and walking tours. On the way home, the Notre Dame contingent worked its way to Assisi, Florence, and Paris for quick, cover-the-basics exposures to those major tourist centers.

In Israel/Palestine there were many lessons to be learned. What was strange to me was that Bethlehem, the location of Jesus' birth, and the Church of the Holy Sepulcher in Jerusalem, the place of Jesus' tomb, were less impressive than many of the so-called minor sites. The main reason, I think, is that the modern pilgrim in Bethlehem and Jerusalem is quickly exposed to the residue of simmering religious struggles among Roman Catholics, Protestants, and various Orthodox groups for control of access to the churches. Each group gets to have a mass on the main altar at an assigned time each day. In between those times, representa-

tives of the groups glare at each other and sometimes blow out the candles lit by pilgrims from the other side. Despite the thrill of being in these historically momentous places, the lingering emotional effect is an unedifying reminder that the Church of Christ is torn asunder by theological disagreements and cultural differences.

Although our first-time exposure to Bethlehem and the Church of the Holy Sepulcher produced mixed emotions, we were fully engaged by Nazareth, Cana, Bethany, Caesarea Philippi, Jericho, and Capernaum. We explored all sides of the Sea of Galilee, including the beautiful chapel on the Mount of the Beatitudes, Capernaum, the Golan Heights, Tiberius, and a modern Israeli kibbutz. We drove to Haifa and visited Mount Carmel. We explored the area of the West Bank and the contested territory around Nablus, Shiloh, and Hebron. In Jerusalem, we walked all around the Old City, from the temple wall to the Dome of the Rock and into neighborhoods divided by religion and ethnicity. One of our favorite places was the Garden of Gethsemane, with its somber chapel and its startling view back over the Old City.

We drove down to the Dead Sea and explored the Herodian fortress at Masada, the place where the last remnant of Israeli resisters was defeated by the Roman army in the 70s AD; most died in a mass suicide rather than surrender. Along the Dead Sea, the lowest point on earth with the highest saline content, we swam (or should I say floated) in the waters without moving a muscle— a great thrill to a non-swimmer like me. We visited Beersheba, a center of the ancient caravan routes, and came in contact with nomadic tribes, people who get around both on camels and in four wheel drive trucks.

Most of the members of our group had religious motivations for coming on the trip. Some of the sisters had taught in Catholic grade schools and high schools. The diocesan priests were interested in updating their theological/biblical knowledge and obtaining firsthand exposure to the topography, multiple cultures, and archaeological evidence from the Holy Land in order to make

them better preachers and religious instructors. The seminarians hoped to make the Bible come alive and help them in their process of discernment. The lay students were more of a grab bag, from those enthusiastically interested in enhancing their educational and religious formation to those who needed an excuse to get away from home for the summer.

I spent the five weeks sopping up as much knowledge as I could. I wanted to become a better teacher and preacher, a more solidly prepared scholar, and a person of faith who would be able to read the Old and New Testaments with fresh understanding and sensitivity. The three weeks in the Holy Land were the most dramatic part of the trip because we were exposed to significant sites with the help of informed and well-delivered commentary.

I was to build on this foundation after returning home. The first thing I read was James Michener's *The Source,* a fictionalized account of a tel in the Holy Land, covering the civilizations that inhabited it from prehistory up until modern times. This was the first of many books and articles and movies that helped broaden my understanding of the complexity of the Holy Land, with its three great religious traditions vying for power and influence and its long memories of events from centuries or millennia past.

During our week in Athens, Father Macowski helped us understand the significance of places of interest in the city, from the Acropolis and the Parthenon to the wonderful archaeological museum and the amphitheaters and gathering places of ancient Greek culture. We went to a folk music and dance show one night under the lights in the area beneath the Acropolis, ate Greek food, visited the zoo, and explored the headquarters of the contemporary Greek government. As in the Holy Land, we enjoyed mingling with the people in the marketplaces and checking out the latest local fashions.

Father Kilgallen helped us understand the challenges Paul faced on his missions around the Mediterranean. His lectures were in preparation for an all-day boat trip to a number of Greek islands and a subsequent bus trip to Corinth, the subject of two

of Paul's most important letters and a major archaeological site. We also stopped at Delphi where we heard how spies from the Oracle used to infiltrate the campgrounds at night and listen to the stories pilgrims told around the campfires. Then they alerted the Oracle so that whoever happened to be playing that role would seem particularly prescient when the petitioners arrived. I found Athens interesting and culturally significant but lacking the variety and spontaneous vitality that we soon discovered in Rome. In Greece, the genuine hearty and persistent allure is in the islands. Subsequent trips have reconfirmed this initial impression.

Our time in Rome was almost overwhelming because there was so much to see and experience. The different levels of ancient civilization, the remnants of early Christianity (such as the catacombs and the early churches), the four great churches of modern Catholicism (Saint Peter's, Saint Mary Major, Saint John Lateran, and Saint Paul Outside the Walls), the reality of the Vatican, the crazy traffic, the mobs of tourists, the old city, the outdoor cafes and restaurants, and the exuberance of modern Roman life—all these were right there for us to savor.

My time in Rome had a deeply religious dimension as well, with all of its churches, cemeteries, shrines, catacombs, seminaries, religious houses, and places of devotion, not to speak of everything to do with the Vatican, the papacy, and the center of contemporary Roman Catholicism. Yet Rome was so much more, with its outdoor cafes, its statuary, its motorbikes, its endless groups of tourists, its shops, its multiple grades of well-dressed police, its fountains, its gardens, and its diplomatic headquarters. All we could do was sample enough to want to return many times in the future, as I eventually did.

After returning to Notre Dame, I handed direction of the College Seminary program over to others and moved out of Moreau Seminary. That fall I became director of the Master of Divinity program within the theology department. It was a major administrative responsibility and I was an untenured assistant professor. The combination flew in the face of prevailing wisdom then

(and even more so subsequently), which held that it was foolish to be engaged in multiple tasks, especially management and oversight functions, prior to gaining tenure. I knew that I was expected to establish my reputation as an effective teacher and a published scholar as well as someone who contributed generously to the common good. Most of the older faculty advised me not to become distracted by the endless demands of administration. Nevertheless, I thought it important for a Holy Cross person to be in the M. Div. job, and I was the best situated to take on the responsibility at that time.

In the end, I was confident that I would be able to fulfill the criteria that were grounds for gaining first a three-year renewal as assistant professor and later promotion to associate professor with tenure. I knew that there were no guarantees, but I had confidence that the leadership of the theology department, of the University, and of the Holy Cross Community would treat me fairly.

A Return to Peru

From December 29, 1982, to January 9, 1983, I participated in a two-week trip to Peru sponsored by the Maryknoll Fathers. Besides me, the Notre Dame participants were Ollie Williams, John Reedy, Bill Berry, Suzanne Kelly, and Sister Marietta Starrie. The trip was directed by Father Peter Byrne, the regional supervisor for the Maryknolls in Peru.

I had first been in Peru in the summer of 1963, under the auspices of Notre Dame's Center for the International Lay Apostolate, for a summer service project led by Maryknoll Father Larry Murphy. During that visit I divided my time between a slum on the outskirts of Lima and the town of Ilave in the Altiplano along Lake Titicaca at 12,500 feet. It had been a transformative experience for me and I was eager to see how much the circumstances might have changed in twenty years.

This new visit was designed to familiarize us with the works of Maryknoll in Peru. We began with some introductory lectures about economic realities and the condition of the Catholic Church. Our first day was spent at the Maryknoll headquarters in a nice neighborhood of Lima. The second day we flew to Arequipa, which lies at 8,000 feet above sea level; our tour there included visits to a homeless shelter and a large parish. Next we took the train to Puno, the major city along Lake Titicaca, and from there drove to Chicuito, about thirty miles up the lake toward Bolivia, where Holy Cross member Diego Yrarrazaval, a specialist on popular religion in Latin America, gave us a tour. While in Chicuito I was afflicted with altitude sickness and ended up losing a full day of activity.

Much of the rest of the trip was spent in the area around Lake Titicaca where the Inca culture is well established and the social and economic disparities of the country are most manifest. We heard from a very impressive German-born missionary bishop, from a Maryknoll priest and sister who work in the region, and from another priest and sister who had been experimenting with living in closer contact with the native people. We also traveled to Unguyo, a trading town about five miles from the Bolivian border, where we participated in a beautiful mass of the Feast of Mary the Mother of God.

Back in Lima, Ollie Williams and John Reedy and I spent a day and a half exploring the work of the Eastern Province of Holy Cross in Lima. We stayed overnight in the slum neighborhood of Canto Grande, explored the local parish on foot, and met some of the people. We also spent time at a neighboring grade school in which one of our priests served as principal.

The trip to Peru was a good break from my duties in the Provost Office. It allowed me to return to some earlier experiences that had been so formative in my vocational story. I had the advantage of being able to compare what I had seen twenty years previously with the new realities of the country.

The interlude reinforced for me the importance of Notre Dame's international outreach and involvement. Despite my lack of fluency in Spanish, in my time as president I would visit just about every country in Central and South America. One motivating factor for these trips was the role of the Catholic Church in the region. My exposure to the culture of poverty was a constant reminder of the inequities of the world and of the developed world's responsibility to seek steps of amelioration. My senses had been touched once again, and I hoped to be able in my new position to keep such concerns as a high agenda item.

Trip to Chile

My first trip to Chile took place approximately a year before I was elected president of Notre Dame. I had a number of motivations for the journey, including a desire to learn more about the apostolic work of the Holy Cross Community there and what types of future involvement Notre Dame might have. General Augusto Pinochet was then president in the wake of a coup that led to the death of his predecessor, Salvador Allende. The coup had led to the execution, detention, or expulsion from the country of thousands of people. Chile was a land under siege, and the Catholic Church was right in the middle of it.

On the trip I was accompanied by Father Carl Ebey, who was serving as Provincial Steward. We were met at the airport by Father Jorge Canepa and Lou Nanni, a friend from Sorin Hall who was serving as a Holy Cross associate in Chile. We drove to Punta de Tralco, a retreat house on the Pacific Coast where the Holy Cross Community was gathered for a few days of summer meetings. I spent an afternoon meeting with people, especially the associates and the Chilean seminarians. The associates are lay volunteers who make a two-year commitment to live and work in various Holy Cross–related ministries. General Pinochet was on everyone's mind. The Catholic Church in Chile had been the

focal point of protest against his regime, and the torture, arbitrary arrest, isolated killings, and climate of fear that characterized it.

In Punta de Tralca I had a conversation about higher education possibilities in Chile with Father Gerry Whelan, rector of Holy Cross–run Saint George's College. Gerry had been rector for four years and had undertaken a number of educational experiments. In the end, the government kicked the Congregation out of the college. It took years for us to get it back. Gerry was convinced that most of the really significant work in Chilean higher education took place in the research institutes that were independently established and thereby free from government control. He advocated that the Congregation establish such an institute with two or three of its own members. In general, he said, there was a spirit of hostility between some percentage of the students and the federal government.

The protest groups in Chile varied from non-violent to radically violent. The non-violent contingent specialized in short, unannounced, public demonstrations that lasted from five to ten minutes. Then the demonstrators disappeared before the police arrived. The radical cadres engaged in bombings, kidnappings, and assassination attempts. Meanwhile, the government under Pinochet used every possible means at its disposal, moral or immoral, to thwart the protesters. All of this has made the average Chilean highly political in conversation.

While in Punta de Tralca, Carl and I spent hours talking with associates, seminarians, and Community members. One of the perennial matters of debate was how important direct involvement in education ought to be. The two Holy Cross high schools, Saint George's and Andacollo, served two different socioeconomic classes. There was general agreement that both schools probably needed a clearer articulation of their respective philosophies of Catholic secondary education. A related issue was that the Holy Cross seminarians all came from among the poorer classes. At ordination, there would be questions about what ministries they would be best suited for.

On our way back to Santiago, we stopped in Talagante to visit at an orphanage that had been run by Father Joe Doherty for twenty-eight years. We found the facilities to be decent but rather old and dilapidated. Administratively, many important decisions were on hold until Joe stepped down as director.

The neighborhood where we stayed in Santiago had 170,000 inhabitants but no high school and no hospital. One morning I visited an economic institute headed by Alejandro Foxley, a Notre Dame faculty member in the Kellogg Institute. We were joined by Rene Cortazar and Lou Nanni and we discussed Chile's strong tradition of higher education and the impact of the coup, when hundreds of faculty and students were arrested and many were exiled. Those who were not exiled had chosen another alternative, the establishment of research institutes apart from the university structure. In 1986 there were about thirty such entities. The government response to them had been harassment rather than direct intervention.

One anecdote captures the palpable tension in the air in Santiago. Father Jerry Papen went down to the center of town one day to buy some Bibles. He purchased them and put them in two boxes. When he got on the subway, he put down one box to pay the fare and forgot it. At the next stop he remembered and turned back. When he arrived at the original station, he found the area around the box cordoned off and six or seven police holding people back. He explained to the police what had happened and they were angry because they had stopped all the trains down the line. All of this resulted from two bombs having been set off in subway stations in the recent past.

I spent one morning at Saint George's College, a strikingly beautiful and spacious campus set right beneath a mountain. It had approximately 3,000 students in kindergarten through high school. Because Saint George's has been one of the largest private schools in Latin America, its graduates are prominent at all levels of Chilean society. In the midst of the Pinochet regime,

the school was not without its challenges: (i) a significant debt had accrued; (ii) there was no quick way to foster a consciousness for social justice among the students; (iii) the return of Holy Cross after years of interdiction had caused anxiety and tension among some of the lay staff.

One morning we drove to a house in a poor neighborhood that served as the residence for six Holy Cross people. Then we toured Andacollo parish and school. The church had been significantly damaged in an earthquake and was only partially rebuilt. Colegio Andacollo was a startling contrast to Saint George's. With 900 students in two shifts, the physical environment was grungy, dark, and depressing. The classrooms were poorly lit and the library was small and poorly stocked. The government subsidized the school according to a formula per student. As a result, teacher salaries were low and many teachers also held jobs at other schools in order to boost their salaries. It was quickly clear that the Holy Cross Community in the years ahead would be challenged by the efforts to oversee and integrate the educational mission at two such radically different institutions serving distinct sections of the population.

Community members shared with me several experiences of the pervasive violence under the military regime. When police raided the poor neighborhoods, they took off their badges and moved through the streets beating people up. They also shot into homes and chapels. Community mail was censored and sometimes stolen.

This trip to Chile helped me to gain a more intimate and personal knowledge of the multiple apostolates of the Holy Cross Community. In later years I would return and also visit other countries where Holy Cross was deeply involved, such as Bangladesh, Uganda, and Kenya. In each case, I would be looking for opportunities for greater cooperation between the University and these regions, whether specifically educational or related to social justice, peace making, or experimental outreach.

Costa Rica Trip

In January 1985 I was a participant in a one-week trip to Costa Rica sponsored by the Association of Catholic Colleges and Universities (ACCU). The goal was to acquaint visitors with the United Nations University for Peace in San José, the capital. Costa Rica, we learned, has a tradition of peace and relative independence. It enviably lacks severe economic and social divisions and does not possess the mineral resources or geopolitical strategic importance to warrant superpower attention. Because Costa Rican presidents can only serve one four-year term, there were five former presidents alive in 1985.

We took a bus trip to the University for Peace on a highway that narrowed down to two lanes and then to a primitive rural road, with frequent switchbacks and narrow bridges and turns. Upon our arrival, Archbishop Román Arrieta Villalobos celebrated mass for the group in Spanish, with the homily in English. He spoke about the circumstances of Latin America, highlighting such factors as poverty, violence, economic dependency, the need to include native populations in the political process, the tendency to make ideologies of Capitalism and Communism, and the influence of fundamentalist Christian groups.

The University for Peace was created in 1980 by the United Nations and has a status comparable to an embassy. The intention was to keep the university small and primarily focused on graduate education and workshops. One of the reasons we were there was the school's desire to network with other universities around the world. The university's theoretical framework had been influenced by the ideas of Thomas Aquinas, Teilhard de Chardin, and Gandhi. One of its first major research projects was on the problem of refugees. At first exposure, the university seemed to me to be underfunded, campus-poor, understaffed, and full of high ideals; only strong leadership and a little luck would be able to make it a real force for good.

We had a presentation by Don Pepe Figueres, the former president who disarmed the country in 1948. Although in his seventies, Don Pepe was quite forceful in his opinions about the absurdity of war and the normalcy of peace. He said he prefers to err on the side of optimism. He had a great sense of humor and exuded the ease of an elderly person with a pride of achievement.

One day we visited a refugee camp in Heredia. Most of the occupants were from El Salvador, displaced by that country's civil war. The assistance provided included emergency aid, legal advice, health treatment, and the development of meaningful work projects. One refugee shared her personal story with us, which included murder and rape perpetrated against her and her family by government soldiers.

This trip in the middle of my third year as vice president was a forerunner of many future journeys. Unlike my previous stays in Mexico, Peru, the Middle East, and Europe, this time I went as a Notre Dame administrator and brought with me a new level of interest in questions of structure and financing and institutional fit. I already knew that I enjoyed seeing new places and learning about different cultures, and I had discovered that there is nothing like being there and having all of my senses touched. Yet now I also had to think about personal relationships and potential future associations. Not only did I need to be open-minded and inquisitive in general, but I also needed to focus on what action to recommend after I returned to campus.

European Summer

Another memorable journey that I took in 1985 was a month-long trip to England, France, Italy, and Greece with Mark Poorman. Mark and I had been good friends since our time at Moreau, when I was on staff and he was studying theology, and we decided that summer was a perfect time to travel. He was preparing to go off

to Berkeley to begin a doctoral program in Christian ethics, and I was approaching the year when the University trustees would decide who would succeed Ted Hesburgh. In Paris, Father Jim McDonald was to serve as our guide, and in Rome Father José Martelli would be our tour director.

One quickly comes to envy the polyglot. While I have formally studied Latin, Spanish, French, German, and Hebrew, I lack a facility for languages. A multi-nation trip inevitably challenges one's skill at communication. Especially consternating are moments that involve purchasing tickets or obtaining quick information. Whatever utopian thinker proposed Esperanto as a common-denominator language must have first gone through the embarrassment of ordering dinner off an incomprehensible menu.

Customs was not a problem on this trip. In most places the checking was perfunctory. I guess we did not fit the profile of smugglers or terrorists. Security, however, was tight at the airports in London, Rome, and Athens. In Athens it took three and a half hours to get the passengers checked through security, there was a half-track guarding the plane, and we had to identify our luggage on the runway before they would place it aboard. But no one complained since memories of a recent TWA hijacking to Beirut were still fresh. I am convinced that the prime value of the security system is psychological. Nevertheless, if it works after a crisis to restore confidence, so much the better.

The night life in the West End of London where the theatre district is located was particularly interesting. There were still many Punkers in England, but their style was more a matter of cultivated display than aggressiveness. The typical group would include individuals with various shades of pastel hair, Mohawk cuts, elongated loops in the ears, and clothing that ranged from the bizarre to the mocking. The Punkers reminded me of the U.S. Flower Children of the 1960s, since they spent most of their time sitting around in public places, obviously enjoying being watched.

The women in English and French cities seemed very modern and liberated. In the smaller French and Italian towns and vil-

lages, however, this was hardly the case. Venice seemed to be a very traditional city with almost all the public roles being played by men. Rome was harder to characterize, since it contained a variety of social subcultures. In Greece, the tendency was traditional with some counterexamples.

The custom of long periods for lunch and dinner in France, Italy, and Greece sets a different tone from the rush of the typical American fast-food meal. Nevertheless, most of the American chains are present in the big cities. It is ironic that we are exporting junk food and importing *haute cuisine.* I liked having the tip included in the bill since it made everything easier to figure out in a foreign currency.

We found European cities to be relatively safe. Even late at night there was no sense of the pervasive anxiety or threat that characterizes so many American urban settings. As a student of crime and police enforcement, I was struck by the almost complete absence of "trouble" or evidence of anyone being arrested or confronted by the police. In the big cities there were plenty of police visible, and in the train stations and airports some carried UZI machine guns, yet I only remember two incidents in all of our travels. One was a group of police running and riding squad cars down a London street in response to an emergency call. The other was a brief shouting match between the police and a drunken Greek on Mykonos that required physical constraint. This is not to suggest that London, Paris, Rome, or Athens are crime-free, but in the central city it tends to take the form of pickpocketing and property theft rather than armed robbery or assault. As a result, one tends to feel safer in terms of bodily integrity than in New York City or Los Angeles.

Europe is full of churches and church history. Some of the greatest examples of human artistry and creativity can be found in the parish churches and cathedrals, yet a pallor of decay hangs over much of it. Many of the churches function more as museums than as vital centers of worship. Perhaps it is hard for an American to appreciate how the old and the contemporary can coexist

in the same culture. We saw many masses along the way as well as people engaging in prayer and rituals of devotion, but the majority of the faithful were older and the clergy seemed one step from the grave. It was estimated that 8 percent of French Catholics practice their religion in a public way. Fewer are baptized, married, or buried in the church than was true a decade ago. In Italy, the state owns the church buildings and provides a salary for the clergy. In Greece, the Orthodox Church is the state religion, although in addition to the large churches there are little shrines (some no bigger than a tree house) scattered throughout the countryside. Most of these were constructed to honor the dead and function like a transplanted mausoleum.

If I were the pope, one of my first priorities would be to evangelize the city of Rome. This center of Catholicism with its hundreds of churches, seminaries, and headquarters of religious communities seems endemically cynical. The hoopla over the pope and the internal struggle for power and influence in the Vatican leave the Romans cold, as if the rumor-mill explains it all away in human terms. We attended an audience with Pope John Paul II in Saint Peter's Square, and despite steamy weather a fairly large crowd attended. About half were Americans. When the pope showed up and rode around in his popemobile, there was clapping and some rhythmic chanting, but after a while, when he spoke in various languages, the crowd grew bored and a good number left before he was finished. The more of a media figure the pope becomes, the greater the danger that he will suffer from overexposure.

I was very moved, however, by our visits to the graves of Pope John XXIII and Pope Paul VI in the basement of Saint Peter's. These two men seem to capture for me the excitement and the controversy of the last twenty years.

We had two medical problems along the way. The first was minor: Mark had some difficulties with his ears and he had to make his way through the British medical system to get some relief. The other was more serious. The day before we were to re-

turn home, we went touring on motorbikes on the Greek island of Mykonos. On our way back from the far end of the island, I noticed that Mark was very uneasy. Back at our hotel he kept complaining about severe pains in his stomach. We tried the low-grade medicines we had with us but nothing provided real relief; we needed professional consultation.

I went to the manager's office and tried to explain what the problem was. He seemed to comprehend and said he would send for a doctor. When the doctor arrived (he spoke fluent English), he determined that Mark was suffering from kidney stones, and he administered an injection which eased the pain, plus some pills to facilitate the passing of the stones. He thought Mark would be all right on the flight to the States and could do the follow-up with his physician back home. Mark eventually passed the stones after our return home.

Another memorable event of the trip was the time we spent in LeMans, France, the founding place of the Congregation of Holy Cross. We were fortunate to have Jim McDonald with us for that pivotal part of the journey since he is fluent in French and knows LeMans well. This was my one and only firsthand exposure to LeMans where Basil Moreau, the founder, is buried and where some of the most important events in the history of Holy Cross took place. We saw the rocking chair where Father Moreau slept in the last years of his life, and we visited the main church and the visitors' hospice run by the Holy Cross sisters. At the time, we had no idea that Basil Moreau would eventually be beatified on the way to canonization.

While in Rome, we had a chance to visit the Holy Cross Generalate (the order's international headquarters), where we were warmly received. We also toured the International High School run by the Holy Cross brothers. This was welcome exposure to other manifestations of the international activity of Holy Cross. Our daily celebration of the Eucharist and our time spent with other members of our community, especially in Paris and Rome, allowed us to reinforce our sense of fellowship in a foreign setting.

Looking back on a life in which I have been privileged to see a good part of the globe, my early ventures to Latin America, the Middle East, and Europe not only gave me the bug for international travel, but they also whetted my appetite for learning as much as I could about the people, culture, and history of the places I visited. I always wanted to be able to bring what I learned into my teaching, preaching, administrative responsibilities, and my vision of the world.

Extracurricular Activities

When I joined the faculty at Notre Dame, I knew that my professional responsibilities would include memberships in one or more societies in my general areas of interest and expertise. I decided not only to pay my membership fees but also to attend the annual meeting when I could. Later, as an officer of the University, I joined the American Council on Education (ACE), which is the closest thing there is to an umbrella organization for higher education, and the Association of Catholic Colleges and Universities (ACCU), which has a mission-based orientation.

After I was elected president I knew it was also important to determine which state-level, national, and international organizations I wanted to participate in. Sometimes I simply followed in Ted Hesburgh's footsteps, but I also saw new opportunities to interact with and learn from other higher educational leaders, and I decided over time to let it be known that I would welcome invitations to take on some of the great issues of the day, such as substance abuse, the promotion of service-learning, the well-being of youth, or matters related to the Catholic Christian community.

I sought to strike a balance between my Notre Dame–specific roles and opportunities for service and good citizenship. I preferred to err on the side of over-activity, since I was surrounded

by a wonderful group of administrative colleagues whom I trusted to make good decisions in my absence. The availability of a Notre Dame plane meant that trips to Indianapolis or Washington or New York City, not to speak of locations farther distant, could be done in half a day. I could realistically attend to on-campus business for much of the work day, be present for a late afternoon and early evening session elsewhere, and still sleep in my own bed.

I did develop a kind of interior barometer that led to my resigning groups if or when I determined that my time was not well spent or when I decided I had made whatever contributions I was capable of. Even in my post-presidential years I have sustained participation in a range of boards and even decided to add one more by joining the board of trustees at Saint Mary's College at the invitation of my friend and former colleague, President Carol Ann Mooney.

Vice-Presidential Years

As vice president and associate provost, I turned my attention to the context of American higher education. I occasionally participated in the meetings of the Indiana Conference on Higher Education, which includes all the colleges and universities in the state, and the Indiana Independent Colleges and Universities, which is restricted to the private institutions. As president I felt obliged to attend an occasional statewide higher education meeting and all the inauguration events at the major campuses, but my time in the provost office taught me to prioritize.

Four groups that I participated in as vice president broadened my frame of reference. The first came when I was asked to serve on, and later to chair, the Higher Education Commission of the Congregation of Holy Cross' Indiana Province. This provided me with an opportunity to better know the University of

Portland, Notre Dame's sister institution in Oregon. It was my initial firsthand exposure to an institution with which I would become deeply affiliated through the years. It was a challenging time for the University of Portland. The school's endowment was relatively small, the operating budget was highly dependent on student enrollments, the facilities were in need of maintenance, and the board of regents did not have a membership capable of major gifts. Even more importantly, the university had absorbed the Multnomah College of Engineering, a secular institution, in 1969, and the board and other constituencies were still divided over how much to emphasize Portland's Catholic nature and identity. In short, Portland at that time was in a survival mode.

Fortunately, since then the university has acquired fine leadership, a much stronger board, a renewed commitment to its Catholicity, record enrollments, and a number of major gifts. Because I came to know the university when times were tough, I have a great appreciation of what its present realities represent.

The second group I participated in as vice president was the Association of Catholic Colleges and Universities (ACCU). Its annual meetings provided an opportunity for me to meet some of the major figures in American Catholic higher education and to attend seminars that touched upon the major challenges facing such institutions two decades after the Second Vatican Council. As president, I attended all the ACCU annual meetings and usually brought a number of other Notre Dame administrators with me. Later I was elected to its governing board.

The American Council on Education (ACE) was then (and still is) the country's most representative and broadly based higher education association—in short, a good place to experience some of higher education's diversity. ACE has a large constituency and attendance at the annual meetings was a bit daunting at first. Over time I learned how to make good decisions about which sessions to attend and how to maximize the interactive potential of the socials and the dinners. Generally, the leaders of Catholic

colleges and universities chose not to attend ACE sessions unless they had a particular role to play, but I was convinced that it was in Notre Dame's best interests to be a visible and enthusiastic advocate on behalf of all of American higher education. Eventually I joined the ACE board and later chaired the organization.

My final involvement as a vice president revolved around the discussions at the local and national level about the nature of a Catholic university. When it became clear that Pope John Paul II was interested in generating a papal document on Catholic higher education, Ted Hesburgh asked me to participate in several sessions on our campus that brought together theologians and other scholars and solicited position papers. Little did I know then how much of my time as president would be spent on the preparation of what became *Ex Corde Ecclesiae,* and on its implementation in the American Church (discussed in the next chapter). This early exposure to the debate served me well later.

My four years as vice president were invaluable in preparing me for the presidential responsibilities I would assume in 1987. While I spent most of my time on campus, learning as much as I could about the complexity of Notre Dame, I also began selectively reaching out beyond the campus. The mix of organizations I chose gave me exposure to some of the central dynamics and sources of disagreement and tension in American higher education in general, in Catholic higher education more specifically, and in the network of schools under the auspices of the Congregation of Holy Cross.

Presidential Years

In assuming the mantle of leadership at Notre Dame, I took over from one of the great figures in the history of American higher education. During his thirty-five years as president, Ted Hesburgh was not only an outstanding leader on campus and with the multiple Notre Dame constituencies, but also was active at the re-

gional, national, and international levels in a host of activities, not just in higher education but in Church service, government appointments, not-for-profit groups, and issue-related movements as well. What this meant for me was that the precedent had been set. No one was going to question whether it was appropriate for the president of Notre Dame to spend time on external activities or to exercise leadership vis-à-vis some of the more perplexing public policy issues of the day.

I instinctively sensed that Ted was able to survive all those years in a high-profile position at least partially because he periodically got away from the fray, so to speak, to enter into worlds other than those that had an exclusive Notre Dame focus. As a new and relatively young president, I had not established a sufficient track record nor mastered enough of the details of the job to be away from the campus to the extent that Ted was at the end of his career. However, I knew I would have the benefit of the doubt as I made decisions about outside activities, and I figured that with the passage of time I could take on additional involvements when they made sense.

From my high school days on I was always an activist, and I enjoyed sustaining multiple forms of service simultaneously. I learned that every new world or subculture provides another opportunity to develop a broader view of reality. I enjoyed team projects, where the energy and capacities of multiple actors contribute toward a common cause. While I had the capability of playing leadership roles, I also derived satisfaction from following the initiative of others.

From 1987 to 2005 I gradually developed a range of board and committee service in six major areas: (i) higher education; (ii) service and service-learning; (iii) intercollegiate athletics; (iv) substance abuse; (v) service of youth; and (vi) Church service. Some of these activities were short term or focused on developing a report or making recommendations to a larger body, but most were multi-year commitments. In some cases, I continue to engage my time and energy in my post-presidential years.

Higher Education

American higher education institutions have been characterized from their earliest days by a propensity to gather together in various associations, societies, boards, and conferences in order to promote their collective well-being and to share common experiences and aspirations. Some of these organizations have been broad-gauged in membership and agenda, and others more specialized. In addition to institution-wide affiliations, there have also been groups made up of board members, presidents, people with different types of administrative expertise, faculty, students, and alumni. And each of these constituencies has often been subdivided by type of institution, mission similarity, and geographical region.

When I joined the faculty at Notre Dame, and even more so after I became an academic administrator, I had plenty of opportunities to get involved with representative groups. Some of these memberships came at my own initiative, and some were by invitation.

Theological Societies

Early on I joined the two most relevant associations of Christian theologians, the American Society of Christian Ethics (SCE), and the Catholic Theological Society of America (CTSA). In the first, I was able to draw upon my ecumenical training at Vanderbilt University. In my early years in SCE, I stood out as a Catholic priest and Notre Dame faculty member. Later, more Catholics would join what had been until the early 1980s a predominantly Protestant group. Active participation in SCE gave me a chance to meet the leading Protestant figures in Christian ethics and to develop a network of professional relations.

SCE was a member organization in the umbrella American Association of Religion (AAR) and its partner group, the Society of Biblical Literature (SBL). Only once did I attend an AAR/SBL

meeting, primarily because it took place in nearby Chicago, and it gave me an interesting insight into the nature of large academic conferences. I decided on a whim to attend a presentation on a topic about which I knew next to nothing, "Medieval Buddhism." I dutifully arrived ahead of time at the designated room, which could have seated up to a hundred people or so. I sat in the first row and waited for the rest of the audience to arrive. At the appointed hour, the emcee welcomed "everyone" and introduced the speaker, who then gave a fifty-minute address. After the talk, the emcee asked if there were questions. Since I was the only one there, I figured that I better ask one even though I had hardly understood anything in the lecture. However, I did remember one technical term that he had used multiple times so I asked him to clarify its meaning. After that scholarly interlude, there being no more questions, the emcee called the session to an end. I cannot help wondering what the emcee and the presenter would have done if I had not been there. I suspect the presentation would have gone on before an imaginary audience, but there would have been no questions from the floor.

With regard to the Catholic Theological Society of America, it seemed natural that I would become a member. In the 1940s and 1950s this organization had been an exclusive preserve of male clergy and religious community members. Photos of meetings in those years show everyone wearing clerical garb. By the 1970s things were changing slowly but surely. Lay women, married men, laicized priests, religious women, and even non-Catholics had begun to seek membership and make presentations at the meetings. In my limited experience, CTSA retained a certain vestige of formality even as the composition of its membership evolved. What was most interesting for me as a Catholic theologian was how different the discussions were at CTSA meetings as compared to SCE. The Catholic instinct to take the teaching authority of the Church seriously inevitably came up against the countervailing desire to rethink foundational questions and to examine how effectively the Church was dealing with the most

crucial questions of contemporary life, especially in moral theology and ecclesiology.

Intellectual camps were more clearly discernible at CTSA meetings, and no area created greater angst about orthodoxy and definitive Church teaching than Catholic moral theology, especially in the areas of human sexuality, biomedical ethics, and war and peace. The presence of a few Catholic bishops at gatherings also affected the tone of the public discussions.

After I became vice president, I never again attended an SCE or a CTSA meeting, even though I continued to read their journals. I remained interested in the debates and the trends and the emerging leaders, but I decided to prepare myself as best I could for coming administrative responsibilities.

Boards of Governance

In addition to my ex-officio membership on the University of Notre Dame Board of Trustees, I have at various times served on the boards of the University of Portland, the University of Notre Dame Australia, Saint Thomas University, Vanderbilt University, and Saint Mary's College. I have also served on an outside advisory board for Our Lady of the Lake University. Each of these involvements has been enriching for me and I have learned much about the shape and diversity of higher education in this country and abroad.

The University of Portland. In my years as chair of the Indiana Province's Higher Education Commission, I came to know well the realities that prevailed at the University of Portland during the challenging time of the 1970s when Portland was in a survival mode.

When I joined the board of regents at Portland in 1985 as an elected representative of the Holy Cross Community, my ordination classmate and good friend, Father Tom Oddo, C.S.C., was Portland's president. When Tom had been elected, I had been able, in conversations with the search committee, to allay their

doubts about his lack of administrative experience, about his progressive theological orientation, and about his ministry in the Boston area to gay and lesbian Catholics. I told them that I was convinced that he would be an effective agent of change (and so he was). Under Tom Oddo's leadership, there was some fundraising success, the student population stabilized, and the university's visibility increased considerably.

After I assumed the presidency of Notre Dame in 1987, Tom Oddo and I looked to each other for mutual support. In 1989, I was stunned when Tom died in a freak auto accident on his way to campus from the Portland airport. A number of us from Notre Dame flew out to Portland for the memorial mass, and after Tom's body was flown back to Notre Dame for burial in the Holy Cross Cemetery, I preached at his wake service in Moreau Seminary and concelebrated at the funeral liturgy in Sacred Heart Church. With his death, I lost a close friend, an ordination classmate, a fellow president, and a great priest.

After Tom Oddo's tragic death, the Portland board faced the challenge of finding a successor, preferably a Holy Cross priest, to sustain and enhance the momentum that had been established. When Father Dave Tyson, C.S.C., became the leading candidate, I was able to give firsthand testimony to the search committee since Dave had served as vice president of Student Affairs in my administration. I described Dave as a first-rate administrator, an effective public speaker, well credentialed academically, and ready for a new level of responsibility.

Dave served with distinction as president of Portland from 1990 to 2003, when he was elected Provincial. In 2003, Father Bill Beauchamp, C.S.C., my long-time executive vice president and good friend was chosen as Dave Tyson's successor. I had the privilege of speaking at his inauguration.

Today, the University of Portland is thriving with record enrollments, high academic quality, attention to its distinctive identity as a Catholic university, a beautiful campus, major investment in new facilities, hallmark athletic success, and a growing

reputation as a school of choice in the Pacific Northwest. I am pleased that our sister institute, the University of Portland, has not only survived past the 1970s, but is now a center of excellence. I have enjoyed collaborating with my three fellow Holy Cross priests—Tom Oddo, Dave Tyson, and Bill Beauchamp—who have led the institution with a strong vision and deep commitment.

University of Notre Dame Australia. It is a rare opportunity in this era of higher education to be involved in the establishment of an entirely new university. But that became my joy and privilege when an unusual set of circumstances led me (and my central administration team) to respond positively to an overture from two visionary Australians to provide assistance in the foundation of Australia's first Catholic university.

In a previously published memoir *An Australian Catholic University: The Original Dream, 1945–1954,* I described in some detail the series of events that led the leadership of Notre Dame to help establish what ultimately came to be called the University of Notre Dame Australia (NDA). It all began when Jim Hesburgh, Father Ted's brother, met an Australian businessman named Denis Horgan who, along with an Australian educator named Peter Tannock, had been involved in discussions with the archbishop of Perth about initiating a Catholic tertiary institution somewhere in the Perth area of Western Australia.

In 1988, early in my administration, I and several other members of the Officers Group met with Denis and Peter over lunch at the Morris Inn. I was immediately taken with the idea (and with the two men) and pledged to come visit Western Australia for the first time on my way back from a meeting in Indonesia. On that first trip Down Under, I began my love affair with Australia and with the Perth project and its farsighted leaders. As a sign of my enthusiasm, I made three trips to Australia in one year.

In January 1990, NDA formally became a legal entity. We agreed to release Dave Link, the dean of our Law School, to serve as the first vice chancellor (president) of the new school. His ap-

pointment was for an indefinite period and we agreed to cover his salary. We also committed to sending undergraduates there as part of our international study options. It was critical to the fledgling institution for us to be so intimately involved with it in its first years, yet I knew that it had to be fully independent and fully Australian as a lay-run, church-related, Catholic university.

In 1994 the first undergraduates matriculated in Fremantle with a total of 570 students. In the same year, NDA decided to establish a campus in Broome, in the far northwest part of the country where the Catholic Church had for decades run missions for the Aboriginal peoples. In 2004 the NDA governing board agreed to establish two separate campuses in Sydney, the largest and most influential metropolis in the country.

As a member of the board of trustees from the very beginning, I maintained a deep interest in the Australian project. I traveled back and forth periodically (fourteen times by 2010) but other ND administrators also visited and many NDA administrators and faculty spent time on our campus as well.

At an International Federation of Catholic Universities (IFCU) assembly in Santiago, Chile, in 1997, as a board member I suggested to Peter Tannock that he should offer to host the 2001 IFCU assembly in Fremantle. It seemed to Peter to be an audacious idea since NDA was still relatively small, but he went ahead and NDA was selected over a Catholic university in Thailand. The resulting meeting was a great success and gave NDA worldwide exposure and Australia-wide credibility as well.

Much of the success of NDA is due to Peter Tannock's extraordinary achievements as vice chancellor. A physically imposing man and former star athlete, Peter sustained a positive spirit even when obstacles seemed insurmountable. He made hard decisions about personnel and priorities. He gave the university a public face in places where it counted most — in the state and federal governments, in the Catholic Church, in the business community, and in higher education. My own relationship with Peter grew in depth and affection through the years.

Today, NDA has 5,000 students in Fremantle, almost 5,000 in Sydney, and 200 in Broome. There are multiple medical, law, business, education, and nursing schools and significant programs in theology, physical therapy, and the humanities. It has attractive urban campuses, a supportive governing board, a good academic reputation, and solid relationships with three separate bishops and their dioceses. All in all, it is an amazing success story.

As I look back on my involvement with the University of Notre Dame Australia, I feel a real sense of satisfaction and achievement. During my presidential years, it was one of my most exciting and rewarding external involvements. Without the backing of Notre Dame, I doubt that NDA would have been established (or at least have prospered so quickly). Our presence was both symbolic (a strong reputational pedigree, the availability of counsel, and public advocacy for the project) and real (the first vice chancellor, a coterie of undergraduates). I was delighted to speak at the inauguration of the campus in Fremantle and at the celebrations of the opening of the two campuses in Sydney. On all of my visits, I have enjoyed interacting with the faculty, staff, students, and administrators and reminding its leadership of how much had already been achieved. ND and NDA (and the University of Portland) are now inextricably linked by their common purposes as Catholic universities.

Saint Thomas University. I joined the Saint Thomas University board in 1997 after being involved with the institution as an invited speaker on several occasions. I knew vaguely that two Holy Cross priests had led the university from 1929 to 1933 during a time of financial crisis. By all accounts, they served ably, but the archbishop of the day and the diocesan clergy preferred to have one of their own as president. Ironically, sixty years later, I, another Holy Cross religious, was given responsibility as a trustee.

The first time I met the present president of Saint Thomas, Father Dennis Dease, I had a wedding at the Cathedral in Minneapolis where he was the pastor. After the rehearsal, he asked

to chat with me. He told me that he had been told by his bishop that he would be the new president of Saint Thomas to succeed long-time leader Monsignor Terrence Murphy. Dennis' question to me was "What is it like to replace a legend?" He knew that I had succeeded the iconic Ted Hesburgh. I responded by telling Denis to be confident and be his own person. The greatest tribute he could pay Monsignor Murphy would be to build on the legacy and positive momentum that he had established.

During my time on the board, Saint Thomas has grown in size, complexity, and reputation while remaining faithful to its mission as a Catholic institution. When it opened a new law school, David Link, former dean of Notre Dame Law School, was heavily involved as an advisor. The undergraduate campus is centered in St. Paul and the multiple professional schools in downtown Minneapolis. It is a regional university with some distinguished programs as well as a large diocesan seminary on its St. Paul grounds.

Vanderbilt University. Since my doctorate degree was earned at Vanderbilt, I always felt a basic loyalty to the university. My experiences had been positive there and I came to know many members of the Nashville Catholic community. In 1998 I was honored by the Divinity School's establishing a chair in Catholic Studies in my name. In the same year, Joe Wyatt, the chancellor, invited me to join the board of trustees which I readily agreed to do.

While there were a couple of Catholics on the board when I joined, I was the first priest ever to serve. At first, I was a kind of noteworthy addition in the eyes of the other trustees (like the first representative of a minority group or the first woman). After they discovered that I was just a normal human being, some of the unusualness dissipated. I was regular in my attendance and a reasonably good social companion at meals. As a group, they respected Notre Dame by reputation, so my word was taken seriously on issues like academic challenges, student life, and athletic competition.

A year after I joined the board, Joe Wyatt stepped down as chancellor and was replaced by Gordon Gee, whom I had known from his previous presidencies at West Virginia, Colorado, Ohio State, and Brown. In my judgment, Joe Wyatt had done an excellent job as Vanderbilt's leader. However, Gordon Gee had a much more visible style of management. With his characteristic bow tie and grin, he seemed to be everywhere. For seven years (2000–2007), Gordon was the face of Vanderbilt, and many good things happened during his tenure. When he announced, surprisingly, that he would be returning to the presidency of Ohio State, the board and the campus community were shocked. Fortunately, a long-term Vanderbilt faculty member and administrator, Nick Zeppos, was available to succeed Gordon and the university has done well in his time as chancellor.

I rotated off the Vanderbilt board in 2008 due to restrictions on the number of successive terms. Subsequently, I have remained involved by speaking at a fund-raising event at the Divinity School.

Our Lady of the Lake University (OLLU). Our Lady of the Lake University in San Antonio, Texas, was founded in 1895 by the sisters of the Congregation of Divine Providence. Originally, it was a college for women students. As the role of the sisters declined and as the neighborhood around reflected changing demographics, the institution began to struggle with declining enrollments, a series of short-term presidents, and a tragic fire. In the midst of these challenges, OLLU decided to assert its special mission to serve the Hispanic community.

When Tessa Martinez-Pollack, a friend of mine, was chosen as president, she invited me to speak at her inauguration. Subsequently, she invited me to co-chair, along with Henry Cisneros (former mayor and former secretary of HHS in the Clinton administration), a once-a-year advisory group which first met in 2006. Over three years, our group, made up of a mix of educational and business leaders, sought to get the administration and board of the

university to focus on what they did well and to try to fashion a distinctive sense of their future aspirations. In 2010, OLLU held a press conference (at which I was one of the speakers) in which they announced an initiative called HENA (Higher Education for a New America), an effort to draw upon its experience in educating Hispanics as part of a mobilization of similar efforts across the country. While OLLU still faces challenges, I have been pleased to have been part of its institutional redefinition.

Saint Mary's College. Saint Mary's College was founded two years after Notre Dame and the two institutions have been closely linked ever since. Father Edward Sorin, Notre Dame's founder, was strongly in favor of the establishment of the college by the Holy Cross sisters, and he helped them find land on adjacent property.

Up until 1961, Saint Mary's had Holy Cross sisters as presidents, the most noteworthy being Sister Madeleva Wolff, who served with distinction for twenty-seven years. Then from 1961 until 1974, the college had a series of short-term presidents—three Holy Cross sisters, one diocesan priest, and two laymen. Much of this turnover had to do with the post–Vatican II decline in religious vocations, the re-evaluation of the priority of higher education among women's ministries, and the increased emphasis in the Church on lay vocations.

For Saint Mary's, the most significant decision in that period had to do with the rejection of a proposed merger with Notre Dame that the leadership of both institutions discussed in the early 1970s. In 1972, when Notre Dame announced that it was going co-educational without its neighbor, some thought that would be the death knell for Saint Mary's. Instead, the college got its second wind and continued its own distinctive style of education.

In my presidential years, I deliberately sought to establish a close relationship with Bill Hickey and Marilou Eldred, two of the lay presidents. Our administrations held meetings each semester, alternating between the two campuses. In 1992, I delivered the college's commencement address and received an honorary degree.

In 1996, I invited Carol Ann Mooney, from the Notre Dame Law School faculty, to join my administration and work closely with Provost Nathan Hatch as vice president and associate provost. In that office she took on many necessary tasks and a few extraordinarily difficult ones. She was especially alert to matters of fairness of treatment and to the University's efforts to increase its gender and racial diversity.

When the Saint Mary's College presidency became open, I was delighted that Carol was chosen. I was pleased to attend Carol's inauguration and, when a year later in 2008 she invited me to join the board of trustees, I was delighted to accept. While Saint Mary's has some continuing challenges, it also has some wonderful assets. I will attempt to assist Carol in her responsibilities with a real sense of pride in the long spirit of cooperation between the two institutions.

Higher Education Associations

International Federation of Catholic Universities (IFCU). The IFCU was founded in 1924 as a predominantly European group of institutions. In 1963, Ted Hesburgh was elected president, and IFCU sought to become an agent of reform and the revitalization of Catholic higher education around the world. In 1967, the so-called Land O'Lakes statement was published after a meeting of twenty-six representatives of American Catholic institutions and Church leaders. While well received among university people, it became a source of controversy in the Vatican. In 1979, Pope John Paul II issued the Apostolic Constitution *Sapientia Christiana* on ecclesiastical universities which set the stage for the development of a comparable document on non-ecclesiastical Catholic ministries. (This would be the backdrop of the work of IFCU during my time on its board as well as of the *Ex Corde Ecclesiae* process with which I was intimately involved and which will be discussed in some detail in the next chapter.)

In 1988 at an assembly in Jakarta, Indonesia, I was elected to the board of IFCU. Over the next decade and a half I would travel all over the world for assemblies (held every three years) and board meetings (once a year). It was a great opportunity to become familiar with the impressive diversity of Catholic higher education from India, Indonesia, and Taiwan to Brazil, Chile, Australia, France, Uganda, and Cameroon. In addition to discussions and necessary decision making, we also had opportunities for cultural presentations, visits to campuses, and organized touring.

In Jakarta, Indonesia, our opening liturgy was spectacular. The local archbishop was the celebrant and preacher. There was a mixed choir of students with organ and drum accompaniment. During the offertory procession, twenty-seven couples in bare feet and brightly hued native dress (most with some form of gold crown on their heads) carried in the gifts. The first couple brought a cage with live doves, while others offered fruit, musical instruments, and a variety of cultural artifacts. Equally impressive in other assemblies were liturgical dancers in native costumes accompanied by drummers in Cameroon, the use of incense and flower petals in India, and the incorporation of native musical styles and dance in Brazil, Uganda, and Chile.

One of the values of having the IFCU meetings in different cultural settings was that all of us had to constantly rethink our notions about the nature of a Catholic university. In many parts of Asia (like Japan and Taiwan) Christians were a small minority. In other places a fair amount of prejudice was made manifest by the government or other religious groupings. In Europe, with a rich cultural heritage, there were few distinctively Catholic institutions.

In 1994 (as a replacement for Beirut which was not a feasible location), the IFCU assembly was held at Notre Dame. After a lot of hard work in preparation, the turnout was excellent, the weather cooperated, the logistics relatively smooth, and the feedback from participants quite positive. The event attracted one of

the largest turnouts ever. In retrospect, our playing host was a great investment. It gave us exposure to a great cross section of leaders in Catholic higher education worldwide that we could never have gained otherwise.

I very much enjoyed my years of service as a member of the IFCU board. I learned firsthand about the richness and diversity of Catholic higher education globally. Those responsible for these institutions have much in common, despite variations in their individual circumstances. A strong IFCU is necessary, in my judgment, to counteract the constant temptation for the Vatican bureaucracy to create an alternate entity that it could more easily control.

Business/Higher Education Forum (BHEF). The BHEF was founded in 1978 to bring together leaders in business and in the academy. Ted Hesburgh was involved in the founding of the organization and he was a faithful participant in its deliberations. He even hosted one of its meetings on the Notre Dame campus a year before he stepped down. Ted was eager for me to keep the tradition of having ND represented on the Forum and I was eager to do so.

During the eighteen years of my presidency I missed only a couple of meetings (due to schedule conflicts). I considered the Forum to be among my most enjoyable external activities. I made good friends in both the higher education and corporate sectors, kept up with trends in the national and international environments, came to appreciate better both the joys and travails of leadership, and spent relaxed weekends away from the fray of on-campus concerns.

One of the roles of the Forum was to issue reports of mutual concern. The vast majority of preparatory that underlay these reports was done by experts from think tanks, usually headquartered in Washington, D.C. These collective reflections focused on matters related to education from primary and secondary to different types of higher educational institutions to the level of

American competitiveness in the workplace to health care, space policy, and basic research.

In January at a Forum meeting in Tucson, a tour was scheduled to the site of the Biosphere II project in the nearby Arizona desert. Biosphere II was promoted by a group of scientists and largely funded by a wealthy Texas philanthropist. The main idea was to replicate as many miniature natural environments as possible within an enclosed dome. A group of volunteers had pledged to live within the sealed enclosure for a full year, deriving all their food, water, and other necessities from materials available within the biosphere. Each of the major climate sections was to be separated off by barriers so that, for example, the desert area and the rain forest area would not contaminate one another.

Our visit came at a propitious time. The physical structure was largely complete so we were able to walk around inside since the biosphere scientists had not yet moved in. An equal number of the volunteers were of each gender and they ranged in age from the late twenties to the late fifties.

When we joined them for lunch, one or two sat at each of our tables. We had lively exchanges as we probed the scientific goals of the project and the motivation of the participants.

After we returned to our hotel, the judgments about the biosphere project took a couple of directions. The business people were skeptical about the long-range sustainability of the biosphere since its construction and original outlay was dependent on large sums of money from one benefactor and it did not seem that tourism would bring in enough income to pay the bill. The university people wondered about its scientific validity since the official explanation of its goals seemed rather diffuse and high minded.

Leo O'Donovan, the Jesuit president of Georgetown, and I had the deepest concerns. Both of us had lived through the relative isolation of Novitiate life (a stage in formation for religious community members) and we were appalled when the participants

admitted they had no clear expectations for behavior in the common life nor any adjudication process for complaints. They seemed to take it for granted that good will and rationality would prevail. They were, after all, adult scientists. However, neither Leo nor I thought it would work, even more so because it was a mix of men and women with presumably widely varying moral codes and histories.

In any case, Biosphere II ended up as a failure. It had a poor financial model and the scientific results proved to be of mixed value. But most of all, some of the participants violated the original agreement that no one could return to the outside world until the year was completed, and the group was riven by rivalries and disputes. So much for scientific utopias that leave out the human factor.

American Council on Education (ACE). Of all the national higher education associations, the American Council on Education was the most prestigious. In my early years, I consistently attended the annual meetings (which tended to be quite large in scale) and sustained our dues-paying membership. However, it was not until I was elected to the board of directors in 1990, and later served as chair-elect and chair, that I fully came to appreciate the value of the organization.

ACE board participation and leadership was a great networking opportunity. I interacted on a regular basis with leaders from every segment of American higher education—private liberal arts colleges, junior and community colleges, military academies, historically black institutions, and large state university systems. Over and over again, I rediscovered how much we had in common as presidents or chancellors despite the wide variation in size and mission of our respective institutions. I also came to appreciate the role of the various higher education associations and their Washington staffs who inevitably became experts on every aspect of public policy that had an impact on our common lives—from the role of the Department of Education and other federal

agencies like NSF, NIH, NEA, and NEH to financial aid awards and the support for university-based research grants.

Among other issues, ACE was in the forefront in emphasizing diversity (by gender, socio-economic background, race, and ethnicity) in our student leaders, faculties, and administrations as well as preserving the range of institutional options within the loosely organized system of American higher education.

Bob Atwell, the ACE president when I chaired the board, had a house in the heart of Georgetown where we usually gathered the evening before board meetings for a social and dinner. I always enjoyed these opportunities for informal interaction with my peers. One evening, for example, I listened in on a discussion among several presidents of historically black institutions where they were quite candid about how, until recently, issues of gender and skin pigmentation influenced who their boards were willing to choose for leadership positions. It had been important, they said, to be a light-skinned male, preferably with closely cropped hair.

On other occasions, presidents opened up about the stresses and strains of the job, including the impact on their spouses and children. When I shared my experience of having an armed intruder come to my office, other presidents told stories that made my brief incident look like a mere unpleasantness.

In my years as chair of the board, I had a bully pulpit for promoting discussion of topics that I considered important like campus substance abuse problems, the development of service-learning opportunities, and prior preparation for a range of potential crises from national disasters and fires to crime and incidents of violence. I was proud to serve in this prestigious leadership role both as a representative of Notre Dame and as a Catholic priest. At the January 1994 annual meeting in Washington, I introduced President Bill Clinton who gave the keynote address. He gave an excellent talk full of concrete points that I was sure that he had absorbed only hours before.

In June 1999 I flew to Italy for a conference co-sponsored by ACE and the Association of European Universities. I had been

invited because of my years of involvement with the ACE board. The site was San Miniato, outside of Florence, on the grounds of a former Capuchin monastery, the rooms of which had been preserved in monastic style with a bed, a small desk, two lamps, a wooden bench with no back, and a dresser. A bathroom was shared with the adjacent room. Right away I knew that I was better prepared for the living conditions than the others present, many of whom were married couples. In the end, we had a stimulating couple of days but not because of the luxury of our accommodations.

The most important role of ACE is to be an effective agent and advocate on behalf of all American higher education. Despite legitimate criticisms about our collective inadequacies from tuition escalation to concerns about the priority of teaching to overinvestment in frills and nonessentials, in the end higher education is one of the real strengths of this country.

Campus Compact (CC). Campus Compact was founded in 1985 by the presidents of Brown, Georgetown, and Stanford Universities and the president of the Education Commission of the States. It represented an effort to counterbalance media claims that college students in the 1980s were excessively materialistic and absorbed in career paths. The hope was that special attention to, and fostering of, the extensive volunteer work going on at America's campuses would spark a greater interest nationally.

My own life story predisposed me toward the values Campus Compact espoused. My three years of summer volunteer work in Latin America, my apostolic work at Saint Elizabeth's mental hospital and an inner-city parish in Detroit as well as working in a student dorm as a deacon and teaching undergraduate students, all convinced me of the importance of well-organized student and faculty involvement in the great social issues of the day.

In the late 1980s I became involved on the Campus Compact board. In 1994 I was chosen as a vice chair, and in 1996 I began a

two-year term as chair of the board. I felt comfortable in this role because there was a coterie of presidents and academic theoreticians who were involved in the organization and who shared similar values and comparable backgrounds.

Campus Compact operated out of Brown University with a relatively small staff. Despite its relatively limited resources, CC sponsored studies, shared best practices, gave annual awards, and sought access to federal and state dollars (like AmeriCorp funding) for specific projects. During my term as chair, we chose Liz Hollander as the group's CEO and helped to develop many statewide compacts, including in 1989 Indiana Campus Compact of which I was one of the founders.

Notre Dame's Center for Social Concerns played a role as a national model for how service-learning might be effectively organized on individual campuses. I became aware in CC that we were one of the few institutions where the social service/volunteer coordinators not only had a substantial, well-prepared staff, but also its own building.

Association of Governing Boards (AGB). The AGB was founded in 1912 to serve the needs of the governing boards of American colleges and universities. With a relatively small D.C.-based staff, it organized conferences, provided experienced counsel to presidents and board chairs, published the journal *Trusteeship,* advocated for best practice in board structures and processes, and represented this distinctive feature of American higher education to multiple constituencies.

In the early 1990s, I joined AGB's board of presidents. Later, I served as vice chair of the organization from 1996 to 1997 and chair from 1997 to 1999. As chair, I worked closely with Tom Ingram, the CEO, and helped set the agenda for our twice yearly meetings. One of the best received contributions of AGB was the list of the top ten issues facing American higher education in a given year. These lists were often used by individual boards as primers for fuller discussions.

After I stepped down as chair of AGB, I was invited to write a column for *Trusteeship* magazine for one year. During that time I wrote six separate columns around 300 words each. They covered topics like leadership in a time of crisis, a defense of institutional variety in American higher education, the role and function of college and university endowments in a time of economic challenge, the role and responsibilities of the presidential assistant(s), New Year's resolutions, and who gets the credit and the blame.

These were opportunities for me to play advice-giver or share what I had learned from my relatively long tenure as president. It was the first time that I had written a regular column since I was in high school. While it was fun while it lasted, I had no aspirations to become the Ann Landers of higher education.

International Association of University Presidents (IAUP). In 1950 the International Association of Universities (IAU) was founded by a predominantly European-based group of presidents. Membership was restricted at first to the top universities in various countries. As time went on, IAU became more international in focus. However, the growth of higher education around the world made the limitations of IAU more manifest. In response, in 1969 the International Association of University Presidents (IAUP) was founded as an alternative vehicle that was intended to be less elitist and hidebound.

In 1990 I attended international assemblies of both groups— the IAU in Helsinki, Finland, and the IAUP in multiple locations in Spain. While I enjoyed both experiences and we maintained our institutional membership in both organizations, my schedule prevented me from attending subsequent such gatherings.

Then, out of the blue, I received an invitation to join the executive committee of IAUP in 1998. I accepted because the timing was right and because I knew that Notre Dame would be one of the best-known American universities involved in the leadership of IAUP. I served in that capacity for one three-year term.

After participating in a three-day IAUP conference in Brussels, Belgium, as a new member of the board, I joined the other members on a real intra-European day with breakfast in Brussels, lunch in Bonn, and dinner in Copenhagen. It was a rather exhausting schedule but quite interesting.

From the hotel, we took a bus to the train station and, after a transfer in Cologne, we arrived in Bonn where we had a meeting with the Minister of Education and two of her deputies over lunch. She described some of the efforts underway to reform German higher education (going from an elite system to a democratic, mass system). From Bonn we took buses to the airport and then flew to Copenhagen, where we had the chance to tour the world famous Tivoli Gardens and to enjoy dinner together hosted by the Danish Ministry of Education. After dinner we flew to Aalborg, about forty-five minutes north, where we began our board deliberations.

Service and Service-Learning

In the same way that my many years of experience in higher education as a student, faculty member, and administrator had prepared me well for participation on a wide variety of institutional governing boards and system-wide representative bodies, so my personal history primed me for a comparable interest in groups promoting service and service-learning.

The Points of Light Foundation (PLF)

In 1990 I was invited by President George H. W. Bush to become a founding director of the Points of Light Foundation (PLF). This organization was related to, but separate from, the honoring by President Bush of individuals and organizations as Points of Light. The vision of the Foundation was to reduce chronic and serious social problems, to increase the quality and effectiveness

of community-service initiatives throughout the country, and to increase the nation's capacity and willingness to provide community service.

In addition to myself, the founding directors were an impressive cross section of leaders from corporate and not-for-profit backgrounds. They included: Ray Chambers (Amelior), John Akers (IBM), Johnetta Cole (Spelman), Marva Collins (Westside Prep), Michael Eisner (Disney), Roberto Goizueta (Coca-Cola), Kim Gross (Stanford Projects), Jim Joseph (Council on Foundations), Maggie Kuhn (Gray Panthers), Brian O'Connell (Independent Sector), George Romney (Volunteer), and Robert Wright (NBC). It was clear that not many would turn down a presidential invitation for this kind of national involvement.

As the work of the Foundation unfolded, I sought to pursue a number of goals simultaneously focusing on business, young people, the media, local networks, computerized information channels, and coalition building with pre-existing service organizations.

While the PLF board normally met in Washington at either the White House or the Executive Office Building next door, in September 1990 we were bused to Camp David, the presidential retreat in Maryland not far from Frederick in the Catoctin Mountains. As a long-time D.C. resident, I had always wondered where Camp David was and what it was like. It turned out to be a large enclosed area surrounded by multiple fences and regularly patrolled by both the military and the Secret Service.

After we passed security and got settled, we met in the cabinet room, attended by both President Bush and his wife, Barbara. Their two dogs were scurrying about beneath our legs during the meeting. I sat at lunch at a table hosted by the First Lady. Afterward, President Bush showed us his equivalent of the Oval Office and pointed out the target practice human outline on the wall that had been used by the former president of Panama, Manuel Noriega, that had Bush's name written on the top and filled with bullet holes in the middle of the torso.

In our four years of existence under the aegis of President Bush, there were a number of achievements. These included the establishment of an office of national service (under Gregg Peters-meyer), the initiation by the White House of Daily Points of Light recognitions, the passage of the National and Community Service Act of 1990, the convening of the first youth leadership forum, and the affiliation with Star Serve focused on students in grades 4–12. In addition, in April 1991, celebrations of service were held over two days in twenty American cities. By 1991 five specific initiatives had been approved.

By 1993, when President Bush had not been reelected, the Foundation which had been separately incorporated, continued to exist. I remained a member of the board until 1999. However, the absence of a direct connection to the incumbent president meant that the board lost some of its cachet and access to resources. While it continued to play an important role in promoting service and volunteerism, neither the board membership nor its capacity to take on new levels of activity was ever the same.

In December 1999, I ended a decade on the Points of Light Foundation board. I was pleased to have assisted in the transition from the halcyon days to the later period when the financial resources were more restricted but the need was just as great. The people I met on the board were uniformly impressive and the staff was of high quality.

The President's Summit for America's Future

In the late spring of 1997 in Philadelphia, the President's Summit on a New Era of Citizenship was held. The general chairman was Colin Powell, recently retired from the military and held in high regard across the political spectrum. Because the event took place after the transition from the Bush to the Clinton administrations, the two presidents were honorary co-chairs. Other notable attendees included former presidents Ford and Carter, Nancy Reagan (her husband was already feeling the effects of

his Alzheimer's), 30 governors, 100 mayors, 145 community delegations, and a group of prominent business leaders.

The Summit was sponsored by the Points of Light Foundation, the Corporation for National and Community Service, and the United Way of America. It was based on the belief that American youth must have access to five fundamental resources to help them live healthy, fulfilling, and productive lives: (i) a sustained relationship with a caring adult; (ii) safe places to learn and grow; (iii) a healthy start; (iv) a marketable skill; (v) opportunities to give back through service.

For me, one of the nice things was that the Summit brought together the leadership groups from a number of my pre-existing activities, such as Campus Compact, Community Anti-Drug Coalitions of America, and the Points of Light Foundation. As so often happens in the not-for-profit social service world, many of the participants knew each other from previous mutual involvements.

The closing event of the Summit, held right outside Independence Hall in a large public square, captured the nation's attention. Because of the presence of so many major political figures, especially the former and present heads of state, security in the area was extremely tight. I glanced up from my seat near the platform a number of times at the police and Secret Service agents with their sniper-scope rifles on the surrounding rooftops. If any trouble had broken out, I would have been right in the midst of the action. At the end of the ceremony, Presidents Clinton, Bush, and Ford and Mrs. Reagan signed a "Summit Declaration of Commitment" on the podium to much applause.

Governor Evan Bayh's Indiana Commission on Community Service

For three years I was a member of a state commission which was established to implement some of the legislation that flowed from President Bill Clinton's National and Community Service Trust Act, particularly the AmeriCorps provision which provided wage, health, and child service benefits and a post-secondary education

award of \$4,725 to young people engaged in one year of full-time community service. During my term on the commission, I felt we were able to establish some momentum within the state. The AmeriCorps initiative continues to this present day as a form of federal- and state-sponsored service with a solid record of success.

Intercollegiate Athletics

In my presidential years I was ultimately responsible for every dimension of our intercollegiate athletic offerings. Much of that task was delegated to Bill Beauchamp, my executive vice president, or to the different athletic directors—Dick Rosenthal, Mike Wadsworth, and Kevin White. However, by invitation, I was also involved at the national level in several other athletics-related groups.

NCAA Foundation

In the late 1980s, the NCAA created a new entity to serve as a kind of philanthropic outreach for the organization. The NCAA Foundation sponsored a number of activities including the subsidization of student-athletes who had dropped out of school before completing their degree work; programming at local campus levels with regard to alcohol and drug abuse, particularly performance-enhancing drugs by student-athletes; programming in leadership development for student-athletes; and media internships for students interested in the coverage of intercollegiate athletic competition.

Funding for the Foundation came in part from the men's basketball contract and in part from corporate sponsors. The board met twice a year and I always looked forward to its deliberations. One thing noteworthy about the board itself was the rich diversity of its members. It had the highest percentage of African Americans of any board I was familiar with. Among the

better known figures on the board were Calvin Hill, Peyton Manning, George Steinbrenner, and Tom Landry.

A nice perk connected to the board's spring meeting was that they always were held at the same location as the site of the men's basketball Final Four and the board members were provided tickets in prime locations. Because we were present for both the semis and the final game, I usually scheduled Notre Dame–related events in the off time. But I was also able to experience firsthand the mega event that the Final Four had become, from indoor and outdoor entertainments to media hype to opportunities for coaches on the hunt for new jobs to make themselves known. My only regret was that Notre Dame never qualified for the Final Four during that time.

In 2002 the Foundation changed its name to the NCAA Leadership Advisory Board. One year later, I stepped down.

NCAA Football Oversight Committee

In its November 2000 meeting, the NCAA decided to establish a committee of presidents to provide oversight and coordination for a study of various issues related to Division I football. When I was appointed to the committee in 2001, I discovered that, although we were explicitly told *not* to discuss a possible NCAA I–A playoff system, we had a number of meeting issues on our agenda. These included subdivision designations, student-athlete welfare, the postseason structure in Division I–AA, financial pressures, the certification of bowl games, the long-term viability of intercollegiate football, and the diversity of football coaching staffs.

The committee was made up of eight sitting presidents, including myself, and six non-voting members which included three conference commissioners, an athletic director, the executive director of the American Football Coaches Association, and another president. We were assisted in our work by the NCAA staff.

After six meetings spread over two years in which we had heard reports from twenty invited guests, we made a number of

recommendations. With regard to postseason football, we proposed an open-market concept with the monitoring of recently adopted criteria regarding the quality of the facilities, the level of gross receipts, sale of a specified number of tickets, and actual average attendance over a three-year period. With regard to financial commitment to the sport, we left that to institutional discretion. With regard to student-athlete welfare, we felt that relevant issues were out-of-season conditioning, academic performance/graduation rates, use of drug supplements, and gambling. Finally, with regard to the diversity of coaching staffs, we urged its adoption as a priority and suggested viable steps to be taken.

NCAA committees are, by their nature, representative of the various schools and conferences that make up the organization. In the course of our deliberations, I found that no NCAA activity is more emotionally charged than Division I–A football. It is the largest enterprise in terms of numbers of student-athletes and staff. It is also the most expensive and exclusively male sport. It is also the biggest source of income, especially for the institutions in the major conferences or independents like Notre Dame. While the BCS formula remains a source of regular controversy, most presidents like the bowl system since it allows half the teams who play in a bowl to end the season on a positive note and, with multiple points of access, many more teams have a postseason opportunity.

The major lesson that I learned from participation on the Football Oversight Committee was that not enough consensus existed within the NCAA to chart a more radical path of reform for Division I–A football. The sheer financial realities connected to football and the dependency on television revenue meant that the will for a new model would most likely only occur if the present structure became unviable.

NCAA Task Force on Gambling

In 2004, Miles Brand, the president of the NCAA, constituted a Sports Wagering Task Force and asked me to serve as chair.

Grant Teaff, executive director of the American Football Coaches Association, was named as vice chair. Bill Saum, from the NCAA staff, was the principal liaison. Other members of the task force came from various appropriate areas of responsibility in higher education and in intercollegiate athletics, including one student-athlete, as well as outside experts from fields familiar with sports wagering.

We had available to us the recently released "National Study on Collegiate Sports Wagering and Associated Health Risks" which provided extremely valuable self-reported information from student-athletes representing a cross section of sports. On the basis of this data, we knew that no college or university could safely claim that they did not have a gambling problem on campus. The good news was that education about the issue seemed to work.

Right from the start, we identified the two major goals of our deliberations as the well-being of student-athletes and the integrity of the game. We were explicitly *not* charged with looking at the general problem of gambling in American society.

The NCAA had two bylaws which forbade student-athletes and other athletic staff from engaging in various activities related to sports gambling and which provided strict sanctions for those who engaged in activity to affect the outcome of a contest or who were involved with organized gambling. There was also a national law that prohibited sports gambling at the state level but was not retroactive and, therefore, did not affect Nevada.

The media interest in our work was quite intensive. I was quoted in a number of print and broadcast outlets with regard to our focus. After a press conference midway through our work, most of the reaction was entirely descriptive or full of statistical data. It became clear that the gambling industry (particularly in Nevada, but derivatively elsewhere) was threatened by our work and afraid of what we might recommend.

We heard testimony from two professional bookies who assured us that once a person was on the line for owed money, organized crime would do anything to recoup their losses. If it

happened to be college athletes who were indebted, one of the recommended ways of paying off was to directly or indirectly affect the outcome of games. I knew that one of ND's former place kickers had become embroiled in gambling debts after graduation and had been involved in persuading two Northwestern football players to deliberately affect the outcome of games. The bookies told us that the mob typically does not threaten individuals but rather their family members, which had a more dramatic impact on their willingness to cooperate.

As we were preparing our first report, there was an aggressive campaign from outside to discredit our work and to cause the NCAA to make sports wagering a lower priority. In the end, instead of our report warranting national exposure and a full court press of publicity, our recommendations were relegated to a press release that appeared after the NCAA convention.

Our recommendations revolved around expanded educational efforts; creating an interactive web site for student-athletes; the expansion of background checks of game officials; a review of the NCAA sanctions; and outreach to federal, state, and local agencies and associations with special interest in, or expertise in, sports wagering.

I learned a lot from two years of involvement with the Task Force on Gambling. It is clear to me that the issue will continue to loom large with a potentially strong negative impact on both student-athletes and on the sports that they participate in. If we do not pay attention, intercollegiate athletics could become like professional wrestling where the outcome is predetermined.

Combating Substance Abuse

President George Bush's Drug Advisory Council (1989–93)

Sometime after George Bush's election as president, I was contacted about my potential interest in serving on a newly constituted Drug Advisory Council. Although not motivated by any

issues related to alcoholism or substance abuse in my immediate family or in my own personal life, as an ethicist, I thought that I might have some analytical skills to bring to the discussion about policy, criminal justice, and amelioration efforts. I also thought that my experience in the context of higher education would be an asset, as well as my years living in a student dormitory and counseling students.

Bill Moss, and later Jim Burke, served as chairs of the council, which had a total of twenty-seven members representing a broad geographical, age, and experience cross section. At face value, it was a prestigious group and the vast majority of them stuck with the council through its four years of existence. Our group worked closely with William Bennett, the director of the National Drug Control Policies.

Six projects were initially proposed. I served on the national coalition subcommittee chaired by Alvah Chapman. In our subcommittee we had a number of sessions where we had reports provided by successful local anti-drug coalitions. We wanted to determine how best to develop a national coalition organization to foster and support such efforts.

I personally was heavily involved in the planning for and coordination of two major National Leadership Forums in Washington, D.C. (on November 9–10, 1990, and on January 9–11, 1992). At the first Forum, we had 450 participants from 172 cities and 42 states. We had an interesting mix of speakers and panel presentations. I gave the keynote address "Anti-Drug Coalitions — A Priceless National Resource." Forum II was even larger, with 740 people from 43 different states. It was the largest meeting of its kind ever held. The presence of President Bush brought a special level of enthusiasm to the gathering.

In addition to the work of our coalition subgroup, progress was also made on the Campaign for a Drug-Free America (to engage the support of other private sector groups in the cause); the Drug-Free Workplace Initiative (to foster policy commitment from

companies and corporations); and further exploration of private prison initiatives (which had mixed support with the council).

After President Bush was not reelected, our council was fated to go out of existence, despite a lot of hard work, numerous meetings, and some noteworthy accomplishments. As a result, our subcommittee stepped up our efforts to create an independent organization to carry forward our task of coalition building. It was to be called Community Anti-Drug Coalition of America (CADCA). Fortunately, we received a grant from the Robert Wood Johnson Foundation to help subsidize the startup. We also put in place plans for National Leadership Forum III to be held in December 1992.

Notre Dame was involved in the work of the Drug Advisory Council, not only by my participation, but also by the work of Golden Dome Productions which videotaped the first two National Forums and produced edited versions that could bring some of the enthusiasm of the sessions to members of the local coalitions who were not able to attend. I subsidized this contribution to the effort from my discretionary budget.

Community Anti-Drug Coalition of America (CADCA) (1992–93)

My involvement with CADCA was a direct result of my participation in President George Bush's Drug Advisory Council. CADCA was spawned by the Drug Council so that there would be a permanent vehicle to support the efforts of community-based anti-drug efforts. We began as a steering committee of the Council with Alvah Chapman as chair. The evolved Coalition had seventeen members and 501(c) 3 non-profit tax status.

CADCA and the Drug Advisory Council had joint responsibility for the planning and execution of National Forum III. Initial funding was obtained from United Way and the Robert Wood Johnson Foundation. Eventually, Jim Copple was named executive director of CADCA and Alvah Chapman served as chair of the board.

I had great admiration for Alvah Chapman, a committed Methodist layman and former CEO of the Knight Ridder newspaper chain. He was based out of Miami, and after Hurricane Andrew devastated the region, President Bush asked him to be involved in coordinating the response. Alvah turned, in his new responsibilities, to the members of the Miami anti-drug coalition, all of whom knew and trusted each other and who represented a cross section of the community, to assist him in the clean-up efforts. He described the response as an excellent example of how people who band together for one purpose can be mobilized for other good works as well.

Forum III took place in December 1992. I introduced President Bush who spoke at one of the luncheon sessions. Other speakers included Vernon Jordan, Jack Kemp, and Tim Russert. There were a number of breakout sessions as well. A total of 679 people participated in the sessions.

While I was pleased to be a figure of continuity from the President's Drug Council to CADCA, by 1993 I decided to step down from the board after serving one year-long term. I felt that the new organization was well led and had some positive momentum. There is no magic formula for deciding how many external activities to sustain simultaneously or when the time has come to resign from any of them. However, I had an internal sense that told me when I had contributed all I could to a particular organization. When I resigned from the CADCA board I did so partially because of upcoming Notre Dame–related activities and partly because I knew that I would have other opportunities to contribute to the substance abuse field.

Governor Evan Bayh's Commission for a Drug-Free Indiana (1989–90)

The first time that I met Evan Bayh I was impressed by him. Before he was elected governor in 1988, he asked one of his staff members, Jeff Modisett, to do an in-depth study of the drug prob-

lem in Indiana and to make recommendations for an administrative approach toward its solution. The ensuing report was the basis for what became the Commission for a Drug-Free Indiana. Jeff Modisett was named chair and a steering committee of fifteen was put in place, of which I was a member. The commission had a staff of nine persons in the central office, with ten regional offices around the state (so it was a major commitment and priority). The final shape of the commission was twenty-five members (five ex-officio and twenty appointed).

Once we gathered as a group, we determined that we would focus on education, prevention, criminal justice, and treatment. On December 7, 1989, we held a Drug Summit in Indianapolis. Then we undertook a series of regional meetings. I traveled to Muncie, Valparaiso, and Jasper and attended the session in South Bend.

One impression I took away from the regional meetings was that, unlike inner cities or cities where they knew they had a problem, rural and small town Indiana were largely in denial. In the end, it depended on how enforcement, medical personnel, and teachers communicated to parents and civic authorities the reality of pervasive drug use in some parts of the youth subculture. If nothing else, we were able to get the drug problem on the agenda for the state as a whole.

After a year on the board, and after we had completed our set of recommendations to the governor and the state government, I resigned from the board. At that point I felt it was more important for me to concentrate my anti-drug efforts at the federal level as part of President George Bush's Drug Council. In that role, I would be representing the citizens of Indiana among other constituencies.

On the basis of activities like the anti-drug groups that I was involved with, I found that the most competent administrators were at the federal level and the least competent at the local level (at least partially because of educational credentials and pay scales). One of the difficulties in dealing with the drug issue was

that education, therapy, law enforcement, and coalition building take place primarily at the local level. Federal and state policies and resources eventually need to be implemented by concrete people in disparate communities.

National Advisory Council on Alcohol Abuse and Alcoholism of NIAAA (1995–98)

The National Institute on Alcohol Abuse and Alcoholism (NIAAA) is a part of the National Institute of Health (NIH) and is the lead federal entity responsible for research in the causes, consequences, prevention, and treatment of alcohol-related problems. It funds more than 90 percent of alcohol-related research in the United States. Among the areas of research by NIAAA that have led to advancements in knowledge have been: genetics (half of the susceptibility to alcoholism is inherited); fetal alcohol syndrome; alcohol and the brain (the causes of intoxication and addiction are based principally in the brain); medication development; drinking and driving (basis for national legislation in 1984); and youth prevention.

Enoch Gordis, the director of NIAAA, and I had met when I served on President George Bush's Advisory Council on Drugs. He sent me a letter inviting me to become a member of the National Advisory Council as a public (non-specialist) member. I was appointed to a three-year term. The primary responsibility of the National Advisory Council, which met three times a year, was to review grant applications to support biomedical research and training activities and to be advocates for the importance of such activity.

I quickly discovered that the number of documents sent ahead of time was huge (about six inches worth) and that the vast majority of the information was given in the most abstract technical language, which would make sense primarily to the experts. My job, as a public member, was not to weigh in on specific

proposals but to listen to debate among the scientists on the council to make sure that they were being fair and impartial as well as open to new approaches and perspectives.

The council meetings themselves were rather rubber stamp since the proposals before us had gone through a rather long vetting process. Overall, I found the actual meetings less than interesting. Nevertheless, I enjoyed the social interaction around meals and the ongoing conversation with the staff about NIA priorities and why alcohol-related research did not receive a bigger share of the available dollars.

The NIH, as a federal agency, is responsible for the presence of large numbers of participants in various agency-sponsored councils, review groups, and ongoing seminars in the Bethesda area. It is part of the American commitment to objective peer review. The NIH campus resembles a well-to-do college with many of the buildings named after former members of Congress, usually the chairs of committees that oversaw the NIH budget.

In my three years on the council, because of insuperable scheduling conflicts, I was only able to make four meetings. When my term of service ended, I felt that I had learned a lot about how the federal research enterprise worked and I was prepared to move on. However, I would soon be invited to serve as a co-chair of a new research effort of NIAAA.

Task Force on College Drinking of NIAAA (1998–2002)

In forming the task force, the goal of NIAAA under Enoch Gordis' leadership, was to break down the barriers between college and university presidents and the research community in the alcohol field. Academic presidents tended to get directly involved in alcohol issues, primarily when there was a campus tragedy or when they were assured that some proposal for amelioration was both theoretically sound and capable of implementation in their particular institution. Many had learned the hard way that, when it

came to social ills, it was better to remain on the sidelines rather than to promise too much. The research scientists, on the other hand, tended to be more interested in research for its own sake than in developing concrete solutions for campus social problems. Their frame of reference tended to be in the decades while that of presidents was relatively short term.

My co-chair of the task force was Mark Goldman, a clinical psychologist from the University of South Florida. The group also included nine other presidents and eleven other researchers. We had eight meetings over three years, not counting committee meetings and a concluding press conference. I also participated with a group of presidents from the Midwest for a discussion of a draft of our recommendations at O'Hare Airport on November 1, 2000.

We broke into two large working groups at our first meeting. These were on contexts and consequences of college drinking and on prevention and treatment. Each of these working groups commissioned reports and held open sessions. Mark Goldman and I, in collaboration with the NIAAA staff, particularly Steve Long and Fred Donodeo, were responsible for the shape and length of the final report. After some debate, we determined that the final title of our report would be "A Call to Action: Challenging the Culture of Drinking at U.S. Colleges." Prior to the publication of our final report, all the major research papers that we had commissioned were published in the *Journal of Studies on Alcohol*. In April 2002, in addition to our main report, we also published three brochures and a handbook which were attempts to summarize what we had learned and to make our recommendations available to a broad audience.

On April 9, 2002, we sponsored a press conference at the National Press Club in Washington, D.C., to discuss our final report, which had a little over thirty pages of text. Among other things, we highlighted the magnitude of college drinking consequences— 1,400 deaths a year; 500,000 injuries; 600,000 assaults; 70,000 sexual assaults; 400,000 instances of unprotected sex; 201 million students driving under the influence; 150,000 health problems. Of

the college age population 11 percent engaged in alcohol-related vandalism, property damage, and police involvement; 25 percent had alcohol-related academic problems; 31 percent abused alcohol and 6 percent were alcohol dependent.

The task force report recommended that college presidents and administrations select research-based intervention strategies in planning campus alcohol programs. It also advocated further research studies to evaluate the effectiveness of the recommended strategies after they had been put in place.

The report adopted a 3-in-1 framework. In order to succeed, schools must intervene at three levels: the individual student, the entire student body, and the surrounding community. The task force rated intervention strategies according to the research evidence available to support them. The most reliable methods focused on changing student's expectations about alcohol use; brief, personalized interventions in places where students were treated for abusive behavior; and programs that modified student expectations about the positive social effects of alcohol. The next best set of methods revolved around increased law enforcement; a focus on drinking and driving; greater taxation of alcoholic beverages; and the formation of a campus and community coalition. The least effective method was knowledge-based interventions (in isolation).

The overall conclusion of the task force expressed a confidence that the culture of drinking at colleges and universities could be transformed by committed, research-based, collaborative efforts that were supported by institutional leaders. We asserted that by changing the culture, these leaders could lower the prevalence of abusive alcohol consumption, thereby diminishing its consequences to the individual, the campus, and the surrounding community.

By the completion of my work as co-chair of the task force, I believed that we had successfully completed the task assigned to us. We had produced a high quality report that had been sent to all college and university presidents and that had been made

available to a broad cross section of interested parties. As one of the presidents involved in the deliberations that led up to the report, I was confident that both sides (presidents and researchers) had spoken frankly from their various perspectives and that we had come to respect each other even when we disagreed about particulars. There was never any rancor or pettiness in our deliberations.

By the end of my combined involvement with NIAAA, I deeply appreciated the quality of its staff and their commitment to service at the federal level. While NIH was a monolithic federal agency in some sense, the institutes within it were addressing many of the most important health-related issues of our time.

Center for Addiction and Substance Abuse (CASA) (1999–)

Joseph Califano, Jr., is a graduate of College of the Holy Cross (1952) and Harvard Law School (1955). He held a number of legal positions within the federal government before becoming a special assistant to President Lyndon Johnson in 1965 and effectively the president's senior domestic policy aide. From 1971 to 1979, he was a partner in the D.C. law firm Williams, Connolly & Califano. In 1977, he was appointed by President Jimmy Carter as Secretary of Health, Education, and Welfare. During his two-year term of service in that position, among other major initiatives, he was responsible for the national anti-smoking campaign. From 1983 until 1992, he was senior partner in the Dewey Ballantine law firm and headed the Washington office.

In 1992, Joe Califano founded CASA with its headquarters in New York City and affiliated with Columbia University. His founding board of directors included a number of distinguished individuals: Jim Burke, Betty Ford, Douglas Fraser, Barbara Jordan, Linda Johnson Rice, Michael Sovern, Frank Wells, and Don Keough.

Early on, CASA received funding from the Robert Wood Johnson Foundation, from an annual dinner, and from private

and corporate benefactors, both to sustain its daily operations and to undertake various studies in the addiction/substance abuse field. Joe Califano was well known from his years of government service and was able to assemble a high-quality staff. It is fair to say that he was the founding father and a strong guiding hand during its first decade or more of operation.

Commission on Substance Abuse at Colleges and Universities (1992–94). I first met Joe when he invited me to serve on a newly constituted Commission on Substance Abuse at Colleges and Universities in 1992. I would end up chairing the commission. The members of the commission contained a mix of leaders from the academy, medicine, the Congress, the judiciary, business, and not-for-profit organizations. In the course of its deliberation (and with the support of Jeff Merrill and others from the CASA staff), the commission examined the abuse of all substances—tobacco, alcohol, steroids, pills, and illegal drugs—at institutions of higher learning. We employed interviews, focus groups, hearings, and reviews of available data and literature.

In August 1993, we issued our first report "The Smoke-Free Campus," which urged colleges and universities to adopt campus-wide smoke-free policies and resulted in a significant number of schools going completely smoke-free.

In June 1994, we presented our second report "Rethinking Rites of Passage: Substance Abuse on American's Campuses." In it, we focused on the dramatic increase in, and intensity of, binge drinking—consuming more than five drinks in one sitting—on America's campuses. While the abuse of illegal drugs—notably marijuana, hallucinogens, heroin, and cocaine—still existed, the evidence was overwhelming that binge drinking was the number one substance abuse problem in American college life. The harmful effects of such activity included death, violence, rape, sexually transmitted diseases, and poor academic performance.

Among the central recommendations of the commission were the need for a collective comprehensive strategy; the need for

education, awareness, and counter-advertising; the development of a national 'alcohol awareness index' by which parents and students could rate colleges; and the need for federal funding for programs and research.

In order to properly roll out the report, Joe Califano and I represented the commission at a press conference in Washington, D.C. We received a good amount of attention from the media and, during the following days and weeks, both Joe and I did follow-up interviews with television and radio stations.

Ten years later, in 2007, I also chaired a follow-through study and report to determine whether the problem of substance abuse had changed for the better or not on America's campuses. The second report was titled "Wasting the Best and Brightest: Substance Abuse at America's Colleges and Universities." This second commission had an equally diverse and distinguished membership. In the work of this commission we used telephone surveys of a representative sampling of students, a written survey of administrators, in-depth analysis of six national data sets, interviews with key researchers, focus groups, and a broad review of pertinent literature.

Unfortunately, the CASA commission found that the culture of student substance abuse had intensified. Students were drinking and binge drinking more frequently and for the purpose of getting intoxicated. In addition, the proportion of students who were abusing controlled prescription drugs had grown enormously, along with the percentage of students who were daily marijuana users and the percent of students using cocaine and heroin.

In response, we recommended various steps to change the prevailing climate through changing students' attitudes and expectations; engaging parents; reducing availability; identifying students at high risk; targeting high-risk times and events; and providing services.

It might seem as though those of us who had served on the two commissions over a decade apart would be discouraged by

the findings. However, I was pleased with the growing recognition about the severity of the problem and the necessity to take ameliorative action. I was convinced that only a multifaceted, sustained effort could begin to turn things around. It was a positive sign to see many people in positions of responsibility looking for solid, feasible approaches that could stand the test of time.

Commission on Substance Abuse in Sports (1999–2000). In 1999, CASA put together a commission to examine the issue of substance abuse in sports. The original intention was to cover in sequence Olympic sports, professional sports, college athletics, and high school sports. Priority was given to Olympic activity because of the Summer Olympics scheduled for 2000. However, once the effort was underway, sufficient funding was not obtained to complete the full study. In September 2002, we issued the report "Winning at Any Cost: Doping in Olympic Sports." We also completed some important interviews with representatives of various professional sports, but we did not have time to finish the round of interviews that we had scheduled nor to finalize a report on the basis of our research.

The commission, which I chaired, was made up of a mix of leaders in athletics, the academy, medicine, Congress, and the not-for-profit community. We conducted an extensive review of relevant literature, held personal interviews and hearings with sports representatives, and consulted experts in fields related to the use by athletes of performance-enhancing substances — a practice known in international sports competition as "doping." In addition, the commission reviewed more than 600 articles in the fields of sociology, law, medicine, pharmacology, toxicology, business, and economics as they related to sports. The backgrounds, histories, and regulatory rules and practices of each of the sports' governing bodies were also examined thoroughly and media reports were regularly surveyed with regard to developments relating to performance-enhancing substance abuse in sports.

The findings of the commission revealed a lot about human nature. The athlete's drive to win combined with the absence of an effective policing mechanism results in an environment that encourages doing anything (including doping) in order to win. The use of performance-enhancing drugs threatened the health of athletes, undermined the integrity and meaning of the sport, and influenced the behavior of children and teenagers who often mimic the behavior of well-known athletes.

With regard to Olympic sports we recommended that nations should hold their athletes to high standards, that an independent international organization should have authority over testing and sanctions, that research should study the long-term consequences of doping, that testing should be made cost-effective, that appropriate U.S. legislation should be strengthened, that athletes should have health passports, and that the banned substance list should be standardized. Since our report appeared, Olympic competition has been compromised in certain sports and testing regimes have been dramatically improved.

Our commission continued to hold hearings after our Olympic report had been issued. We focused initially on professional athletics. It quickly became clear to me that professional sports with strong players' unions had created a situation where the commissioners and the owners had less control over the issue of performance-enhancing drugs and related matters than they would have liked to have. This was especially true with regard to Major League Baseball and the National Basketball Association. Unfortunately, our commission ran out of funding and no subsequent reports were forthcoming.

Commission on Substance Abuse among America's Adolescents (1995–97). In 1995, CASA constituted a Commission on Substance Abuse among America's Adolescents. I chaired the commission whose members included a cross section of academic leaders (at both the high school and college level), a member of Congress, a judge, a football coach, and a business leader. We spent two years in our

research and discussions and, in 1997, produced a report titled "Substance Abuse and the American Adolescent."

We found that smoking, drinking, and the use of illicit drugs (especially marijuana, which was much more potent than it was in the 1960s) had increased as these substances became more available to teens. Furthermore, the age at which children were first experimenting with abusive substances had never been lower. One factor contributing to this pattern was the glamorization of smoking, drinking, and some drug use in the media.

The CASA study was able to isolate smoking, drinking, or using marijuana from other problem syndromes and propose that the statistical relationships were powerful. The trajectory from smoking to drinking to marijuana use to the use of hard drugs was common among teens. While controlling availability needed to be a national priority, we also saw it as critical to help teens develop the skill and the way to say no and to not want to use drugs. The responsibility for creating a drug-free environment lay with parents, teachers, peers, clergy, doctors, and the trend-setting entertainment, fashion, and advertising industries. In the final section, the report made suggestions for fulfilling the responsibility for parents, schools, religious institutions, the entertainment and fashion industry, the medical community, and the government. Some of these recommendations directly targeted substance abuse. Others involved broader efforts to reduce factors that placed teens at risk. Most of the recommendations were not expensive or complicated. Above all, they required a shift in attention, attitude, and time.

Joe Califano and I once again presented our report at a press conference in Washington, D.C. We received a fair amount of media attention and gave a number of telephone interviews in the subsequent weeks. But the attention span of the American public is always limited. Our real goal was to reach out to American parents of teenagers who genuinely needed to be concerned about the health and well-being of their offspring. I knew from my experience that only repeated iteration of our fundamental message could be of significant impact across time.

CASA Board (2004–). After serving as chair of three CASA commissions, in 2004 I was invited to become a member of the CASA board which has a mix of business and political leaders, entertainment figures, higher education administrators, and experts in the substance abuse field.

CASA is funded by federal, state, and local government grants, by fees for service, by foundation grants, by gifts from individuals and corporations, and by the proceeds from an annual dinner in New York City. I made it a point to attend these dinners when I could. One year I was seated at the annual dinner with the leadership group from the cable channel HBO. An attractive woman turned out to be a regular on the hit show *The Sopranos.* Her date was a former big city homicide investigator who ran an agency that provided protection for Hollywood stars and other high-profile individuals. Another year I was with a group of financial gurus from New York. For some of them, I seemed to be the first Catholic priest that they ever shared a meal with. Despite the different worlds that we inhabited, I could usually find common ground with my tablemates at such events.

In addition to board meetings, I have also participated in CASA conferences. In February 2000, I chaired a panel on the role of religion in the recovery process at a conference held at the Ronald Reagan Presidential Foundation in Simi Valley, California, on the topic "Substance Abuse in the 21st Century: Positioning the Nation for Progress." In October 2003, I was a panelist on the topic of church and synagogue involvement in facing substance abuse at a conference held in New York. Then, in February 2008, I participated in a conference in Washington, D.C., on the topic "Sobering Up the High Society: Substance Abuse and Public Policy."

From 1992 on, CASA has built a major library holding on issues related to substance abuse, created an on-line network, run workshops and conferences, issued periodic reports and books, and sponsored various commissions. One of the most effective vehicles for gaining attention at meetings and press conferences

is the use of color imagery from brain scans which capture, in vivid detail, the impact on the center of human consciousness of various substances.

Drawing on the research of CASA, Joe Califano himself has authored three important books—*Women under the Influence* (2006); *High Society* (2007); and *Parent Power: The Key to Raising Drug-Free Kids* (2009). Each has been geared to the widest possible audience.

Service of Youth

The Boys & Girls Clubs movement traces its origins to 1860 in Hartford, Connecticut, where three women provided a place for young boys who were often cold and hungry, especially in the New England winters. Gradually, a loosely organized network of such facilities was established. In 1901, the Federated Boys' Clubs was created, which later changed its name to the Boys Clubs of America. In 1990, the Boys & Girls Clubs of America was established to better reflect the commitment to all children of whatever gender.

I had never been a member of a B&G Club in my youth, although I vaguely remember visiting an inner-city club in D.C. with one of my friends. In the late 1990s, having finished my service on a couple of boards, I was invited to become first a trustee at the regional level and later governor at the national level of the B&G Clubs organization.

The organizational structure of the B&G Clubs movement is akin to that of a federation. The national organization, which is headquartered in Atlanta, is led by a president (since 1996, Roxanne Spillett), assisted by a highly active and talented staff. The board of governors has formal responsibility for the national operation and regional and local boards for their respective spheres of operation. The annual national convention brings together representatives from all levels and serves as a pivotal time for sharing

experiences, examining issues that affect young people, honoring individuals and groups for special levels of achievement, and shaping the collective sense of commitment and responsiveness

During my time on the board of governors, the B&G Clubs organization has gone through a period of unprecedented growth and development. It was especially driven by efforts to serve in new settings — on Native American lands, in public housing projects, on American military bases, and in inner-city public schools. From 2002 to 2007, the total number of clubs grew from 3,302 to 4,314. The greatest growth in numbers by age group has been with the thirteen to eighteen year-olds, manifesting the increased outreach to teenagers. The result is that over 400,000 youth are served on a daily basis by the local clubs.

The board meets regularly in Washington, D.C., and New York City, but the annual convention tends to move around the country. While I served for a short period on the local St. Joseph County Club, I have also enjoyed visiting local clubs in Benton Harbor, Valparaiso, and Portage to experience firsthand the variety of populations served. The local clubs offer programming that varies from athletic participation and recreational activities to tutoring, mentoring, leadership formation, life skills, and art shows. Some clubs, in addition, offer a hot dinner in parallel with food provisions and lunch in the local public schools.

In the fall, connected to one of our board meetings, we have a Youth of the Year dinner at which five regional winners share some of their life stories. Their accounts are always deeply moving since their local club personnel have helped them overcome severe obstacles in their family lives and social circumstances. I always came away somewhat amazed at the resiliency of young people given the right set of opportunities. On the morning after the dinner, at the Congressional breakfast, one of the five is chosen as Youth of the Year and represents the organization at various events.

I have enjoyed working with Roxanne and her staff as well as coming to know the other governors. The governors are lead-

ers from a broad cross section of American life — business, communications, entertainment, sports, government service, and the professions. Among the better known board members, at least to the external world, have been Hank Aaron, Colin Powell, Denzel Washington, Ken Griffey, Jr., Mel Laird, Arnie Burns, and Condoleezza Rice.

One year at the Congressional breakfast I was sitting at a table with Colin Powell and Denzel Washington. Part way through the meal I noticed that Denzel seemed unusually nervous and sleep deprived. He told me that he had been up all night preparing for his big talk. He explained that he was an actor, not an orator. I found that comforting since I have been a frequent orator (a role in which I am usually relaxed), but only under duress, an actor reciting preassigned lines.

As part of my service as a governor, I have made presentations to groups of local club administrators in the Midwest, to a nationwide gathering in Orlando, and at the headquarters in Atlanta. On each of these occasions, I have drawn upon my expertise in ethics and upon my administrative experiences in higher education.

There is no other youth-serving organization that has the national sweep, resource base, or demonstrated level of success of the Boys & Girls Clubs movement. The national leadership is always examining trends to try to stay current with the needs of America's youth. Today, there is progressively more attention being devoted to academic success and high school completion levels (both major indicators of potential for lifetime employment and participatory citizenship).

Church Service

In many ways, my life as a priest and Holy Cross religious is a form of service within the Catholic Church. I consider all of my external activities as somehow related to priestly ministry, whether

within Church institutional contexts or without. Obviously, when I celebrate the Eucharist or the other sacraments or counsel a grieving person or lead a pilgrimage, the priestly role seems more explicit. However, I personally have not found any great identity problem or crisis of conscience when functioning in non-Church settings.

My primary forms of explicit Church service have been at Notre Dame, within my religious congregation, on the boards of other Catholic institutions, in occasional talks on behalf of Catholic schools, hospitals, or charitable organizations, and, when invited, on the boards of other Catholic institutions or representative bodies. In this chapter, I will focus on two. In the next chapter I will provide a more expansive account of my years of participation in the *Ex Corde Ecclesia* process.

The Sister Thea Bowman Black Catholic Educational Foundation (1989–94)

Sister Thea Bowman, the granddaughter of slaves, was born in Yazoo City, Mississippi, on December 29, 1937. While still a young girl, she began a spiritual quest that, at age nine, led her to become a Catholic. Soon she was enrolled at Holy Child Jesus School staffed by the Franciscan Sisters of Perpetual Adoration. Impressed by the life and work of the sisters, at fifteen she joined the community by entering St. Rose convent in LaCrosse, Wisconsin. There she was given the name Sister Thea. Later in her life, she received a doctorate in English literature and linguistics from the Catholic University of America. After finishing her formal education, she helped found and served on the faculty of the Institute of Black Catholic Studies at Xavier University in New Orleans, the only black Catholic university in the Western Hemisphere. In 1987, she helped organize the Black Catholic Congress. Sister Thea is credited with having incorporated African rituals and dance, as well as African-American folk songs, into the mass in this country.

I first met Thea Bowman in the late 1980s and was immediately struck by her charisma, her optimism, and her deep spirituality. When she was diagnosed with cancer, her physical appearance began to change but her spirit was not dampened. Six days before she died of cancer on March 30, 1990, Notre Dame announced that Thea had been awarded the Laetare Medal, our highest honor. She received the medal posthumously.

In October 1989, Sister Thea, Mary Lou Jennings of Stowe, Vermont, and the Rev. Thomas F. X. Hoar of Winooski, Vermont, established the Sister Thea Bowman Black Catholic Educational Foundation to provide financial support for black students at all educational levels. The Foundation was set up to provide an opportunity to receive a quality education at one of the many Catholic institutions of higher education. The intent was that scholarship awards would range from $2,500 to $5,000 on a year-by-year basis, dependent on the donations received by the Foundation. The scholarship awards could be applied toward tuition, room and board, or books.

The Foundation began with great enthusiasm and a warmhearted desire to open up opportunities for black Catholic students in high school to continue their education in Catholic tertiary institutions. It got started with a small budget, a volunteer staff, and more professed enthusiasm than short- and long-range planning.

In 1989, I had my first meeting with Mary Lou Jennings. She described the vision of the Sister Thea Bowman Foundation, which had recently been launched at a special liturgy on the campus of St. Michael's College in Winooski, Vermont, concelebrated by five bishops. It was determined that the chair of the board would be Archbishop Eugene Marino of Atlanta, the highest ranking black bishop in the United States. Eventually, when I agreed to join the board, it had five university presidents as well.

Right from the start, it became clear that fund-raising would be the biggest challenge for the organization. While the intentions were grand, the resources were limited. At one of my first

meetings, the board agreed to a scheme whereby the Foundation would attempt to raise $700,000 through the sale of "Thea Paper," a gift wrap with Sister Bowman's picture on the cellophane wrapping. Purportedly, the Knights and Ladies of Peter Claver, two different African-American fraternal societies, had already committed to selling 200,000 rolls of the wrapping paper. The Foundation then hoped to sell 300,000 rolls. This whole idea seemed strange to me, especially considering the logistics, but I did not want to squelch the enthusiasm of the participants at the meeting. In the end, the paper project was embarrassingly unsuccessful.

In the face of this, I asked Bill Sexton, our vice president for University Relations, to provide some advice and assistance. Bill soon recognized that the Foundation was a back pocket operation with volunteer staff and few personnel or financial resources. In 1990, we hosted the board for a meeting at Notre Dame. The gathering went reasonably well, even though there were no breakthroughs in fund-raising success. In the subsequent years, I attended one more meeting of the board in person in Washington, D.C., but afterward I sent one of my assistants to represent me. I was reluctant to completely withdraw, yet I was not sure that board participation was a good use of my time and often the dates were incompatible with my schedule. In 1993, I finally resigned.

In the end, I decided that it was more effective for me to focus on recruiting, admitting, financially supporting, and counseling African-American students directly at Notre Dame than investing time and energy in the Thea Bowman Foundation. Our internal resources were far superior and, thank God, we were able to make speedier progress with regard to such efforts than we might have if we had relied on the Foundation as such. If Sister Thea had lived, perhaps things would have turned out differently. She was an extraordinary woman who is fully deserving of being remembered through a Foundation devoted to better access for

African-American high school students into Catholic institutions of higher education.

Bishops and Presidents Committee (1988–92)

The Bishops and Presidents Committee was established in 1974 to promote collaboration between bishops and presidents. The National Conference of Catholic Bishops (NCCB) and the United States Catholic Conference (USCC) picked the bishop members and the ACCU selected the president members. The committee is chaired by the bishop head of the NCCB/USCC Committee on Education. Sitting *ex officio* on the committee are the executive secretary of ACCU and the USCC secretary of education.

I was chosen by ACCU as one of the president members in 1988. Almost from the start of my involvement with the committee, the proposed papal document on Catholic higher education loomed large. In October 1988, Pope John Paul II, during the *ad limina* visit to Rome of a group of American bishops, stressed the importance of the Catholic identity of Catholic institutions of higher learning.

During my four years of participation on the committee, I was also involved as a delegate in two meetings in Rome as part of the preparatory process that led to the papal document *Ex Corde Ecclesiae,* as well as a member of the *Ex Corde* Implementation Committee, which was made up of a mix of bishops and presidents. This meant that I usually had more firsthand knowledge of the international process and the steps toward national implementation than most of the other members of the Bishops and Presidents Committee.

The committee discussed other matters as well—the role of Catholic graduate schools, the financial health of some Catholic colleges, the role of campus ministry, and tensions over academic freedom—but the dominant topic of interest was the papal document.

The tone and tenor of the meetings of the Bishops and Presidents Committee was always cordial. Generally, I enjoyed getting to know the bishops and spending time in discussion with my higher education colleagues. However, the committee had no explicit mandate and, therefore, no one external to our deliberations was awaiting our proposed courses of action. The most important potential work of the committee was taken over by the other entities created by the Vatican and the Conference of Bishops.

Conclusion

The activities described in this chapter were not "external" in the sense of being disconnected from my administrative responsibilities at Notre Dame, yet they were all voluntary, required neither by my job description nor by explicit instructions from those who hired me. They sprang, rather, from my native interests, from my perception of my God-given talents, from my experiences earlier in life, and from my conscious desire to be a servant-leader.

I was fortunate in following Ted Hesburgh as president in the sense that he set the precedent. As long as I could properly attend to my fundamental responsibilities, both on and off campus, no one objected to my presence in multiple other worlds or to the travel that went along with it. In fact, my colleagues seemed proud that Ted's visibility and representative role was bearing good fruit in my own ministry. It was appropriate for Notre Dame to have a priest president who was interested in other worlds and who could bring those perspectives back to deliberations on the campus.

If I erred at all, it was in terms of over-involvement. Yet I did learn that some groups that initially intrigued me were simply not a good fit. I also sensed the point when I had contributed what I had to offer and was ready to rotate off of boards. By the later years

of my presidency, I had learned how many external activities I could sustain simultaneously. That meant that if I wanted to accept a new invitation, I had to complete an old commitment first.

I feel privileged to have been invited to play the roles that I did. Along the way, I met some extraordinary people, both on the boards and the staffs and among those they served. Equally importantly, I believe that we achieved a significant measure of good. For that, I thank all those who were part of our common enterprise.

CHAPTER 7

From the Heart of
the Vatican

Among my activities, none was more demanding in terms of time
and energy than my years of service during the various stages of
preparation for and interpretation of the 1990 papal document
on Catholic higher education, *Ex Corde Ecclesiae* (From the Heart
of the Church). Prior to 1965, the Church had made no attempt to
articulate a general statement of principles that would apply to
Catholic universities throughout the world in all the diversity of
their cultural contexts. While individual popes had spoken fa-
vorably about the importance of Catholic education and a few
had been instrumental in helping found Catholic universities, it
had not seemed necessary to go beyond those hortatory comments.
Even the 1917 Code of Canon Law skipped over this topic entirely.
In the United States, only the Catholic University of America was
founded with the direct involvement and support of the country's
Catholic bishops and the Vatican.

In 1949 the International Federation of Catholic Universi-
ties (IFCU) received official recognition from the Vatican. Then
in 1963, under Ted Hesburgh's leadership, IFCU became an inde-
pendent association. In the wake of the spirit of reform follow-
ing the Second Vatican Council, IFCU decided to formulate a

statement on the distinctive purposes of a Catholic university. From 1965 until 1990 when *Ex Corde Ecclesiae* appeared, there were numerous attempts to develop a statement that would both reflect the realities, hopes, and challenges of existing institutions and win the support of Church hierarchical leaders. While there were agreements about many aspects of a distinctive sense of mission and identity, different sides in the conversation were preoccupied by more divisive issues such as institutional governance, academic freedom, the role of the local ordinary, and the traditions of the academy.

In 1967, Ted gathered twenty-six representatives of nine major Catholic universities on property owned by Notre Dame at Land O'Lakes, Wisconsin. The group included members of the episcopacy, scholars, and leaders of religious communities. The document that grew from this meeting—"Land O'Lakes Statement: The Nature of the Contemporary Catholic University"—quickly gained legendary status, because of both its sweeping, positive view and the opposition it generated in some quarters. Most American Catholic educators welcomed the statement for its emphases on academic freedom and institutional autonomy as well as for the great emphasis it placed on the study of theology and the need for interdisciplinary dialogue.

While the Land O'Lakes statement received considerable attention, those who formulated it were all from North America. The challenge was to achieve a similar level of consensus for a document with worldwide application. In 1973 IFCU disseminated "The Catholic University in the Modern World," a statement that reflected the values of academic freedom and institutional autonomy expressed in Land O'Lakes, but also acknowledged that in different parts of the world and in different academic cultures there are various ways of being "Catholic." This document lacked juridical force, but that was seen by most American commentators as a positive element. Despite its generally favorable response, Cardinal Gabriel-Marie Garrone, then prefect of the Pon-

tifical Congregation for Catholic Education, saw a need for further elaboration.

In 1974, the Vatican sent a letter to all Catholic university presidents seeking their help in developing a new academic law for ecclesiastical faculties. Even though this would not apply to the vast majority of American Catholic institutions of higher education, some anxiety was expressed because of references to the role of theology departments in general. Moreover discussions were underway in some of the more prominent American Catholic universities about questions of lay governance. In 1979, an apostolic constitution, *Sapientia Christiana,* was promulgated that put into place a new academic law for ecclesiastical faculties. That same year, Pope John Paul II spoke to a gathering of Catholic college and university presidents at Catholic University in Washington. His upbeat tone allayed some of the fears that *Sapientia Christiana* had generated.

Meanwhile in 1974 the National Conference of Catholic Bishops established a joint Bishops and Presidents Committee to promote mutual understanding and acknowledge the importance of American Catholic higher education. As a result of conversations in this committee, the Bishops Conference issued a 1981 statement, "Catholic Higher Education and the Pastoral Mission of the Church," which covered topics ranging from identity and mission to the role of theologians and bishops to concerns about ethical formation, campus ministry, adult learners, and the role of religious congregations. Overall, that document was well received.

During the same time frame, efforts were underway to revise the 1917 Code of Canon Law, and in 1978 a first draft of proposed new canons was circulated. American Catholic university leaders responded to those canons having to do with Catholic higher education. Finally, the Revised Code was promulgated in 1983. The neuralgic points in it had to do with the consent by the competent ecclesiastical authority to bear the name Catholic university

and the necessity for those who teach theological disciplines to have a mandate from the competent ecclesiastical authority. Some canonical experts questioned the applicability of such norms to Catholic colleges and universities in the United States.

Three years earlier, the Pontifical Congregation for Catholic Education had undertaken the formulation of a document akin to *Sapientia Christiana* that would be applicable to all Catholic universities. It was said that after the New Code of Canon Law was promulgated, the document would give detail and depth to its applicable canons. Thus began the formal process that led directly to *Ex Corde Ecclesiae*.

In 1983 the first, restricted draft of a *Schema* on Catholic higher education was circulated to *periti,* or experts. In 1985, a revised draft was circulated to all bishops and university presidents. The bishops' responses were sent on to Rome; the responses of the presidents were synthesized and reported to the Pontifical Congregation for Catholic Education. The Bishops and Presidents Committee was also active in the response and served as a bridge between the two groups.

In 1986, Sister Alice Gallin, O. S. U., on behalf of the Association of Catholic Colleges and Universities, sent a "Synthesis of Responses" to the proposed *Schema* to the Congregation for Catholic Education. The responses represented 110 of the 235 Catholic colleges and universities. While there were some negative comments about the *Proemium* of the proposed document, most concerns were directed at the section on "Norms." For example, the synthesis said, "In the United States . . . the university must protect academic freedom and judicial due process for faculty, have nondiscriminatory policies toward students and faculty, and recognize the legal autonomy and responsibilities of boards of trustees. A college or university cannot relinquish such basic characteristics without losing its status in American civil and constitutional law." It went on to say, "Our presidents are very sensitive on the issue of being 'Catholic,'" and further, "the real crux of the document is perceived by many to be the assertion of a power on the

part of the bishop to control theologians . . . and to assure 'orthodoxy' in their teachings."

Shortly thereafter, a separate response to the proposed *Schema* was forthcoming from the presidents of fifteen leading Catholic universities of North America: Catholic University, Saint Jerome's (Canada), Villanova, Dayton, Saint Louis, San Diego, Georgetown, Notre Dame, Detroit, Boston College, Fordham, Marquette, Santa Clara, DePaul, and Laval (Canada). The presidents went right to the point, saying that "the publication of this *Schema* would, in our judgment, actually cripple the present efforts of our North American universities to fulfill the mission the *Schema* describes." They went on to say, "[T]he single most important problem in the present document is this recurring insistence that any authentic Catholic university must be under the jurisdictional control of ecclesiastical authorities. . . . It is important to affirm the Catholic identity of our universities, but it is also important that they be authentic universities." Finally, they added, "If theology is to be granted the same academic integrity of other disciplines, theologians also must enjoy authentic academic freedom."

After I was elected president of Notre Dame and before I assumed the responsibility in July 1987, I was focused almost totally on transitional tasks. While Ted Hesburgh was still in office, he conferred with me about all matters that had relevance beyond July 1. Among the things he organized early in the transition was the "Colloquium on Theologians and the Magisterium," which took place on campus in January 1987. He appointed Father David Burrell, C.S.C., a former chair of Notre Dame's theology department, to oversee the planning for the colloquium, and he invited three groups of participants—theologians, bishops, and academic administrators—who seemed to him "well-equipped to go some way towards articulating the middle ground in which we must live and work, as well as to make concrete proposals for collaboration." He asked three persons from each of the three groups to make presentations regarding their expectations for the respective roles of the other two groups.

The participants included nine bishops, fourteen theologians, and fifteen academic administrators. Among those who had a connection to Notre Dame were William McManus, former bishop of Fort Wayne–South Bend; Paul Waldschmidt, C.S.C., auxiliary bishop of Portland and a former president of the University of Portland; David Burrell, C.S.C., former chair of theology at Notre Dame; James Burtchaell, C.S.C., and Richard McBrien, both of the Notre Dame theology department; Jack Egan, founder of Notre Dame's Institute for Pastoral and Social Ministry; Ted Hesburgh; and myself.

In the discussion about the role of the theologians, there was broad support for the definition of a theologian as "one whose focus is on the apostolic faith, promoting the Church's understanding and proclamation of the Gospel, whose theological service to the Church receives public recognition, who is willing to exchange commentary and criticism of theological work, and who relates to hierarchic authority with the respect that is appropriate."

In discussions about the role of academic administrators, several points were emphasized. One was a need to articulate and affirm to the institution's various constituencies the nature and values of the academic enterprise, especially the research function, the freedom of the academician, and the Catholic identity and mission of the institution in service to the Church community. There was also a responsibility to support and protect the theologians of the faculty, always with a preoccupation in favor of their orthodoxy and communion with the Church, especially in areas of research that might lead to conflict with received ecclesial teaching. There was a need to initiate collaboration and dialogue with the diocesan bishop and the local church on a formal and informal basis. Finally, there was a desire that the resolution of conflicts be defined, including the possibility of the consideration of such cases by a committee or body at the national level.

This colloquium was my first opportunity to hear firsthand the reaction of a cross section of American Catholic educators

to the proposed *Schema*. It was also my first interaction, as Notre Dame's president-to-be, with people who would soon become my colleagues and friends in leadership positions in Catholic institutions. As a theologian myself, I knew that most of my peers, both at Notre Dame and in other Catholic research institutions, were fearful of what we suspected was an effort driven by the more conservative forces in the Catholic Church to take back some of the reforms of Vatican II. We feared that Rome did not really understand the American cultural context, which is so different from that in Europe. The intention of the colloquium was not to issue a document but rather to promote conversation and to strategize.

An international meeting was held in Rome in April 1989 to discuss the latest draft of the proposed *Schema* on Catholic higher education as submitted by the Pontifical Congregation for Catholic Education, headed by Cardinal William Baum. Approximately 160 delegates were invited, including representatives of episcopal conferences, religious congregations, institutions of higher education, and Vatican dicasteries. Representing the United States were eighteen presidents chosen by the Association of Catholic Colleges and Universities, four bishops chosen by the Bishops Conference, two members of religious congregations, and assorted other observers and advisors. The American group invited Avery Dulles, S.J., and Monsignor Fred MacManus as *periti*. I was one of the presidents.

At our first meeting, the American contingent was briefed by Jim Sauve, an American Jesuit who had been assisting the Congregation for Education in drawing up the new *Schema* draft. It struck me as odd that we had not received an agenda, a list of participants, or a schedule before we left home. I would soon learn that the Vatican has its own ways of proceeding.

We met in the Synod Hall, which is beyond the gates that restrict access to the heart of the Vatican, a location suggesting that we were insiders involved with important matters. But it was soon evident that most of the participants were clerics and

most of the women present were in the American delegation. The Synod Hall was quite modern, with the latest audio-visual equipment, comfortable padded seats, and translation booths with earphone coverage in English, Italian, French, and Spanish. The sound system worked well and the translators kept up except when the speakers talked too quickly. There were two television screens in front of the moderator's desks so that the speakers were seen in a frontal view no matter where they were seated. The room was tastefully decorated, with a predominance of wood, carpet, and drapes. A large crucifix and a smaller Madonna with Child hung on the upper wall in the front.

I was assigned to a group that took up the role of theology in a Catholic university. The consensus among of the presidents was that the narrative section of the *Schema* was unnecessary, but if there had to be one it should be considerably shorter and more general in formulation. I suggested that we focus on the relationship of university administrators to the local bishop or national hierarchy, and on the role and importance of the theology department in the university. My group was a microcosm of the assembly. The presidents from various places in the world were rather uniformly unenthusiastic about the need for a document and were especially critical of the second section and its normative and potentially juridical quality. The bishops were rather quiet. The Vatican representatives seemed to relish taking on the assignment of fashioning some universal statement. One was supposedly a member of Opus Dei and seemed disturbed by the drift of our conversation. Another came to one of our sessions with books of canon law and kept quoting from internal church materials.

During the course of the day my emotional state varied. Sometimes I had a sense that none of this had anything to do with reality and I wondered why I was there. Then I would feel a surge of obligation to speak about the situation of Catholic higher education in the States and how crucial I consider it to be. In one intervention I described the changing situation of theology depart-

ments and of the whole discipline of theology as we experienced it (more diverse—lay, male and female, married, single) and how the tradition of academic freedom has served us well. I really believed that Catholic theology was now stronger in the United States than anywhere else in the world and that Notre Dame had a major role to play.

The alternation among languages frustrated all the participants eventually. In our group, no one language sufficed. If the president or secretary reprised a contribution, it always seemed truncated. Speakers who gave the same talk in more than one language often embellished it in the second version. A couple of the group members had a propensity to grandstand, which got tiresome the third or fourth time.

One difficulty was that we kept referring to Catholic "universities," yet only a small percentage of Catholic institutions are full-fledged research institutions and most of them are in North America and Europe. These were most vulnerable to a charge that the Church suppresses legitimate avenues of research, a condition known as the "Bob Jones Syndrome," or the conviction in the world of the academy that "Catholic university" is a contradiction in terms. In many countries (e.g., France, Belgium, Italy, India, Canada, Spain) Catholic institutions receive state support, which can either compromise their independence or marginalize them in a broader state system; while in a country like Poland, the Church protects the academy from excessive state interference. This is why it was so hard for the Europeans to comprehend the American system.

The Vatican position seemed to be this: The Church teaches in a variety of ways, all of which manifest Christ's dictum to "teach all nations." It is the responsibility of the local bishops and higher authority within the Church to assure that what is presented as Catholic doctrine is authentic and reliable, and the best way to achieve this is to have universal standards enforced by the local bishop. The proposed *Schema* should lay out these principles and describe how they should be implemented.

There were many problems with this position. First, it presupposed that the university was an instrument of the Church or derived its origin or rationale through Church sponsorship. In fact, the university seems to be a human organization devised to structure the pursuit of knowledge; through the centuries it has developed a structure and methods of procedure which are seen to make sense on their own terms. A Catholic university is not a parish or a diocesan agency or a catechetical center or a seminary; it is a university. "Catholic" modifies "university," and not vice versa. Any attempt to reverse this priority would automatically call into question its seriousness as an academic institution.

The second problem had to do with history and development. In the United States it was not the Church hierarchy as such that established and supported Catholic higher educational institutions (except in a few instances), but rather religious communities of men and women and, more recently, lay people. By an appropriate subdivision of responsibility, Catholic educators focus on what they know best and the result is evident—a high-quality, diverse, geographically distributed system that is the best in the world. The continued financial support of Catholic lay people is one of the best tests of its perceived value to the Church community.

The third problem had to do with civil law, academic freedom, government grants, accrediting agencies, predominantly lay boards, and all the other features of American Catholic higher education that resist encroachment by outside forces, whether under Church auspices or otherwise. There is a delicate line between influence and interference, between informal means of communication and consultation and formalized procedures of direct involvement. It would not take much pushing for the present balance to be destroyed or for schools like Notre Dame to be involved in an endless round of court cases, faculty strikes, and disenchantment among Catholic parents. In a previous version of these meetings, Ted Hesburgh had a cardinal tell him, "If you

can't get money from the government, you can get it elsewhere." Easy to say for someone who never had to implement a five-year fund-raising campaign.

What these reflections are intended to suggest is that those of us representing Catholic higher education were not trying simply to protect our own hides or maintain our prerogatives. We really felt that the present spirit of the document formulation could seriously harm—or even destroy—what generations of our predecessors worked hard to build.

On the second day of our meetings, Pope John Paul II had his first outdoor audience of the year. On the third day, security was tight since the pope was hosting both Lech Walesa from Poland and the prime minister of Ireland. That day the bishops held a separate meeting. I spoke to our group of the precarious balance achieved in the United States, where predominantly lay boards in collaboration with religious communities were committed to preserving both Catholic identity and academic freedom in the face of pressures from the left and right, in society and the Church. The resources necessary to being a full-fledged research university are daunting, I explained, and only four or five Catholic universities had the potential to participate at that level. For their Catholic identity to be called into serious question from Rome would surely harm this precarious balance.

The coffee breaks were a chance to check up on what was going on in the other groups and the exchange was rather frank. Who knew who overheard what snatches of conversation? I guess wars have started over less. On the other hand, there was a real spirit of civility overall, and I heard no one lose his temper or become noticeably hostile or personally offensive.

Our American delegation met at 3:30 p.m. each day at the Columbus Hotel. Four of the six working groups had elected an American as president, which meant four Americans were on the steering committee, and they reported a consensus in all the groups about dissatisfaction with the normative section. American

opinion was taken seriously, if only by the force of numbers. I really sensed in my group that my comments had been reacted to by the others and that they had had an impact.

At our first plenary session since the first day, all of us were buoyed by the commonality of themes. I was proud of the four American presidents, who gave excellent reports on behalf of their groups. Common themes: hard to capture the complexity of Catholic higher education in a document; questionable whether there should be a normative section but if there is one it should be general, inspirational, positive, and short; there should be greater ecumenical sensitivity and a more affirmative approach to non-Catholic institutions of higher education; the description of pastoral care should incorporate worship, counseling, spiritual development, service, and integrative approaches to culture; canon law should be left out, since it presupposes a different context and will confuse the university community. Whatever the Vatican's Congregation for Education expected to happen when they called us to Rome, a momentum had now been established. The participants had been frank, thoughtful, and focused. Whether the final product would reflect these opinions was another matter.

The plenary session provided an opportunity for responses from individual participants. Although most of the Americans were inclined to hang back at that point because we had had such visibility as a group, I was impressed with the sincerity and openness of the speakers. There was a yearning for support, encouragement, and respect. Catholic universities in whatever culture clearly had a special and distinctive mission.

I made a major intervention to stress the importance of the principle of subsidiarity and to oppose a suggestion from Bishop Adam Maida (then bishop of Green Bay, later Cardinal Archbishop of Detroit), who seemed to favor a kind of accrediting board to assure the Catholicity of colleges and universities. I then offered comments on the importance of Catholic research universities and the components such as academic freedom that assured their credibility as full-fledged universities. There was some ap-

plause when I finished, and later on the other Americans and many others told me they agreed with my sentiments. I also spoke about the importance of the International Federation of Catholic Universities as a center of cooperation and international exchange.

At a meeting of the American group I spoke of the Kafkaesque quality of the sessions. It was not clear who was in charge, who would write the final document, what role our deliberations would play, or whether we should try to produce a final report. Nevertheless, I felt that we were having an impact on those present as observers and participants. We could only do our best and live in hope.

On the morning of the fifth day our group went around again to get a sense of how to proceed. One agreement was that the IFCU, as the most representative international body of college presidents, should be consulted in the next stage of development of the document. I proposed a recommendation about how the principle of subsidiarity would lead to a different kind of statement in the document. It won unanimous support after the words "according to the nature of the Church" were added. The recommendation then read, "In the text of the *Schema,* whenever a description is provided of the respective levels of responsibility for Catholic identity and mission among university administrators, local Church authorities and other Church officials, the principle of subsidiarity *according to the nature of the Church* should be acknowledged and maintained. In particular this would suggest that whenever possible, collaborative and informal procedures are to be preferred to juridical ones." I waited to see if it would win support at the plenary meeting.

The president of Leuven University in Belgium was the most outspoken member of our work group. A layman and a lawyer, he had had several run-ins with the Vatican in recent years, especially in the area of biotechnology research, and he spiced his comments with anecdotes about this or that encounter. We Americans always seemed moderate in contrast.

At a plenary session it was announced that a fifteen-member interim commission would follow up the present meeting and help prepare the next draft of a document to be proposed to the *Plenarium* meeting of the Congregation for Education. The interim group would have a chance to look at it when they returned to Rome in September. The Secretary of the Congregation specified that we should elect the members of the interim commission according to the following division: three from IFCU, two from the bishops, three from the United States and Canada, two from Latin America, two from Europe, two from Asia and the Middle East, and one from Africa. This seemed to me to be an excellent step, since it provided a clear mechanism for following through on our deliberations. When the American-Canadian group met we elected Father Joe O'Hare (Fordham), Sister Sally Furay (San Diego), and myself. Don Monan (Boston College) was the alternate. I was not eager to be gone from the campus in September but I felt obliged to do my part in the following stage of preparation of the document.

As things began to wind down, I felt that we had accomplished quite a bit. The American group had been cohesive, friendly, reasonable, and frank. Altogether, six of us on the commission were active on the IFCU board. None of us knew what impact our recommendations would have in the end. However, I knew that I personally would be returning in five months or so.

At our closing session, a vote was taken on our summary propositions. Only presidents and bishops were eligible to vote, and most of the propositions passed unanimously. The pope arrived in the Synod Hall a little after 12:30 p.m. There were a few security people but they were not prominent. The bishops in our group had dressed in their robes with their red beanies and were generally seated in the first two rows. Spouses of participants had been invited so our contingent was somewhat larger. The Secretary of the Congregation opened with a few words of greeting and a rather fulsome summary of our meeting. Pope John Paul then read from a prepared text for about thirty minutes. The contents

were generally positive and supportive. He made reference several times to the need to harness or channel the results of scientific research in a direction promotive of the human good. His most common refrain was "the dignity of the human person." Most noticeably, there were no words of complaint or critique directed to us. The final stage of the visit was one long photo opportunity, with each of us in turn coming forward to shake the pope's hand and have our picture taken.

Later on, our group had a press conference with reporters from the Associated Press, the *New York Times,* the National Catholic News Service, the *Los Angeles Times,* the *National Catholic Reporter,* the *National Catholic Register,* and *Time* magazine. Obviously most of them were searching for a hot story about conflict and confrontation. They were probably disappointed. The results of the meeting turned out to be more positive (at least in the short run) than the American presidents had anticipated. While there were conservative pressures to keep things under control, the Congregation surprised everyone by voting openly on the summary propositions and establishing the interim commission.

Yet I had very ambivalent feelings about the Vatican as an institution after this, my first sustained exposure. Surely the papal office and the role of the bishop of Rome as the spiritual leader is one of the riches of Catholicism. Unity of faith is a call of the Gospel, and all of us benefit from the efforts to facilitate the work of evangelization, catechesis, pastoral care, worship, and teaching. And there is no doubt that a church of 700 million adherents worldwide requires a bureaucracy to foster its life and organize its efforts. Nevertheless, anyone who has studied the history of the Church knows that power can be alluring, even religious power.

We have had good and bad popes, thriving and corrupt periods, martyrdom and pomp and circumstance. The present period in Rome reflected a more conservative style than prevailed right after the Second Vatican Council. Opus Dei and other Europe-based movements had gained a measure of legitimacy and importance in the Vatican. A kind of clerical culture was reasserting

itself in the seminaries and religious houses. Women were still on the periphery at the Vatican, and many of the functionaries seemed to fear saying anything controversial lest their career path be impeded. It all seemed a long way from the more informal, collaborative, lay-involved style of the States. In notes I made at the time, I opined that it would probably be the Church of the Third World that determined the future shape of Catholicism.

The Second Vatican Meeting

I was excited to be one of fifteen elected representatives at the follow-through meeting in the Vatican in September 1989. By then, the *Schema* had gone through four or five revisions, and this was to be the final stage of drafting for what would become *Ex Corde Ecclesiae*. We knew before arriving in Rome that after our meeting there would be the *Plenarium* of the Pontifical Congregation for Catholic Education to review our document and then send it on to Pope John Paul.

Instead of meeting in the modern and comfortable new Synod Hall where we had met in April, we were moved to the old Synod Hall, which once functioned as the Vatican granary. Entrance was through a passageway in the immense, solid stone and brick wall that rings Vatican City. Towering over the inner courtyard were buildings that rose perhaps ten or twelve stories like a medieval castle or ancient walled city. From this vantage point, the Vatican seemed more like a prison or a fortress than a portal to the world. The feeling was of permanence, impermeability, resistance to change.

In addition to the fifteen delegates there were fourteen experts or members of the Congregation at the meeting. Because Cardinal Baum, the head of the Congregation, was ill, Archbishop José Saraiva Martins (Secretary of the Congregation) chaired our plenary session. The three American delegates were Father Joe

O'Hare, S.J. (Fordham), Sister Sally Furay, R.C.J. (Provost, San Diego), and I. We came to the meeting committed to preserving the consensus view of American Catholic university presidents. Our preference was still to have no document at all, but we saw the new draft as a significant improvement. In our judgment, the most sensitive points revolved around the relationship between a Catholic university and the institutional Church, particularly with regard to the role and function of the theologian. I knew that Joe O'Hare was particularly adept with the written word (as a former editor of *America* magazine) and that Sally Furay was a civil lawyer. When people asked me about my background, I said that I was a theologian, which usually got their attention, considering the discussions that we were engaged in.

In addition to the fifteen elected delegates, the group included eight members of the Congregation for Catholic Education, one representative of the Vatican Secretariat of State, and five invited experts, one of whom was Adam Maida. The other experts were European. We spent most of the opening morning taking turns in offering general reflections on the new text. There was a bit of parry and thrust, with the presidents generally applauding the tenor of the draft but urging a loosening of some language, while the more conservative spokespeople fretted about a need for more formalized instruments of Catholic identity and about the prerogatives of the local bishop. By the end of the morning it was clear that the majority of us considered the document a fairly good response to the April discussion but with unresolved tensions in the text. For most of us, the heart of the document revolved around the articulation of the notions of institutional autonomy, academic freedom, lay control, the importance of research, and the role and function of theology in a university setting.

We broke into three working groups and I volunteered to serve on one that had some of the more controversial material. Our group met around a commodious boardroom-style table in a second-floor room that seemed to be a repository for ancient

pieces of art. Immediately on the wall in front of where I was sitting were two fifteen foot high statues of Saints Peter and Paul which at one time stood at the entrance to Saint Peter's. I think they were passing on a subliminal message.

On the second day, after we all had a chance to comment on the texts in Part I, we started with the Norms, but had to break to move to the plenary session. The discussions there were polite, slowed down by the need to translate. It became clear that the other two groups had completed their initial work, so it was decided to have the secretaries duplicate the amended texts and make them available for the afternoon session. Our group would meet earlier to try to catch up.

Monsignor Baldanza, one of the top figures in the Congregation, motioned me aside during the break and informed me that the Congregation was hearing positive things from the American bishops about Notre Dame relative to the Catholicity question. It was not quite clear whether that was intended to be a compliment or a reminder that he and Ted Hesburgh had not always seen eye to eye. I told him about all the good things that were going on and how important the Catholic identity of the University was, and we parted on a positive note. All I could think was that, like many bureaucrats, his perception was formed by the number of complaints he received. As far as I knew, neither he nor anyone else in the Congregation had ever spent time on our campus—hard to believe when considering the prominent role we play in Catholic higher education. In the end, I was happy that we were in Rome's favor, whatever the reasons.

The afternoon session was rather frustrating. Our group had turned to the normative document because it presumably had a higher status in the life of the Church and tended to have juridical consequences. Many would read the final document for the first time by turning immediately to the Norms and understanding the rest as preamble.

Bishop Maida introduced a change of wording in Article 2, which hinged on the distinction between a "public juridical per-

son" (a fully certified entity of the Church, like Catholic University in D.C.) and a "private juridical person" (his interpretation of the status of Notre Dame since 1967, when we moved to a mostly lay board of trustees). From the perspective of a canon lawyer, he argued that this provided a symmetrical and orderly descriptive framework which acknowledged the lack of direct ecclesiastical control over the life and resources of private juridical persons. I had to admit to myself that I was suspicious of such seemingly simple descriptive categories, but on the face of it I had no grounds to protest.

Eventually, we joined the others for a plenary session. Because the three groups had worked separately, even though reports were given by the secretaries, we had not agreed upon a format for moving on toward completion of our work. Some wanted to have each of the small groups review the work of the other two groups and subsequently reconvene. Others preferred a large group conversation right from the start. Another point of division was whether we should review and approve specific texts (a kind of writing by a committee of the whole) or whether we should identify the central points and leave the drafting to one person or a small group. It was finally resolved that we return to small groups in the morning, chart our progress, and then decide.

The first problem was that whatever we decided as a group had no guarantee to make it through the *Plenarium* in October, to say nothing of the pope's final draft. At best, we were consulters, yet here we were spending our time on the minutiae of a proposed document. The second problem was the combination of a seemingly democratic, or at least representative, process with the presence of an almost equal number of Congregation functionaries and invited experts. To be enthusiastic about such a configuration required both a clear order of procedure and high levels of trust. In this instance, most presidents of universities did not want a document in the first place or, as a backup position, preferred no normative section. Therefore, when the conversation became juridical and/or canonical, all my instincts were to resist measures

that seemed either coercive or contrary to the best interests of American Catholic higher education.

The third problem was that, except for the presidents in the group, no one appeared to have an experiential base of any breadth for speaking about Catholic universities throughout the world. No business enterprise or government agency would allow decisions to be made at home base without visiting in person the concrete institutions being discussed. As a result of this poverty of experience, the discussion proceeded in a highly abstract and deductive fashion (e.g., proposing the attributes of an ideal Catholic university), or it viewed the debate over the nature and structure of a Catholic university as one instance of some broader trend (e.g., the individualism, secularism, hedonism, consumerism of Western society since the Enlightenment). In the afternoon, I took a long walk around Rome to put things in perspective.

Next morning there was a noticeable sense of progress and we were able to concentrate on the most critical points. By noon we had finished our task as a small group. Our afternoon plenary session turned out to be much more positive than I had expected. The presidents and secretaries had produced a written text of all seven articles in the normative section as well as a reformulation of the section on the relationship between bishops and theologians. After rather peaceful discussions, we voted on the seven articles one by one.

Emotionally, the participants had a sense that consensus had been achieved. The members of the Congregation seemed happy that a workable text was produced in the allotted time. Joe O'Hare was an excellent reporter of the results of the steering committee, combining sincerity and equanimity with humor, so that any tension was diffused. All three presiding members of the Congregation, while displaying a certain deference to the bishop participants, had as their agenda the completion of the assigned task without major confrontation or public squabble. Long-range questions remained about what would happen next,

of course, yet I was convinced that this stage of the discussion had gone well, and most of that was attributable to the role we played as delegates

Certain thoughts ran through my mind in retrospect. The range and diversity of Catholic higher education around the world is one of the great achievements of the Church. In one of my interventions at the meeting I urged the Congregation to do two things. One, I proposed that some scholar or group of scholars undertake a historical study of Catholic higher education from the High Middle Ages to the present. Second, I suggested that we collectively focus on those parts of the world, particularly black Africa and Asia, where there is a great demand for Catholic education but either insufficient resources or hostile governments. Notre Dame's involvement in Notre Dame Australia was one example of how such ventures might be begun.

I also thought about the need to promote positive interaction between university administrators/governing boards and the National Conference of Catholic Bishops. The Bishops and Presidents Committee, of which I was then a member, would play a crucial role in consultation with the Association of Catholic Colleges and Universities.

Joe, Sally, and I joined Bishop Adam Maida and Bishop James Malone for dinner on my last night in Rome. We gathered at a typical Roman restaurant in the old Jewish section of the City near the Capitoline Hill. It was a relaxed opportunity to review our work at the Vatican and talk of many things. Even a heavy shower that drove us inside from the patio did not detract from the enjoyment of the evening.

Ex Corde Ecclesiae

After my involvement in the two meetings in Rome, I felt a sense of expectation (tempered by some anxiety) about what the final

text of *Ex Corde Ecclesiae* would say. In fact, most of its component paragraphs rather closely resembled our final draft in the second Rome meeting, and there were no total surprises. Still, as with all documents that appear in multiple languages, a lot depended on the interpretation of specific sentences, especially in the normative section.

The title *Ex Corde Ecclesiae* means "From the Heart of the Church." The title of a papal teaching document is commonly derived from its first few Latin words. The text has an introduction and two long sections. Part I discusses the identity and mission of a Catholic university. Part II proposes general Norms and four transitional Norms. Most reactions to the introduction and to Part I were positive. For example, in the introduction the pope makes reference to his own experience as a student and teacher in Poland and cites the importance of an "ardent search for truth" and "learning to think vigorously, so as to act rightly and to serve humanity better." He also mentions fondly his many meetings with Catholic educators during his international trips.

In the section on identity and mission, he describes some of the complexities of the modern Catholic university and its multiple constituencies. I found paragraph 28 especially important for two reasons: first, because it takes up the relationship between the bishop and Catholic institutions of higher education in his diocese, and second, because I helped compose the language that made it into the final document. It reads:

> Bishops have a particular responsibility to promote Catholic universities, and especially to promote and assist in the preservation and strengthening of their Catholic identity, including the protection of their Catholic identity in relation to civil authority. *This will be achieved more effectively if close personal and pastoral relationships exist between university and church authorities characterized by mutual trust, close and consistent cooperation, and continuing dialogue.*

My contribution is in italics. (Gratefully, this type of relationship prevailed in my own interactions with Bishop John D'Arcy in our local area.) This passage would be much quoted as time went on.

In a paragraph on the relationship between bishops and theologians, much is said about their respective roles, but the pivotal line is, "It is intrinsic to the principles and methods of their research and teaching in their academic discipline that theologians respect the authority of the bishops and assent to Catholic doctrine according to the degree of authority with which it is taught." This section, in connection to the normative section about the same topic, would be at the center of discussion for the next ten years.

In a section about the general Norms, it says explicitly that they

> are to be applied concretely at the local and regional levels by episcopal conference and other assemblies of Catholic hierarchy in conformity with the Code of Canon Law and complementary legislation, taking into account the statutes of each university or institute and, as far as possible and appropriate, civil law. After review by the Holy See, these local or regional 'ordinances' will be valid for all Catholic universities and other Catholic institutes of higher studies in the region, except for ecclesiastical universities and faculties.

This language allowed for some wiggle room vis-à-vis different cultures and legal systems. It also set in motion the effort at the regional level that led to the establishment of the *Ex Corde Ecclesiae* Committee.

In the normative section, Article 4, paragraph 3, received the most attention, not just upon publication of the document but in later debates as well. It reads, "In particular, Catholic theologians, aware that they fulfill a mandate received from the Church, are to be faithful to the *magisterium* of the church as the authentic interpreter of sacred Scripture and sacred tradition."

Implementation Debates

On December 15, 1990, Archbishop Daniel Pilarczyk wrote to Catholic colleges and universities announcing that the National Conference of Catholic Bishops had established a committee to review *Ex Corde Ecclesiae* and aid in its implementation in the United States. The members included the bishops of Washington, Mobile, Detroit, New Orleans, Columbus, Springfield–Cape Girardeau and Youngstown; the presidents of Rosemont, Catholic University, Dayton, New Orleans, Mount Saint Mary's, Notre Dame, Boston College, and Carroll College; and six resource persons, including three nuns, two priests, and the attorney for the U.S. Catholic Conference.

A month later the Congregation for Catholic Education issued "Directives to Assist in the Formulation of the Ordinances for the Apostolic Constitution *Ex Corde Ecclesiae.*" The directives had the quality of most bureaucratic documents; they were insistent, specific, and legalistic in tone. The document's drafters may have believed that an appropriate response would be forthcoming quickly, but that was not to be the case. In the last section of the directives, there was a reminder that (i) the ordinance as applied to regional circumstances must be sent to the Congregation for Catholic Education for review and a determination of whether they conformed to the Apostolic Constitution; and (ii) once the ordinances were approved, the universities were to incorporate both the general Norms and the ordinances into their own statutes.

With regard to point (i), at the end of the first long stage of discussion and approval of ordinances at the national level, they would be sent back by Rome for further revision. With regard to point (ii), the existence of independent, predominantly lay boards meant that this directive would never be implemented.

In a related matter, I wrote a note of congratulations to Archbishop Pio Laghi, who was moving from Apostolic Pro-Nuncio to the United States to become head of the Congregation for Edu-

cation at the Vatican. Laghi was a consummate diplomat with a career in the Vatican ambassadorial corps that spanned a number of countries. In the following years, I would interact with him on many occasions—on campus, in Rome, and at international meetings. I was always convinced that his time in the United States allowed him to appreciate the distinctiveness and strength of American Catholic higher education. I believe that behind the scenes, he helped to slow down the implementation process in his conversations with other Vatican bureaucrats.

At the first meeting of the *Ex Corde Ecclesiae* committee in September 1991 we chose Bishop John Leibrecht, then the chair of the USCC Bishops and Presidents Committee, to chair our committee as well. One of the first things that struck me about our committee was its high level of formality, especially among the bishops. Many of them addressed one another as "your eminence" or "your excellency" or whatever, even though they had known each other for decades. In my interaction with the bishop members, I either called them by their first names or just used "bishop" or "archbishop" or "cardinal." It was a small thing, but the formality was clearly intended to reinforce implicit notions of power and authority. Most of the bishops called me Monk in return, since that was how I introduced myself. As for the presidents and advisers, we all used first names with each other.

Another dimension of this dynamic just below the surface was the fact that, in the final determination of recommended ordinances, only the bishops would have a vote. The presidents' role was entirely advisory. I admit, however, that in our deliberations we operated more as a committee of the whole and we all had the opportunity to express both our opinions and our vote.

I had to miss the second meeting of the committee in January 1992 but was present for a September meeting in Washington that began with dinner hosted by Cardinal James Hickey, the archbishop of Washington, at his residence. This was a nice gesture of hospitality. Cardinal Hickey was always quite friendly to me, at least in part because I am a D.C. native and went to

Carroll High School. By temperament he was mild mannered and soft spoken; by inclination he tended to be very conservative, and he referred to canon law in situations of doubt.

Bishop Leibrecht announced that the Congregation for Catholic Education had set a deadline of December 31, 1991, for submitting ordinances. However, they were willing to extend the deadline for another six months, which meant that the full body of American bishops would have to receive them by June 1993 and the administrative board three months sooner. (This setting of deadlines and granting of extensions would go on for nine more years. When I went to IFCU meetings, I would find that nothing had been done by other national conferences because they were all waiting to see what the Americans would come up with. Rome seemed to be more concerned about theology in the United States than elsewhere, which was a kind of backhanded compliment to the growing influence of American Catholic theology.) The members of our committee agreed to a good faith effort with regard to deadlines, although many of us at the meeting advocated a process of wider consultation. I said that *Ex Corde* had taken a long time to germinate and it would profit by every step of the consultation process.

The September meeting began with presentations by three theologians. Lisa Sowle Cahill (Boston College) looked at the "mandate" in the context of *Ex Corde Ecclesiae*; Joseph Komanchak (Catholic University) pictured the theologian's task as both ecclesial and cultural, and Avery Dulles, S.J. (Fordham), stressed the notion of *communio* between Catholic universities and the Church. These presentations set a good tone for the ensuing conversation. Cahill, Komanchak, and Dulles were all highly regarded Catholic theologians who represented a cross section of opinion, from progressive to conservative. The fact that they were invited in the first place was a reminder that the bishops' group depended on the scholarship and theoretical formulations of theologians in arriving at the balanced judgments and the proper exercise of their prerogatives in the life of the Church community.

I was unable to attend the next meeting in January 1993, as were four other presidents. Before the members of the committee at that session was a seven-page text from Father Bill Byron with additional suggestions from other members. Bishop Leibrecht indicated that the document was being proposed as the one to be sent out to bishops, provincials, and college presidents. After extensive discussion, several amendments were proposed. In the midst of the debate, there was a question about whether the presidents on the committee had a vote. Some bishops said yes, at least before the vote on the final document, but others said no, the presidents were only consultants. The consensus was to continue having the presidents vote. At the end of the meeting, Bishop Leibrecht expressed hope that there would be a draft of the proposed ordinances ready to send out after the next committee meeting, and that the period of consultation would be ended by the fall of 1993.

The next meeting took place in March. A few days later, I sent a summary in a memorandum to the Notre Dame Officers Group, an excerpt of which follows:

> The *Ex Corde Ecclesiae* Committee has been meeting for approximately two and a half years in an effort to offer some applications of the original document to the American cultural setting. . . . It is the intention of the committee to send out the material to all bishops and to all Catholic colleges and universities. It will be the responsibility of the presidents of these institutions to make the material available to the founding religious community, if there is one, as well as to the boards and other representative bodies of the institution.
>
> It is my candid opinion that of the proposed ordinances, numbers four and five, which deal with the mandate for Catholic theologians, will generate quite a bit of negative reaction. We voted down, by a close vote of the bishops, proposed ordinance number eight which would have made the possession of a mandate necessary and as a prior condition

to the issuance of teaching contracts in a Catholic institution. The other ordinances have problems as well. They are not as immediately controversial as the ones I have mentioned. . . . When the time comes, it will be very important that the University put together a responsible and frank reaction to the proposed ordinances.

In April 1993, Bishop Leibrecht sent the committee members a proposed mailing to be sent to bishops and Catholic higher education presidents throughout the country. In the draft were eight proposed ordinances. This mailing completed the first major stage of the committee's work. Since the deadline for responses was December 31, 1993, the bishop members clearly expected that the end was in sight. But that was not to be.

From the beginning to the end of our work, John Leibrecht was a model committee chair. He was likeable, fair, and down-to-earth. He had been a school superintendent and knew quite a bit about American education. He seemed to have no personal ambitions to move from his diocese to a more prominent posting, so he was not susceptible to ecclesiastical game playing. He trusted the process, even if it seemed glacial to some of the bishop members. Those of us in higher education, on the other hand, were accustomed to committees taking years to resolve difficult issues.

Cardinal Hickey was the most manifestly conservative of the committee members. He was never unfriendly, but he simply saw the world from a different frame of reference. His main ploy was to make reference to canon law. Then he would turn to Bishop Maida, who was a canon lawyer and, though more restrained than Cardinal Hickey, was clearly on the same side. Archbishop Lipscomb had a doctorate in Church history and was a very nice person who appreciated the complexity of the issues we were dealing with; he had spent many years trying to find viable processes to resolve doctrinal disputes. Archbishop Schulte and Bishop Griffin were relatively quiet in our debates; neither seemed especially engaged in the topic, perhaps because they had other things on

their minds. Bishop Malone was the closest thing the presidents had to an ally. I considered him to be a pursuer of compromise and common ground.

After Bishop Leibrecht sent out the draft, a wide variety of consultative processes were put in place. The professional societies prepared to weigh in, as did the college and university communities. Even before I formally solicited responses, I received some.

Meanwhile Benito Lopez, chair of the ACCU, wrote to Bishop Leibrecht offering a synthetic summary of five regional meetings sponsored by ACCU. He captured the spirit of the meetings this way: "It is our consensus that in their present form the proposed ordinances do not offer constructive assistance in dealing with real problems we confront and, instead, could create new problems for our institutions and our bishops." Among the concerns expressed was the effect of the ordinances on the interior life of the institutions. The ordinances were viewed as overreaching and lacking clarity, and the meetings showed a general discontent about the language of the ordinances.

It did not take long for the bishop members of the commit- . tee to realize that the Catholic higher education community was, by a large majority, opposed to the ordinances as written. They also began to realize that the process of consultation was probably going to be more protracted than they originally imagined. It became clear that the president-members of the committee were in fact representative of their constituency.

By the now-outdated deadline of December 31, 1993, the committee had received a huge amount of material reflecting the intense interest in and concern about the proposed ordinances. Some of the responses were long and detailed, others were but one page long, but it was apparent that the vast majority of the college and university people were opposed to the ordinances, at least in the form in which they had been proposed. During the same period, law firms rendered opinions, Catholic journals devoted issues to the ordinances, and the popular press occasionally

interviewed interested parties. In addition, the leadership of the ACCU and a number of other Catholic organizations provided responses. It was clear that one way or another we had mobilized the diverse and complex world of Catholic higher education in the United States to provide an honest appraisal of the ordinances.

In the fall of 1993, Notre Dame was host to a meeting of the presidents of Holy Cross–related institutions and Holy Cross religious superiors. Superior General Father Claude Grou, C.S.C., in particular urged that all recognize the importance of solidarity and of communication at all levels of leadership in Holy Cross. He asked those present to help the Congregation's leadership understand the difficulties being faced.

On February 2, 1994, Bishop Leibrecht addressed the annual meeting of the ACCU. He was the only bishop present and he tried to convey what he understood to be the perspectives and concerns of the bishops. He said the bishops' working guidelines were that the number of ordinances should be limited; that the ordinances must eventually prove acceptable to the full body of U. S bishops and to Catholic colleges and universities; that local implementation is preferred to national; and that, after experience with the promulgated ordinances, a review should take place and the ordinances amended as necessary.

From my point of view, Bishop Leibrecht's talk was an excellent summary and went a long way toward dissipating some of the tension in the air. He answered questions straightforwardly and with openness of mind. He was a man-in-the-middle who was trying to finish the tasks assigned to him by not alienating any of his constituencies.

By February 1994 it was evident that the consultation process was having vigorous participation all around the country and that the committee needed more time to complete its work. In a committee conference call in August we agreed to hold our next meeting in June 1995, at which time we would review comments from the dialogues already underway and redraft ordinances on the basis of this feedback.

In August 1994, I participated in a conference call of the *Ex Corde Ecclesiae* implementation committee. The topic was the timeline for future work and dates for committee meetings. Bishop Leibrecht was under pressure from two sides: the presidents wanted the conversation to be expanded and prolonged; the bishops wanted to get it finished. Bishop Leibrecht proposed that the implementation committee meet in January to review comments from the dialogues and draft ordinances related to the themes addressed in the dialogue. Then between January and June 1995, the bishops and presidents would be invited to dialogue specifically on the mandate issue, after which the implementation committee would meet to draft the ordinances.

In a related matter, on May 22, 1994, the Vatican Congregation for Catholic Education and the Pontifical Councils for the Laity and for Culture had produced a document titled "The Church's Presence in the University and in University Culture." The claim was made that this document had its origin in a process that began in 1987, but most of the presidents saw it as an attempt to influence the implementation process and to encourage pastoral initiatives on the part of the bishops. This document avoided any judicial recommendations but instead was composed of descriptive and hortatory sections. It included a positive section on the apostolate of the laity, especially of teachers.

By the time of our January 1995 implementation committee meeting, Father Terry Toland, S.J., had been hired as a full-time consultant. He was a former college president and had great credibility with the presidents on the committee. One of his assignments was to facilitate some of the local dialogues. Another was to summarize the feedback that we were receiving.

With each passing committee meeting, Don Monan and I became the most vociferous among the president members. Sometimes Don played the bad cop role and I assumed the good cop role. Bill Byron and Brother Ray Fitz were also active participants. When it came to the question of the mandate, the major Catholic research universities had the most at stake, and Notre Dame

and Boston College were the only two represented on the committee. Alice Gallin, although not a president, was always an articulate ally.

In our January discussions we concentrated on the issue of the mandate. Don Monan pointed out that even though the final wording of the ordinance was relatively mild, the opposition to it by theologians and institutions was virtually unanimous. He recommended that the mandate not be included in the table of contents of proposed ordinances. Fred McManus picked up on a discussion that took place about "presumed mandate" as a result of the hiring process. Bishop Malone, in line with this approach, said that in the case of an egregious problem, the bishop could withdraw the "presumed mandate." I then described the hiring process for Catholic theologians at Notre Dame, indicating that part of the process was a determination of whether the candidates' training, work, and disposition would make them Catholic theologians. I suggested that the hiring process we used would satisfy the concern that the mandate language attempted to validate. The important thing was to respect the good will of those who hire and promote, trusting that they take seriously the Catholic identity and mission of the institution.

The idea of a presumed or implicit mandate began to gather support among both presidents and bishops. As it gained some traction, our conversation within the committee continued. Parenthetically, I should point out here how much progress had been made in the course of our deliberations. Unlike the beginning of the process, when the bishops and presidents were far apart in their opinions, by 1995 a real consensus had begun to emerge. After much consultation and listening, both groups had clearer ideas of what was at stake and how we hoped to proceed. Some of this was attributable to the leadership of Bishop Leibrecht, but the other bishops on the committee had, in fact, listened well at the local and regional meetings and had done their homework. No one knew how Rome would react after we finished our work, yet we remained hopeful. At the same time, the presidents, boards,

and faculties of Catholic institutions had engaged in serious discussion about the nature of their Catholic mission and identity, some for the first time in a formal way. This was solid fruit of the years of deliberation.

In February 1995 Bishops Leibrecht and Malone made a report on the progress of the implementation committee at the annual meeting of the ACCU. The two were excellent choices, since both were highly respected by the presidents and capable of handling themselves in the give-and-take of such a gathering.

Bishop John D'Arcy, our local ordinary, by disposition did not enjoy the twice-a-year national meetings of bishops. However, he was a real trooper with regard to the *Ex Corde Ecclesiae* discussions as they unfolded. He intervened twice in the bishops' March 1994 meeting with kind words about how he and I had developed a relationship of mutual trust and respect. He advised his fellow bishops to take their time in this process.

In August 1995, the implementation committee held a conference call to discuss the draft of a response to be titled "*Ex Corde Ecclesiae*: An Application to the United States." By the end of the conversation, there seemed to be general acceptance of the document, if not total agreement with all parts of it.

While I missed that call, being out of the country at the time, I felt that the most important stage of our committee conversation had been completed. We had gone from widespread disagreement to relative consensus. We had also come to respect each other's opinions and to find commonality in our concerns. I was now confident that if we could find wording that would win approval from the U.S. Conference of Bishops, we would have successfully completed our task. Much would depend on the bishop members of our committee and their willingness to lobby their friends on the Bishops Conference, just as we had had to assure our fellow presidents in the ACCU. If, at the last minute, disgruntled American bishops decided to make a power play with Rome, there was little that we could do about it. In that worst case scenario, the conversation would be far from over.

In August Bishop Leibrecht sent out the draft of the "Application" document. He requested that bishops and college/university representatives, including trustees and faculty, meet together to discuss the paper. After a final vote by the NCCB, the document would be sent to the Congregation for Catholic Education for final canonical recognition.

In January 1996 the *Ex Corde* committee met to sift through the feedback to the latest version of our draft. Archbishop Lipscomb asserted that the bishops were generally satisfied and he expected the draft to be accepted with minor alterations. Bishop Leibrecht felt that the mandate was still the biggest issue. When we turned to objections, I offered that a consensus had emerged in the committee that the route chosen was best suited for the American context of Church and higher education. I pointed out that the feedback received by the committee from bishops, presidents, and university committees indicated that they are willing to live with the document and implement it with great seriousness.

In February 1996 Bishop Leibrecht wrote to the bishops, presidents, religious community sponsors, and Catholic learned societies promising that a newly revised document would be sent to everyone in late summer so that further dialogues could take place before a vote by the full assembly of bishops at its November meeting. In June Bishop Leibrecht made opening comments at the National Conference of Catholic Bishops meeting in Portland, where he reviewed the process that had taken place and established a positive tone, saying, "The intention of our committee is to give you a document that really is pastoral in its approach. I cannot emphasize that enough. Some of the more positive reactions we have heard, not only from yourselves but also from the institutions, come because this pastoral mode is being picked up."

He went on to focus on the mandate issue. The new direction that has emerged says two things: (i) the institution itself has to be aware of and responsible for hiring professors who will be faithful to the *magisterium,* and (ii) if something goes wrong,

the bishop needs to step in with a procedure agreed to by everyone that will address the problem. He concluded by saying that the mandate was still the neuralgic issue before the committee, which hoped its present formulation was a workable solution.

At a June meeting of our committee the tone and tenor was generally positive. Some, like Cardinal Bevilacqua, believed that the committee was on the wrong track. It was predicted that there would be a floor fight at the November bishops' meeting to strengthen the mandate section, but that the document would probably receive the necessary two-thirds vote of support.

In August Bishop Leibrecht sent out the newest draft of the Application document and indicated that the committee welcomed comments.

The implementation committee held a dinner in Washington prior to the bishops' vote on November 13. I was not able to attend, but I felt that after many years of debate and redrafting, we had collectively come up with a final text that we could all live with, bishops and presidents alike. I was hopeful that we could move on with our lives. I had found our trustees, administrators, faculty, and student body all quite professional in how they contributed to the conversation. If nothing else, we had undertaken a rather thorough analysis of what it meant to be a Catholic university and how we could best fulfill our respective responsibilities.

The document on the implementation of *Ex Corde Ecclesiae* was passed at the NCCB meeting by a vote of 224–6. As Bishop D'Arcy explained in a subsequent memorandum, the decisive favorable vote was facilitated by an indication that the NCCB would continue to discuss the mandate issue. He wrote, "It would seem that such a large vote, which is not often achieved, augers well for the reception of this document in Rome."

In early December I wrote to Bishop Leibrecht thanking him for his leadership and his patience. I felt that he played a special role in the successful completion of our task.

While all of us knew that the bishops' vote was not the final step, we were hopeful that approval from Rome would be a mere formality. So we were shocked on May 6, 1997, by a letter from Bishop Anthony Pilla, president of the NCCB/USCC, to Bishop Leibrecht. It informed us that the Congregation for Catholic Education headed by Cardinal Pio Laghi had reviewed the implementation document and sent it back for another draft. To me, it was clear that conservative forces in the American Catholic Church, particularly some of the bishops who had been critical of our draft, had gone directly to Rome instead of fighting a losing battle at the bishops' meeting. This would not be the first or last time in Church history that such tactics would be attempted.

Once the word got out, the more liberal spokespersons began to see the whole thing as a conspiracy to discredit what our committee had achieved. I, on the other hand, even though I was disappointed, did not think the battle was lost. As long as our committee continued to exist, I figured we had a reasonable chance of preventing egregious changes and of moderating whatever formulation of a "mandate" process that some were trying to reestablish. I was enough of a process person to know that participation is everything, and that relationship building and good arguments can often carry the day.

Meanwhile, the NCCB had established a subcommittee, chaired by Cardinal Bevilacqua, to make recommendations to our implementation committee about two matters: appropriate use of canonical language where necessary and comments on the mandate issue. This seemed to be a way of giving voice to the conservative forces within the bishop's conference, Cardinal Bevilacqua being a noteworthy representative. I think it is fair to say that even the bishop members of our committee were not pleased by the new dynamic. None of our remaining meetings would be characterized by the same level of mutual respect that we had attained after so many years of working together. I sensed that we presidents now had reliable allies among the committee bishops.

In the midst of all this turmoil, we were hosting on the Notre Dame campus a workshop for new bishops. On June 4, 1997, Bishop D'Arcy and I participated in a panel discussion on the implementation of *Ex Corde* on the fourteenth floor of the Hesburgh Library.

After a meeting in Rome in June 1997 between several bishop members of the implementation committee and Cardinal Laghi and his staff, Bishop Anthony Pilla, head of the U.S. Bishops Conference, appointed a subcommittee chaired by Cardinal Bevilacqua, that was to prepare new formulations of contested wording in the normative section of the implementation document. The other members were all canon lawyers.

In August I participated in a committee conference call in which there was recognition that it might not be possible to complete a new document prior to the November 1997 meeting of the bishops and that June 1998 might be a better target date. Cardinal Maida pointed out that so far no other country had requested recognition of ordinances; they all seemed still to be waiting to see what happened in the United States.

In the subcommittee discussion, the concept of *communio* began to be emphasized once again. For Cardinal Bevilacqua, that concept could be an important key to a proper and acceptable understanding of the *mandatum* canon. (I personally have always been suspicious of Latin terms that somehow do not seem to be translatable into good English. They easily become playthings in rhetorical battles so that the real sources of disagreement can be masked.)

In January 1998, we received a memo from the subcommittee with a new draft of the Application document. Cardinal Bevilacqua indicated that the theological concept of *communio* was the overriding guiding vision of the draft document, and especially of the *mandatum* canon. As we expected, the most significant change in the draft from the subcommittee revolved around the question of the mandate—who was expected to seek it, how it would be granted, and on what grounds could it be taken away. This issue

would be at the heart of our deliberations once the subcommittee got together with our committee.

That meeting happened later in January and in many ways it was an uncomfortable gathering. The presidents were not pleased that our hard work of so many years had been squelched, yet we were committed to limiting the harm of the direction proposed by the subcommittee, especially the excessively juridical language of the ordinance section. We knew that we would have a dogfight on the mandate question. For Bishop Leibrecht the challenge was to keep us on track one way or another.

In August I attended the second combined meeting with the canonical subcommittee. By its end, it was clear that the two groups held two contrary views of what was at stake and how to proceed.

In October, the president members of the implementation committee received a memorandum from Bishop Leibrecht indicating that the bishop members of the implementation committee had decided to send the subcommittee draft *as is,* without any additions.

As might have been expected, the first part of 1999 was a time of lively discussion of the draft in Catholic publications and at the meetings of Catholic higher education associations. In February Cardinal Francis George addressed the ACCU meeting, proposing that the proper understanding of a mandate was the statement of a relationship, not direct control. It was a juridic recognition that a Catholic theologian teaches in communion with the Church.

In March I participated in a conference on *Ex Corde* put together by Monika Hellwig for the presidents of the major Catholic research universities (San Diego, Catholic University, Saint Thomas, Villanova, Dayton, Loyola of Chicago, San Francisco, Fordham, Saint Louis, Georgetown, Detroit Mercy, Santa Clara, Dayton, Marquette, Loyola Marymount, Boston College, and Saint John's). We discussed the third draft of an alternate to the subcommittee's draft. In June the implementation committee and subcommittee met in Washington but I was unable to be present.

Meanwhile, I was receiving oodles of material from Catholic colleges and universities, from bishops, and from other interested parties. Generally, the representatives of colleges and universities, the academic societies, and the religious communities involved in higher education made one last attempt to argue that imposing a mandate for Catholic theologians could do real harm to the place of theology in the contemporary Catholic university. Some of the bishops' responses were appreciative of these concerns; others simply wanted to adapt the new formulation and move on.

On November 5, Bishop D'Arcy, along with Bishop Dan Jenky, C.S.C., met with the presidents of Catholic colleges within the diocese of Fort Wayne–South Bend for a final dialogue before the bishops' meeting. He mentioned that he had spoken recently to the boards of trustees of Notre Dame and Saint Mary's College. He identified the key area as the theology department and the mandate.

On a trip to Rome in May 1999, Dick Warner and I met for thirty minutes with Cardinal Laghi and his assistant, Archbishop Joe Pittau, both of whom I knew quite well. When we got around to discussing *Ex Corde,* Cardinal Laghi stated that if more time was necessary before the U.S. bishops could agree on a document, that was fine with him. He also mentioned that the bishops and the presidents should be in substantial agreement with regard to the implementation before final approval was given. After Cardinal Laghi left us, Archbishop Pittau reiterated the fact that the bishops and the presidents must agree on an implementation document and that it would not be helpful if the two groups were not in agreement.

Final Vote

On November 17, 1999, I attended the part of the bishops' meeting where the final vote on the amended text of the implementation

document took place. I was present as a representative of both the implementation committee and the ACCU. I felt that there was little more we could do prior to the vote and that our next challenge would be how to deal with its implementation if the bishops chose to approve it, and if it then received final approbation from the Vatican. I was rather sober in my expectations, however, and as things turned out, the meeting was not one of my happier experiences.

As the debate progressed, most of the bishops who spoke offered rather predictable reflections. What drew my attention were the contributions of a couple of bishops who seemed to me to be currying favor in line with their ambition for higher levels of responsibility within the firmament of bishops.

When the vote was tabulated, the bishops approved the 1999 draft with minor modifications by a vote of 223–31, with one abstention. Presuming the final approval of the document by the Vatican, it was specified that a full year be devoted after the final approval for discussions between bishops and Catholic theologians, administrators, and board members. These conversations were intended to focus on the implementation of the document.

During the discussion before the final vote, Bishop D'Arcy had this to say,

> I believe that the question before us is one of the most important and most difficult issues to come before us in my 25 years in the Conference . . . I would like to speak on the *mandatum* as treated in the present document. I believe that it does too much and too little. It does too much because it has become not the means to an end but the end itself. It seems that is all we talk about. What we need is what the Congregation for the Doctrine of the Faith calls reciprocity between bishops and theologians because of their interrelated goals. The *mandatum* has become an end in itself rather than a means to obtain this reciprocity. . . It does too little. It would not of itself create a strong Catholic theology department. That is

done by the chairman, with whom the bishop should have a good relationship. Relationships are the question here . . . the *mandatum* of itself will not create a full, Catholic theology department.

The final approved version of "*Ex Corde Ecclesiae*: An Application to the United States" was much different in tone and content from the version that had been approved by the bishops in 1996. The real debate lay in the Particular Norms that had generated the most controversy all along. The main improvement from some of the earlier juridical formulations was in the use of qualifying language such as "taking into account their own statutes" and "as far as possible and appropriate, relevant provisions of applicable federal and state laws, regulations and procedures" or "as much as possible, conform their existing statutes to such norms" or "to the extent possible, the majority of the board should be Catholics committed to the Church."

The norms specified that the president should be a Catholic (even though a footnote specified an approach if the president was not). And they prescribed that Catholic theology should be taught in every Catholic university, even though the real issue was whether such departments should be theology departments or departments of religious studies.

The longest part of the normative section was devoted to the *mandatum*. While specifying that Catholics who teach the theological disciplines are required to have the *mandatum* granted by competent ecclesiastical authority, the accompanying footnote attempted to clarify what a *mandatum* is ecclesiologically—the recognition of an ecclesial relationship between the professor and the Church. It went on to say that it was the responsibility of each professor to seek it and not the responsibility of the Catholic university as such. If a professor chose not to seek a *mandatum* (or it was not granted), it was up to the university to determine what action should be taken, in accordance with its own mission and statutes.

In the main text, the document called the *mandatum* an acknowledgment by Church authority. Those who receive it teach in their own name, not in the name of the bishop or of the Church's *magisterium*. It reflects the expectation that authentic Catholic doctrine will be taught. Further specifications were provided: the *mandatum* was to be granted by the bishop of the diocese in which the Catholic university is located (granted personally or through a delegate). Once granted, it remained in effect unless and until withdrawn by competent ecclesiastical authority. And it should be granted in writing.

Much of the rest of the document received less attention. After the initial shock wore off, the higher education people became focused on the material in the conclusion. Here it specified that the norms would become effective one year after the document's acceptance by the Holy See. Then there would be a five-year process to review and evaluate the implementation and a ten-year review by the NCCB.

In May 2000, less than a year after the November 1999 vote of the bishops, the Vatican Congregation of Bishops signaled official recognition of the document. Then, on June 1, the National Conference of Catholic Bishops through its president, Bishop Joseph Fiorenza, decreed that the Application document would be in force on May 3, 2001.

A year later, Monika Hellwig sent a memo to ACCU member presidents, pointing out that the next question was how the new ordinances were to be implemented. All of us involved in Catholic higher education were intent on trying to minimize the harm they might do. The worst case scenarios would be open rebellion among our theology faculties on one side or a witch hunt by super-orthodox Catholic groups on the other. I personally hoped that if we all kept calm, we could advocate for a process that would have us conform to the minimum expectations laid out in the ordinance (and in the footnotes) but not much more. I suspected that the vast majority of American Catholic bishops did

not want a public fight on their hands. They were prepared to satisfy the requirement and then move on to other matters.

Monika also informed us that Bishop Wuerl, the new chair of the bishops' Education Committee, had appointed a *mandatum* committee, to be chaired by Archbishop Pilarczyk, with Cardinal Bevilacqua, Bishop Wuerl, Bishop Doran, and Bishop Braxton serving as members. There was also to be one representative from ACCU, appointed by the bishops, to serve as a consultant. Others might still be appointed with additional areas of expertise. At first glance, the *mandatum* committee seemed stacked against us with a heavy canon law orientation and the presence of Cardinal Bevilacqua, who had opposed the 1996 vote on the implementation document.

At its June meeting the ACCU board agreed that the organization and its member institutions needed to work with bishops both locally and nationally to try to resolve some of the more difficult matters. One strategy was to facilitate regional conversations among presidents, bishops, board members, and theologians.

At the October 2001 meeting of the Notre Dame Fellows, a resolution was issued that reviewed the history of the establishment of the Fellows and of the Board of Trustees in 1967 with the approval of the Holy See, as well as the status of these entities in civil law; it also referred to the embodiment of the Catholic character in the statutes of the University. In three concluding resolutions, they asserted that (i) the University shall at all times retain its essential character as a Catholic institution of higher learning as presently provided in the Statutes of the University; (ii) there is no need to amend or change the Statues or Bylaws to incorporate norms of *Ex Corde* in order to ensure the Catholic character of the University; (iii) that incorporation of such norms would not be consistent with the fiduciary obligation of the Fellows.

In September, a report from an ad hoc committee of the Catholic Theological Society of America appeared. Titled "Theologians, Catholic Higher Education and the *Mandatum*," it proved

to be very influential in assisting Catholic university constituencies and many others to understand what was at stake in the implementation of the mandate and to understand potential ways to achieve the goal intended by the ordinance.

Another part of the report looked at the canonical status of a *mandatum*. Among the points of clarification were these: the requirement applies only to Roman Catholic theologians in Catholic colleges and universities; it applies to the individual and not to the institution; it would be appropriate to apply only to tenured professors, whatever their rank (this did not win general acceptance); it applies only to those who teach "theological disciplines"; it is not retroactive (this did not gain approval); the Church's canonical system provides a special protection for its theologians; criteria and procedures for granting the *mandatum* must be agreed upon nationally, they must not be ambiguous, ideological, or idiosyncratic; before a bishop withdraws a *mandatum* or refuses to issue one, a panel of recognized theologians should be consulted (this did not win general acceptance, at least in the initial granting of the *mandatum*).

The report was invaluable both because of the clarity it provided on theological and canonical grounds and because it helped Catholic theologians in Catholic institutions of higher education to imagine a way different than the worst case scenarios that some had imagined. In the time before the Application norms took force for the United States, the minimalist instincts of the report began to gain support. If the *mandatum* were considered necessary in canon law, it was still possible to implement it in a way that the least possible harm was done. This was to be achieved by having bishops and Catholic theologians keep the request for and the granting of the mandate as a private matter between the bishop and the theologian.

When steps were actually taken to implement the *mandatum* at the local level, the vast majority of American bishops refused to provide lists of who had requested and/or been granted the

mandate. As a result, it was impossible to know from the outside what percentage of a given faculty was *mandatum*-certified and what was not. This was despite the effort by certain conservative Catholic organizations with a strong ideological agenda to gather the information, including names.

In the Diocese of Fort Wayne–South Bend, Bishop D'Arcy, after meeting with the Notre Dame theology department, sent a letter of invitation to request the *mandatum* to all Catholic theologians who, he thought, would be so disposed. I was never provided with a list of those who received the *mandatum,* although Bishop D'Arcy did indicate to me that he was pleased with the high percentage who applied. I also heard from multiple sources that he bragged at bishops' meetings that he was confident Notre Dame had a higher percent of *mandatum* recipients than any other Catholic research university.

Thoughts in Retrospect

In one fashion or another, I spent almost fifteen years of my life in some type of involvement with the preparation for *Ex Corde Ecclesiae* and its subsequent implementation in the American context. In the process, I learned a lot about myself, about the way that the Roman Catholic Church functions as an administrative entity, and about the role that Notre Dame needed to play as a Catholic research university.

On the positive side, I believe that Notre Dame—along with the vast majority of Catholic colleges and universities in the United States—has arrived at a much clearer understanding and articulation of what makes us distinctive. In our curriculum, in our residence life, in our worship, in our research priorities, in our hiring, in our policy formulation, in our extracurricular activity (including the service we render), in our formal and informal relationship to the local bishop (and to the national and universal

Church), and in our sense of clarity of purpose, I am convinced that we fulfill, within human limits, the most inspiring formulations of *Ex Corde Ecclesiae* about the nature and vocation of a Catholic university. Like all large families, we sometimes disagree among ourselves about specific matters, yet the overall momentum of our common life constantly reinforces the commitments called for in the Apostolic Constitution.

The role that Bishop John D'Arcy played during this whole process was admirable. When I began my term of service as Notre Dame's president, the two of us established the type of "close personal and pastoral relationship . . . characterized by mutual trust, close and constant cooperation, and continuing dialogue" that *Ex Corde* called for; we respected each other's prerogatives, kept each other informed about potentially controversial issues, and sometimes agreed to disagree. While John D'Arcy did not enjoy bishops' meetings, he gave a number of noteworthy interventions at such gatherings when the implementation of *Ex Corde* was being discussed. On those occasions, he always spoke favorably about Notre Dame, about our theology department, and about his relationship to me. For this I was grateful.

During the numerous meetings that I attended—in Rome (twice), in Washington (eleven times), at ACCU gatherings, at IFCU meetings, at special sessions in the diocese, with other Holy Cross religious, with the Notre Dame trustees and fellows and administration, with the Notre Dame faculty, and with many other constituencies—I came to have a better sense of the lay of the land in Catholic higher education. I came to recognize the real leaders and the most articulate voices. I also had the opportunity to make Notre Dame better known, to fashion operative coalitions, and to develop new friendships.

On the negative side, I found myself put off by some aspects of contemporary Church life that I got to see up close and personal. I disliked the utter formality and hierarchical preoccupation of some of the participants in the conversation. I resented the lack of respect for process that led to the rejection of the 1996

application document by the Vatican, presumably at the instigation of some players on the American scene who were unhappy with the results. I found myself put off by the character assassination and rumor-mongering of some of the American archconservative organizations. And, as the implementation discussion continued, I did not like being considered a turncoat by some liberal spokespersons within the Academy.

The irony of the outcome, at least in the short term, is that most of the fears projected as a result of the implementation of *Ex Corde,* especially the requirement of a *mandatum,* have not been borne out. The *mandatum* has remained a private matter between the bishop and individual Catholic theologians. No master lists have appeared, either on individual campuses or nationally. So far, no one has had a *mandatum* taken away (at least publicly). Overall, the scene on Catholic campuses has been relatively quiescent. However, anyone with a knowledge of Church history will be aware that what appears on the books with normative status can always come back to be a source of difficulty when circumstances change or new actors appear on the scene.

I am pleased that things worked out as well as they did. It makes the many hours that I gave over to *Ex Corde* something I can be proud of. I and the other presidents were only consultants who lacked a determinative vote, but our presence all through the process, I am convinced, helped achieve a much better result than would have been the case otherwise. For this I am thankful.

The Process of
Presidential Succession

In May 1982 the University trustees persuaded Ted Hesburgh to stay on as president for five more years despite his previously indicated willingness to step down. The board added the stipulation that the next generation of qualified Holy Cross priests be placed in major administrative roles. Five years hence, they would become part of a pool of possible successors.

In my years at Notre Dame, there had always been speculation about who was on the hot list to become the next president. Early on, it was said to be one of the 'B's—Ernie Bartell, Tom Blantz, Jim Burtchaell, and Dave Burrell. When Jim Burtchaell was elected provost (and effectively became the implicit chief overseer of the daily life of the institution), he seemed to jump to the top of the list. After Jim resigned as provost (once Ted Hesburgh told him on behalf of the trustees that he would never be president), the question of succession returned to the level of speculation and rumor.

Tom Blantz had been vice president of Student Affairs and was a highly regarded professor of history. Ernie Bartell had been president of Stone Hill College and was a former chair of the Notre Dame economics department and director of a federally

based higher education program in D.C. Dave Burrell had been long-time chair of the Notre Dame theology department and, for a short time, the director of the Tantur Ecumenical Institute in Israel. These three seemed the most likely candidates, although a few other names popped up now and then. The main issue with the three 'B's was their age. Earlier in their careers, they might have been likely prospects, but since Notre Dame now had the tradition of a long-term president, it was possible that the trustees would dip into the next age cohort.

Meanwhile, I was enjoying life as a teacher/scholar/pastor/ preacher with some administrative responsibilities in the theology department. Then my life took a profound change: Provost Tim O'Meara invited me to join his office as vice president and associate provost. In accepting this offer, which I was pleased to do, I became the number two person in the provost office and the fourth officer of the University in the operative pecking order of the day.

Tim and I had had little prior contact. One of the things he told me when we first discussed my new responsibilities was that I would be taking over many of the tasks that Father Ferd Brown, C.S.C., had attended to when he held my position. That included certain aspects of the academic budget, coordination of the promotion process for library and professional faculty, and coordination with the directors of the library and the Snite Museum. I was also provided a great degree of leeway to get to know the University as a whole — its faculty, its major administrators, its administrative units, and its physical plant, not to mention its major deliberative bodies and alumni. I became an *ex officio* member of the Officers Group and was invited to attend all trustee meetings. I also began to assume my share of alumni club events.

At the same time that I was preparing for my transition, two of my Holy Cross peers were making transitions of their own. Bill Beauchamp, a delayed vocation and one year younger than I am, had just been ordained and appointed assistant to Father Ned Joyce, C.S.C., the executive vice president. Dave Tyson was ap-

pointed executive assistant to Father Ted, and two years later became vice president for Student Affairs. Bill Beauchamp became executive assistant to both the president and executive vice president.

It was rumored that Mike McCafferty (from the Law School) and Ernie Bartell (then at the Kellogg Institute) were considered part of the same pool of candidates as Dave, Bill, and I were. In reality, the three of us constituted a cohort that had received similar invitations at the same time, and the next four and a half years would find us constantly interacting and eager to establish a spirit of mutual support. In the early years of our new assignments, the time when an eventual decision about the next president would have to be made seemed like decades ahead. It was not a preoccupation with me; it was simply a future possibility that occasionally popped into my consciousness.

There were many lifestyle changes that my new responsibilities entailed. While I continued to live in Sorin Hall, I had to shift my hours of sleeping and waking from the student-oriented ones of my first years in Sorin. Academically, I would continue to teach, but only one course a semester. Furthermore, I would need to dress up in a clerical collar for office hours and official events, a decided change from my normal informal appearance. Finally, I expected to travel more, both to fulfill my responsibilities and to broaden my base of knowledge about Catholic higher education.

The summer of 1982 was an exciting time as I gradually began to rethink all the major components of my life. I resigned as assistant rector of Sorin and became a priest in residence in the hall. I resigned as director of the undergraduate program in the theology department and effectively moved to a part-time teaching load. I began to develop a year-long calendar so that I would be available to attend officers meetings, trustee meetings, special university-wide events, and other occasions where my presence was expected. I bought some new black clothes so that I would at least look presentable.

One of my first professional decisions was to choose a secretary. I had taken it for granted that I would inherit whoever had served previously, and when I met Annette Ortenstein, the incumbent, she seemed liked a good and competent person with a backlog of invaluable experience. I asked her to continue on and we remained a team from 1982 until 1993, when she retired. Annette possessed a deep voice that was particularly pronounced when she answered the telephone, which sometimes confused callers. At the end of each workday, she used to say to me, "I'll see you tomorrow, God willing."

My immediate reporting line was to Tim O'Meara as provost of the University. The physical setup of our quarters on the second floor of the Main Building was a fairly large anteroom with the provost office straight ahead, my office to the left, and the offices of Sister John Miriam Jones (assistant provost) and Isabel Charles (assistant provost) to the right. I quickly developed a good relationship with Tim, John Miriam, and Isabel. In my four and a half years as associate provost, the basic personnel in the offices remained the same.

Tim was a chaired professor of mathematics before becoming provost. In that role, he kept late hours and was infamous for calling up deans and other administrators for unscheduled late-night sessions to talk about budget, personnel, or other such matters. He also had a habit of keeping the door to his office slightly ajar so anyone in the lobby could hear bits and pieces of conversation. As a stickler for confidentiality, I always thought the practice was odd, but in retrospect I suspect there was an explanation for letting conversation filter out—it was a way of keeping the interactions in his office professional and issue focused.

The four administrators in our office held scheduled meetings among ourselves but generally the content was task oriented. We were never a core of special advisors or an internal think tank; Tim preferred to meet with us individually about things that were on his mind. I was a source of wisdom in his eyes on matters related to theology, the Catholic Church, and the Congregation of

Holy Cross. All of us in the office participated in the meetings of the Officer Group and the provost's advisory committee, which discussed faculty who were up for tenure and promotion, and eventually voted on each case.

Some of the most emotionally engaging matters for the budget subcommittee of the Officer Group revolved around building the budget for the following year. Tim had developed a relatively esoteric budgeting system that no one else seemed to quite understand. This gave him a lot of leeway, in a pinch, to pour resources into the academic side of the University vis-à-vis the other units. Ned Joyce, at least on paper, was the executive vice president, and Tom Mason was the vice president for business affairs, but the real determiner of the University's spending priorities was Tim. Among other things, he was a big advocate of achieving and sustaining faculty salaries in the top 20 percent for our type of university nationwide. This was always a great bargaining chip in his relationship to the faculty.

One of my priorities as associate provost was to meet one-on-one with every member of the faculty, both to get to know them personally and to hear their views about their departments and colleges and about the University in general. Some were absolutely candid, others more reserved. Some had no idea what I was up to or what my motives were; others were happy just to have an officer of the University meet with them. In these sessions I did not take notes, although occasionally I would jot down an important point. My intention was to gain an overall impression and to derive some sense of the faculty as a whole. The most embarrassing moments in my interview schedule occurred twice when, sleep-deprived because of late nights in Sorin, I actually fell asleep in the middle of conversations. I was not sure how long I was in the land of Nod, but when I came back to reality, the other party was simply staring at me.

A second priority was to visit all the separate units and facilities of the University. As a former student and long-time resident, I cockily assumed that I knew the institution rather well.

To my shock, I discovered whole offices that I had never heard of or thought much about—like risk management and the computer crisis control group and the locksmith, the nursery, the sign shop, and the seven campus water wells. Little by little I began to build a backlog of familiarity with the people and social systems and facilities which supported the academic and residential activities of Notre Dame.

A third priority was to participate in the trustee meetings as an observer and get to know its members and their spouses. The winter meetings in Florida were especially conducive to relaxed interaction. My first winter meeting trip was to Key Biscayne, Florida. In the first week of February, there was a 99 degree temperature differential between South Bend and Florida, and I was quickly convinced that such sacrifice for the cause was to my liking. I also went to the social events connected to the on-campus meetings of the various advisory councils and the alumni board. These experiences before I was elected president helped me make a smoother transition later.

Another priority had to do with the "town-gown relationship." Legally, Notre Dame is not in South Bend or Mishawaka, but rather in Saint Joseph County. Yet most of our employees and some of our students live in one of those cities, and we are in a symbiotic relationship with their governmental entities for just about every dimension of our common life, from sewage and roads to restaurants and shopping malls and schools and snow-removal and law enforcement. As a student of urban life and a self-confessed city slicker, I was inherently interested in how we could enhance the relationship between Notre Dame and its surroundings. So Bill Beauchamp, Dave Tyson, and I received Ted Hesburgh's permission to form a campus-based committee to pursue this goal.

We began by meeting with the local mayors and county commissioners, with various business leaders and those responsible for promoting economic development, and with a mix of neighborhood leaders and the heads of not-for-profit organizations.

Once we got past the venting of previous bad experiences and misperceptions, it became clear that there was a great fund of good will that we could tap into. For a variety of reasons, neither Ted Hesburgh nor Ned Joyce had found enough time among their concerns to focus on Michiana. Bill, Dave, and I came with a new enthusiasm and a mandate from the top to pursue whatever initiatives seemed to offer the best opportunity for progress in our mutual quality of life. In later years, my early involvement in the town-gown strategy group would prove to be the source of new levels of Notre Dame investment in the community, from the South Bend Center for the Homeless and the Robinson Community Learning Center, to Project Future, the Saint Joseph County Boys & Girls Clubs, the Chapin Street Health Clinic, Northeast neighborhood renewal, and the multifold activities of the Center for Social Concerns.

One of the things Tim O'Meara said to me when I became associate provost was that, while I would remain a tenured member of the theology department and thereby in the College of Arts and Letters, I needed to strive deliberately to embrace the academic needs of the whole University. It was good advice. As the modern university has evolved, particularly in the American context, the tendency has been for individual faculty members to have a greater loyalty to their area of specialization than to the department, college, or university in which they work.

I was not daunted by having a new title or becoming an officer of the University. Even the speculation, as the years went on, about being part of the pool of potential successors to Ted Hesburgh was not a real burden. The hard thing for me was finding the proper balance among the different roles I had happily played during my years as a faculty member and hall staff person. I wanted to continue teaching and I intended to keep living in Sorin as priest in residence. I also desired to preserve my liturgical role on campus—in Sorin, in Sacred Heart Church, and in the other dorms. On paper I was still a member of the theology department, yet it seemed inappropriate for me to attend departmental faculty

meetings. In many ways, this was a blessing. I would have plenty of meetings to attend in my new job, but at least for the first few years I had so much to learn about the University as a whole that I actually enjoyed the presentations and discussions.

For Holy Cross religious at Notre Dame who live in the dorms, there is a kind of built-in tension between their responsibilities in their residential, academic, and other roles and their membership in the Corby Hall Community for prayer, meals, and mutual support. This dilemma is further exacerbated when one becomes an administrator, with its additional sets of social and other obligations. From the time I became a vice president, I committed myself to being as faithful to the Corby Community for the various aspects of the common life as my other obligations would allow. From feedback I received through the years, other Holy Cross religious seem to have recognized this priority on my part.

By personality and temperament I incline to be informal. I have never been big on titles or appearance or the accouterments of privilege. When I moved into the provost office, the main thing I asked for was a new chair. As a Holy Cross priest I was provided an automobile and I gladly accepted the one I was given. I had a discretionary fund in the office account which I tapped into for what I considered important reasons, mainly charitable causes and special occasions. I had a travel budget to cover professional trips. I did purchase from my personal budget two new black suits and some clerical shirts—for the first time since I was ordained, I would be dressing in clerical garb on a daily basis.

When I was an administrator in the theology department, I never had a secretary. Instead, I used to seek the assistance of one of the departmental staff or else took advantage of the secretarial pool. One way or another, I always completed necessary work, including various types of correspondence, and I used to wonder how full-time administrators kept their secretaries busy. When I made the transition to the provost office I found out. Annette Ortenstein had served a number of administrators during

her career at Notre Dame, and having worked with my immediate predecessor in the office, she knew from experience the main tasks that needed to be attended to—creating a calendar, processing mail, dealing with phone calls, typing reports, handling visitors, dealing with crises, interpreting administrative dynamics, and above all, creating a professional, friendly work environment. I quickly discovered that I had a proficiency in dictating letters and reports. I used a hand-held recording device and Annette transcribed from the tape after I was done. For most things, this worked well for both of us.

From the time I became a full-time administrator I established the practice of receiving in the office the *South Bend Tribune,* the *Chicago Tribune,* the *Chicago Sun-Times,* and the *New York Times.* I have always been a big newspaper reader, and now I incorporated my passion for keeping up with the news into my new life. I also subscribed to a variety of magazines—religious journals, news magazines, professional journals, and general interest periodicals. The *Chronicle of Higher Education* and related magazines also became part of my regular reading. As an inveterate book reader, I began to expand my areas of interest into higher education materials—institutional histories, biographies of major leaders, memoirs, theoretical discussions, reflections about the distinctiveness of Catholic higher education, and analyses of past and future roles of the federal and state governments. Meanwhile, I was trying to keep up in my field of Catholic moral theology, in theology in general, and in other areas of professional interest.

One of the most unpleasant jobs I was given while in the provost office was to reassign some fifty parking places that belonged to those who for years had used spaces around the perimeter of the Old Fieldhouse when it was decided to tear down the facility and build a memorial fountain surrounded by green space. I consulted with the person in the police-security department who normally handled such necessary, if unexciting, decisions. He told me frankly that whatever we did, we would make more enemies than friends. All faculty, staff, and administrators

(not to speak of students and alumni) feel it is their sacred right to park next to where they work or live. First, we had to establish a pecking order. Then we had to decide whom to bump from other spaces so that the new lot-less group would have somewhere to go. When the final decisions were announced, it was indeed true that few were happy. My involvement in this parking reallocation was a great lesson—in some situations there is no good answer. Simply decide as fairly as possible and move on.

On paper I was responsible for the implementation of the provost office budget, but most of the actual work was done by Fred Baumer, the controller, and Otho Bendit, one of his key aides. My direct involvement came when I had to sign off on budget forms submitted by each academic unit. I did become fairly proficient in the use of an adding machine, but I was never really interested in numbers themselves, especially at the level of detail that the accounting operation required. This was not a part of my job that I relished, but I figured I would do the best I could and trust the judgment and experience of the professionals who assisted me.

One of my direct reporting lines was from Bob Miller, the director of University Libraries. It was my job to sign off, as Tim O'Meara's delegate, on library hires and promotions. When I periodically met with the staff to hear their concerns, it was manifestly clear that a certain type of personality is attracted to library work. Generally, they were proud of their contribution to the academic mission of the University but felt underappreciated. Among them were those who worked closely with faculty and students and those who operated primarily behind the scenes. There were disagreements about the future use of technology, about the proper relationship between the branch libraries and the main library, and about whether, in the ideal library, all the books would be in or on loan. Most of the library faculty and staff were female and this had had some influence historically on how they as a group fit into the academic pecking order.

One of my other areas to supervise was the Snite Museum of Art under its director, Dean Porter. The University's collection of art materials had grown substantially since the time of Father Tony Lauck, C.S.C., its first director. Only a relatively small percentage of the holdings was on display at any given moment. On the one hand, the challenge was to keep acquiring new pieces to enhance the quality of the collection, while on the other hand, the Snite needed to remain a venue for traveling shows and periodic displays of Notre Dame faculty work.

Dean Porter was a gregarious, upbeat person who could charm the needles off a cactus (a relevant image since he often painted outdoor scenes in the Taos region of New Mexico). The workforce in the broader field of art is notoriously temperamental, and Dean had to mediate disputes now and then. My role on occasion was to help the museum improve its relationship with the academic department of art, art history, and design. The museum always wanted the department faculty to utilize the art in the Snite collection as an integral part of their teaching. Some of the faculty, contrariwise, hoped to have a greater influence on the museum's acquisition and special event policies.

As a member of the provost's advisory committee in the tenure and promotion process, I had my first exposure (except as a candidate for promotion myself) to the complicated, multi-layered system by which faculty are evaluated. Later on, after I became president, I would receive all of the packets from the different levels of evaluation, including from the provost and his advisory committee, and render final decisions. My time in the provost office proved invaluable in my presidential years.

The packets vetted by the advisory committee included a summary of courses taught, student teaching evaluations, publications, research grants, lectures or invited talks, professional engagements, awards, and internal and external evaluations of scholarly productivity. Votes of the departmental tenure committee and the departmental chair and the appropriate deans were also

among the information we received. The first challenge was to find the time to read all that material. The deans were a part of the committee, so we could listen to their oral assessments of faculty within their colleges. In the vast majority of cases, the outcome was clear, either pro or con, once we read the explanatory material. The challenge was to handle those cases where there was a mixed vote at the departmental level, or disagreements between the department chair and the dean, or a strong research record but abysmal teaching, or vice versa. As was happening all over America, higher education administrators were especially sensitive to concerns about bias or procedural unfairness for members of underrepresented groups such as women and minorities. To a lesser extent, but still importantly, non-Catholic faculty sometimes expressed concern that their contributions would be underappreciated in a Catholic university context.

Any evaluation process is subject to inconsistencies, misunderstandings, and the other limitations of the human condition. Yet in my years on the provost advisory committee, I felt that every person under consideration for promotion received a fair hearing. The internal discussion that took place was free and open. If we felt that we needed more information, we sent the dean back to get it. There were two votes taken, with about a month in between. Sometimes, from the first determination to the second, there was a major swing in opinion. There was no pressure to have a certain percentage of yes and no votes. It just turned out that some candidates did not pass the University's standards, which become more rigorous at the time of deciding tenure than they were at the time of first renewal. None of us felt good about having to say no to someone who had served our community for up to six years, but because the awarding of tenure is a kind of lifetime protection with large financial implications, we knew that we acted on behalf of present and future generations of students and faculty peers.

As a vice president, I regularly attended the meetings of the Officers Group. By this time Ted Hesburgh had been president for

thirty years, so there was a kind of tradition-laden format for the meetings. Several officers gave reports, there were budgets and major construction projects to be approved, and we dealt with some of the mechanics of administration. Ted was the dominant figure in terms of rank and prestige, but Tim O'Meara basically set the agenda and assigned responsibility for reports and follow-through. What I soon learned was that Notre Dame was really run in its daily operation by Tim, who regularly met with Ted about all the major matters. In a sense, Tim was Mister Inside and Ted was Mister Outside. Ned Joyce still oversaw the trends in spending and investment income and played a major role in athletics (an area where Tim O'Meara had no interest), but Ned was by then a step removed from the role that he had earlier played in the life of the institution. Both Ted and Ned were heavily involved in national (and in Ted's case international) organizations and both played pivotal roles in fund-raising and alumni relations.

By the time policy matters reached the Officers Group, they had been heavily vetted by Tim and Ted and, presumably, by Ted and Ned. As a result, I always had the sense that while our meetings were necessary for overall morale, they were not critical for their influence on particular outcomes. The major decisions were determined by a process of top-level consultation that seemed to work well, so who were we to complain? I, in fact, knew of other institutions where the consultation process was excellent but the outcomes were less than the best, so it was clear to me that as long as Ted was in place, there was no sense of urgency about changing the functioning among the officers.

One major discussion that I remember from an officers' meeting was about a proposal to expand the football stadium and partially fund the project by selling skyboxes to companies and individuals. It was Ned Joyce's dream to expand the stadium before he retired, and he sought the advice of consultants who had been involved in other stadium expansions. The main problem with their slick presentations was that they did not account for the tradition-laden, principle-driven nature of this University. Once

we opened the meeting for discussion (a relatively rare event), it quickly became clear that the direction of expansion envisaged by the consultants had no chance in a Notre Dame environment. Ted soon saw the drift and recommended that the expansion topic be tabled. It was not to be resurrected until years later, after I became president.

A humorous incident connected to officer meetings took place one sunny spring afternoon. In the meeting, Ned Joyce among others had been complaining about the cost to reseed the grass on the quads which students were using for touch football, Frisbee tossing, and other spontaneous fun. He suggested that we put out a letter reminding the students about all the dedicated space for athletics that existed on the perimeter of the campus. After his peroration, Dave, Bill, and I looked at each other as if to say, "Good luck." As we walked home from the Center for Continuing Education, we came upon the South Quad, where we stopped and looked left and then right. I would guess there were several hundred students lying on the grass, sunbathing, playing some game, or otherwise celebrating spring. We all had a laugh and went on our way. So much for administrative edicts.

As part of the pool of potential successors to Ted Hesburgh, I attended the social events connected to the meetings of the College Advisory Councils during home football weekends. Most of them went by like a blur. Learning the names (of couples, not just the advisory council members), recognizing the faces the second or third time around, getting used to the time commitment on weekend evenings—all these took some adjusting to. As with any large group, I hit it off right away with some, often because I had pre-existing relationships or because we had friends in common. At first I wondered whether political differences or varying opinions about aspects of Catholicism would put me on the spot, but seldom did anyone bring up controversial matters in these social gatherings; and if they did, I developed graceful ways of changing the subject.

The funny thing was, the closer we got to the time for a decision about the next president, the more individuals or couples would go out of their way to let me know I was their preferred candidate. Of course, I had no way of knowing if they said the same thing to Bill and Dave. In any case, it was a bit socially awkward deciding how to respond.

One of my more interesting responsibilities in the provost office was dealing with Canon Astrik Gabriel, the director of the Medieval Institute. He was a respected scholar, a member of a relatively small religious community, Hungarian by birth, and a genuine character. He loved food and fine wine and had legendary status in many of the local restaurants, from which he would be periodically banished because he had insulted the chef, the maitre d', or the manager about the quality of the repast. On occasion he would show up in the visitor's cafeteria in the South Dining Hall with a group of student lackeys who then spread a tablecloth on one of the wooden tables so the canon could dine in style.

Canon Gabriel was large in girth, and one time at Holy Thursday services in Sacred Heart he was concelebrating. After communion, as he was walking back to his seat in the area beyond the altar, he accidentally knocked over the credence table full of bottles of wine and liturgical vessels. He glanced briefly at the mess and then, with nary a trace of concern, walked on as if to suggest that someone must have put the table there by mistake.

Prior to my election as a vice president, Canon Gabriel would not have known me from Adam. But once he had to report to me, he spent great energy cultivating the relationship. He visited my office a couple of times a year, usually to pass on small gifts. He sent me postcards from his foreign trips. He made mention of me in the preface of some of his scholarly treatises. After he retired as Medieval Institute director, the University agreed to provide him with an office, a room on campus, and a budget to cover scholarly travel expenses. In return, he agreed to give an annual gift of rare medieval manuscripts from his collection.

Each fall he would come to my office with great fanfare to make the presentation. After this happened a few times, I became convinced that some of the documents he passed along were simply being recirculated from the Library. It was not worth the hassle to check, since we had agreed to take care of him whether they were or not. When Canon Gabriel finally died, Notre Dame lost one of its truly unique characters.

In the football season, we had to host University guests in the box seats below the press box. This meant that I had to dress up for games, something I had never done before. It also entailed trying to keep our guests as upbeat as possible, no matter what was happening on the field. In December 1983, Notre Dame played Boston College in a frigid Liberty Bowl game in Memphis. When the official party arrived at the stadium, we found ice covering the concrete under our seats and on the stairs, and it was precarious to move about. It proceeded to precipitate during the game, a mix of snow, ice, and freezing rain. They kept the field playable, but after halftime the stands started to empty out. Some of the ND official party went out to the buses to warm up and never came back. Meanwhile, Ted, Ned, and Tim and Jean O'Meara were comfortably in the press box, but Bill, Dave, and I were in the stands along with a few remaining stalwarts. The only way we could stay warm was by dancing to the band music. A few fans even lit fires around their seats.

The fact that Notre Dame ended up winning by one point against a Doug Flutie–led BC team made it all worthwhile. I did learn the lesson, however, that bowl games in December and January, outside of Florida, Arizona, and California, can be colder than expected. There is wisdom to sitting in the press box.

Priorities and Commitments for Excellence (PACE)

Prior to my election as vice president and associate provost, I had served on the PACE committe. In November 1982 Tim O'Meara

presented to Father Hesburgh the so-called PACE Report, a long-range planning document intended to guide the University's growth and development for the next decade. That began a cycle of planning documents, ten-year external accreditation reviews, and fund-raising campaigns—a process with which I would grow familiar in subsequent years.

My participation in the PACE committee deliberations was a real gift. It allowed me to have access to reams of documentation, to participate in discussions about every dimension of University priorities, and to get to know not only the major administrators in a personal fashion but also a cross section of faculty who would play a role in later priority discussions. It became clear to me by the end of the PACE process that, no matter how many conversations and deliberations were held, someone would have to make the final decisions and, inevitably, some of the participants would feel that their views and concerns did not receive a proper response. By instinct and training, I am a process person, preferring consultation and debate. Yet when PACE was finally published, I knew that every unit of the University would interpret its significance from a prism heavily influenced by their local concerns. In future years, that reality would never change.

The PACE Report contained thirty-eight recommendations. The section on mission was a strong reaffirmation of the importance and centrality of Notre Dame's Catholic identity as seen through the characteristics of sacramentality, mediation, and communion. The longest section focused on teaching and research. With the passage of the years it is possible for me to look back on the PACE Report and situate its influence on future Notre Dame development and planning.

Teaching and research. The report articulated a greater emphasis on faculty research while at the same time wishing to preserve our traditional strength as a place of quality teaching. One of the ways to achieve this goal over the next decade would be a significant reduction in faculty teaching loads. While this made great sense,

it was also extremely expensive since new faculty had to be hired to cover the required number of courses.

Undergraduate-graduate balance. The reputation of Notre Dame was historically carried by its undergraduate programs, with some attention to the Law School and a few areas of research in the graduate school. What PACE envisaged was a new emphasis on graduate education, one that would require a heavy financial investment in infrastructure at the level of endowed professorships, new centers and institutes, further development of the library and the computer center, and new facilities. The hope and the promise was that this would not be at the expense of commitment to undergraduate education. Building the endowment was one way to pursue both goals simultaneously, as was the distribution of priorities in the next fund-raising campaign. Because the majority of Notre Dame graduates had undergraduate degrees (including those among the trustees and major potential benefactors), the new emphasis on graduate and professional education was not an easy sell. That would continue to be the case during all my years as president.

Catholic mission and identity. As trustees looked toward the time when Ted Hesburgh would be succeeded, they felt it important to emphasize once again matters related to the Catholic character of the institution, and especially the role of the Congregation of Holy Cross within it. The PACE Report did the same, but not all parts of the University had the same understanding of what this entailed or how critical the issue ought to be. For example, when it came to recruiting and hiring Catholic faculty, the broader professoriate diverged quite a bit on how much freedom individual academic units should have in the process. This issue would be a neuralgic point for the next two decades and beyond.

Core curriculum. In the 1960s and 1970s, a number of prominent American colleges and universities moved away from the notion

of required areas of study, or core curriculum, for undergraduate students. Notre Dame never did. PACE affirmed the traditional stance but it also called for reevaluation of how best to achieve the University's distinctive academic and mission-related goals within the assigned curriculum. Each of the later long-range reports would chart a similar path, and after extensive discussion, minor changes would be made in the curriculum. No one was ever able to develop a consensus of support for any radical new direction.

Financial aid. From the PACE Report on, financial aid became a critical fund-raising goal. It was the main means by which academic standards could be raised and various forms of diversity could be achieved. This was an area of new attention that quickly gained momentum, and one that I would enthusiastically embrace in my presidency.

The Library. PACE recommended doubling the library endowment and strengthening well-established collections. In a sense, the report reflected the prevailing uncertainty about the future direction of University libraries. Since then, the development of online services has led to a kind of schizophrenia about whether collection development and/or computer-generated databases are the real future. Since no one knows for sure, there have been pressures to do both, which is inordinately expensive.

Undergraduate enrollment. PACE recommended maintaining undergraduate enrollment at 7,300 during the 1980s, but reevaluating the percentage of men and women. In fact, the numbers of undergraduates have continued to rise despite this and later recommendations to maintain the status quo. The wisdom has been that a few more here or there can help to ease pressures on the budget. As for gender composition, it has come close to 50–50. Later disputes would revolve around the desired percentage of Catholics, of undergraduate minorities, and of international students.

In summary, PACE raised some new issues for the first time in an official document of the University and gave increased emphases to others. Most of the paths it charted would prepare the way for similar emphases in later planning. University-wide planning can be a tedious, multi-year process, and the outcome is always more of an art than a science.

The Vice-Presidential Years

In my first year as a vice president, there was concern in the Faculty Senate about that body's role in university governance. This would become a perennial issue through most of my years as president. The main problem was that the senate was a deliberative body without executive authority. When Ted Hesburgh made his annual visit to the senate, he concentrated on matters related to Catholic character, faculty research, and the undergraduate curriculum. In Tim O'Meara's annual visit, the topics were more pragmatic — salary and benefits, the tuition benefit plan for faculty children, and concerns about classroom space. Other senate concerns revolved around child day care, financial aid, the honor code, and the role of athletics.

While I did not have any direct role with the Faculty Senate during my years as a vice president, I did serve on the Academic Council, and in fact was responsible for sending out the minutes of those meetings. Much of the council's time was devoted to various aspects of the PACE Report as it was evolving. In particular, there was lively discussion of the roles of teaching and research, the concept of "marginal" departments and programs, the importance of financial aid and academic advising, the role of athletics, and the qualifications for faculty hiring. Long after PACE, these concerns would continue to preoccupy the council.

The council also elected a committee to undertake a mandated five-year review of Tim O'Meara's performance as provost. In general, Tim was popular with faculty leaders; while always

espousing raising academic standards, he was seen as giving priority to faculty salaries. He was also a layman and a distinguished mathematician, favorable qualities in faculty eyes. Perhaps the most whimsical topic addressed by the council was whether to authorize a change in the wording of the Victory March to incorporate gender-neutral language. About such matters, emotions tended to be highly charged.

My Notre Dame committee assignments included serving on the Committee on the Responsible Use of Alcohol, which Bill Beauchamp chaired and on which Mark Poorman and Dave Tyson also served. The funny thing was that when the final report—which became known as the Beauchamp Report—was issued, my name was left off by accident. When some students unhappy with its contents gathered in protest in front of Corby Hall, chanting Bill's name in a derogatory fashion, I called him on the phone to alert him to the possibility that they might soon appear outside his residence in Alumni Hall. After wryly chiding me for disaffiliating myself from the work of the committee, he took my advice and moved into the Morris Inn for the night. In retrospect, the Beauchamp Report recommendations had a positive effect on campus and were the first in a number of later steps to improve the overall campus environment with regard to the use of alcohol.

In April 1983 I submitted to the Academic Council the final report of the University Curriculum Committee. Two areas in modern university life that have the potential to evoke great passion and emotionally charged opinion are changes in the calendar and changes in the curriculum. Notre Dame had preserved a core undergraduate curriculum through all the revolutionary days of the 1960s and 1970s, and much of the reason had to do with our identity as a Catholic university. We had large departments in philosophy and theology, for example, because of this commitment. While theoretically people were open to discussing new configurations of courses, once they began to weigh the practical consequences, support for structural changes usually began to wane. My involvement with the Curriculum Committee was a

great introduction to the reasons for inertia when it came to curricular changes. Most of the alterations that were finally approved had to do with the content of courses rather than the departments that offered them.

By the summer of 1984, I had spent two years in my new responsibilities. I knew the parameters of my main responsibilities and had developed a rhythm in the job. I also knew that the time for selecting Ted Hesburgh's successor was fast approaching. Despite the increasing attention that Bill, Dave, and I were receiving (and the accompanying scuttlebutt), our own personal dynamics were healthy and mutually supportive. Sometimes, we had to laugh about the comedic dimensions of our situation. There really was nothing we could do but strive to perform well in our assigned task and learn as much about the University and its people as we could. In my professional life, I was named by Pope John Paul II as a consultant to the Vatican Secretariat for Non-Believers, an appointment that ended up being an insignificant responsibility since all of its business was transacted at a distance.

Among the highlights of 1985–86, Joan Kroc donated $6 million to establish the Notre Dame Institute for Peace Studies, and a new fund-raising campaign was launched with a goal of $295 million. I knew that if I were elected president, fund-raising would be a major part of the job. It was not something that I had set out to do with my life, but I was not afraid of the challenge either. That spring Don Keough was elected chairman of the board of trustees, and Andy McKenna was elected to the newly created position of vice chairman. These two men would play a major role in my years as president.

As part of my responsibilities in the provost office I served as chair of the University Honesty Committee. Students considered the two most common types of cheating to be copying and colluding on outside assignments, but they believed that an honor code would not work because students would be hesitant to turn in their peers. The faculty reported that they preferred to deal with dishonesty cases in a personal fashion because they considered

penalties for cheating to be too varied and too lenient. In the end, the committee chose not to recommend a strict honor code. This issue, however, would surface a number of times in the following years, and gradually a modified honor code would be established.

Transition Year

In April 1986, Tom Carney, who chaired the board's nominating committee, sent a letter to members of the faculty promising consultations in preparation for choosing the new president. He formed an advisory committee consisting of all faculty members of the executive committee of the Academic Council for the academic year 1985–86 who were not members of Holy Cross. The provost would chair the committee. In a follow-up letter, Tim O'Meara invited faculty to write him concerning potential candidates. A six-month clock had started to run until the November trustees' meeting, when the choice would be announced.

With these formal announcements, it was clear to Bill, Dave, and me that now we were more than just targets of rumors and gossip. Instead, we would be among those evaluated by multiple constituencies in the University. The prospect of the coming year was both exciting and daunting. As it turned out, the next six months passed in a flash, or so it seemed.

As I began my fifth year as vice president and associate provost, I looked forward to the final resolution of the question of presidential succession. In August I took a two-week vacation, with the time split between D.C. (where my mother and my sister Joanne lived) and Connecticut (where my sister Mary and her husband John lived). We engaged in the usual mix of family time, short trips to interesting sites, and occasional forays to eat out, play miniature golf, or go to a baseball game. While the whole family was fully aware of the pending decision about the presidency at Notre Dame, it was not a preoccupation for any of us. The prevailing attitude was if it happens fine; if not, life will go on.

When the academic year began in late August, I continued my round of meetings with faculty and administrators, with heavy emphasis on dorm rectors in the first part of the semester. Because a number of seminarians had asked me to serve as their spiritual directors, I made time for monthly meetings with them. In the time before the formal election, the campus community was relatively quiet. Most faculty were busy either speculating about the outcome or trying to figure out how to influence the faculty committee that was part of the process.

I met with the trustee's search committee for the first and only time on October 1. They asked me a range of questions, and afterward I felt that I had done reasonably well. Later in October I had lunch one day with Andy McKenna in the Morris Inn. As was his wont, he was feeling me out. Finally, on November 12, I met with Don Keough and Andy McKenna at the Morris Inn. At that point, I found out that I would most likely be elected two days later, though with no guarantees. Mostly they were interested in finding out whom I would choose to serve in the other top positions of my administration. When I named Tim O'Meara and Bill Beauchamp, they seemed satisfied.

When the trustees met in the Center for Continuing Education building on November 14, there was excitement in the air since the board had never before elected a president. Back in 1952 when Ted Hesburgh was appointed, it was a decision of the Indiana provincial and his council. In those days, the local Holy Cross Community gathered in chapel for the reading of obediences, as assignments were then called. Ted's name was announced as the successor to Father John Cavanaugh, C.S.C. Afterward, Ted was handed the keys to the Main Building, and that was it.

In my case, at the appropriate moment Bill Beauchamp, Dave Tyson, and I were asked to leave the trustees' meeting and move to a room that functioned as a holding area. The three of us tried to keep a sense of humor about it all, especially since there

was nothing we could do now to affect the outcome. I have no memory of how long the board discussion took. The next thing I knew, Don Keough and Andy McKenna came into the room and congratulated me as the sixteenth president of Notre Dame. Dave and Bill graciously gave me words of encouragement and support. Then I was led into the auditorium, where the trustees stood and applauded. It was quite a moment.

I cannot say that I was surprised, since Don and Andy had suggested as much two days before. I was, however, extremely grateful and honored and humbled. I knew that the trajectory of my life had taken a drastic turn.

From the outside, some seemed preoccupied with the challenge I would face in taking over for a legend—a Holy Cross priest who had served with distinction on and off the campus for thirty-five years. Ted held iconic status among the Notre Dame constituencies, and he was well known in the broader worlds of the academy, of government, and of American leaders. Yet I honestly was not daunted by the opportunity I was being afforded. My five years in administration had convinced me that the University was healthy financially and otherwise ready to pursue a new level of academic excellence, staying faithful at the same time to its distinctive mission as a Catholic institution.

I also felt instinctively that Notre Dame was ready for change. In his last decade or more, Ted had entrusted the daily operations of the University to the successive provosts, particularly Jim Burtchaell and Tim O'Meara. There was no doubt who had the final authority, but Ted seemed comfortable with being visible when and where he needed to be—in fund-raising campaigns, with trustees and advisory councils, at orientation, Junior Parent Weekend, commencement, and during reunion weekends.

What this meant for me was that Notre Dame was a complex institution that functioned well with a president who delegated while he concentrated on fundamental things on campus and a host of interests elsewhere. I figured that that would make

the transition easier as I learned the ropes and tried to establish my own personal way of doing things.

In the eyes of the trustees, the most reassuring thing was that I intended to retain Tim O'Meara as provost. They seemed to figure that things would not fall apart as long as such an experienced administrator was remaining in place. With the retirement of Ned Joyce as executive vice president and my choice of Bill Beauchamp, another relatively young major administrator, the presence of Tim seemed to loom large in their eyes. I had, of course, worked for Tim for five years and I knew his strengths and weaknesses well, as he did mine. I was confident that we could properly redefine our relationship in the new configuration of things.

With regard to the members of the Officers Group and other major administrators, I thought that I could use the interval between my election and the date of my formal ascendancy, July 1, to meet with them individually and decide whether or not I wanted them to continue. The board itself seemed less concerned with an immediate determination of this matter once the question of the top three officers was resolved.

After the board meeting, Don Keough, Ted, and I met with the media representatives present. I had been cautioned by the campus media advisers to keep my remarks brief, to say more about Ted than myself, to thank Tim O'Meara and Bill Beauchamp for their willingness to serve, and to try to convey a proper mix of confidence and humility. Whether I succeeded or not is up to others to decide, but I was sure that I had not made any major glitches.

The rest of the day was full of telephone calls, pats on the back, and congratulatory messages. At some point I decided to just enjoy it all, knowing that such adulation would never last. I was most excited to share the news with my mother and my sisters, and as a Holy Cross priest, I especially appreciated the words of friendship and support that came from my fellow Community members.

A month later, my hometown newspaper, the *Washington Post,* ran an article by William Gildea titled "Mayor of Turkey Thicket, President of Notre Dame." It was an approach to my election that focused on my athletic background and my continued involvement with undergraduate students in a basketball setting. It was a bit of a tongue-in-cheek approach to a purportedly serious topic.

Inevitably, I followed the coverage of my election in the local and national press and on radio and television. There were no blogs in those days and no cell phone networks. While the media attention was positive, it was clear that most commentators did not know what to make of me. I am sure that some thought it odd that candidates to succeed Ted Hesburgh were limited to priests of the Indiana Province of the Congregation of Holy Cross. But within that pool, they knew as much about me as they did any of the others.

The things they highlighted were the details that made me stand out from the typical new university president—that I had been a scholarship basketball player, that I lived in a dorm and was accessible to students, that I was a popular teacher and a tenured professor who had written two books and many articles. Nothing in my past could answer the question about how I would be as the leader of a complex institution or as a fund-raiser. Nor was it clear what my administrative style would be. On the positive side, I was an insider, a three-time Notre Dame graduate who had spent most of his post-ordination career at the University. With regard to the knowledge of local people and places, it appeared that I would have a head start.

There was no inkling in the media that my selection was unpopular. Presumably, the trustees had sufficient confidence in my potential that they were willing to give me the benefit of the doubt. The same was true of Bill Beauchamp as the successor to Ned Joyce. Once the initial round of interviews was through, attention turned back to the celebration of Ted Hesburgh's thirty-fifth and last year as president. The various constituencies of the

University wanted to make sure that their love and respect for Ted were publicly manifest.

That meant that my job was to retreat from the limelight and concentrate on preparing myself as well as I could. Despite the bets among some of the trustees, I had no intention of moving out of Sorin Hall. I did decide not to teach that spring. I had been given the luxury of a little over six months between my election and my formal assumption of office, and in multiple ways I sought to ensure that the time would be productive.

The remaining part of the fall semester of 1986 was a combination of fulfilling my existing responsibilities and beginning to adjust to the new reality. I was not yet president, yet most of the Notre Dame family inevitably saw me in a new light. I needed to keep a low profile but also respond to invitations from the media to broaden the image of me that was available from my *curriculum vitae*. Furthermore, the other members of the Officers Group were curious about my intentions—especially how they might fit into the new regime.

I had a couple of meetings with Tim and Bill to discuss important long-range matters, and I began having lunch with the sitting deans. One of the involvements that I never thought about much at the time was how the congregations at the liturgies I celebrated in Sacred Heart and the students at the dorm masses might view my homilies as indicators of how I would function as president. I had become accustomed as a former athlete, long-time teacher, and frequent celebrant of masses and the other sacraments to being a public person. It was not as if I had emerged out of a cocoon. It was just that people who did not know me well were more curious than they were before.

By December I had begun to participate in parts of the Fly-In Weekends, those special fund-raising events at which we hosted six to ten couples on campus for personal time with the central leadership of the University. Once the Christmas season rolled around, I began making stop-in visits (sometimes connected to

meals) with various campus groups as they celebrated the season. I did accept some media interviews. All the interviewers were trying to broaden the range of knowledge about my personal background and about my opinions on major issues. I tried to keep things general, both because Ted was still president and because I did not want to arrive prematurely at conclusions about controversial issues. I felt it was better to keep a certain sense of mystery while I was in waiting.

On December 11, Ted, Ned, and I drove up to Chicago for dinner at the home of Cardinal Joseph Bernardin, the archbishop of Chicago. It was an opportunity for an informal chat with a man who would become one of my real heroes as a Church leader. Because of the large number of Notre Dame alums in Chicago and their importance in lay leadership roles and as financial benefactors for the archdiocese, it was important that the archbishop of Chicago and the president of Notre Dame have a positive, mutually respectful relationship. Ted and Ned were quite gracious in facilitating the evening's get-together. I spent much of the Christmas and New Year's holidays at home in Washington. It was a time to be together with my mother and family.

My appearance on the CBS TV show *60 Minutes* brought Morley Safer and a camera crew to campus, and for a full week they followed me everywhere, including meals with students. I was asked where I normally hosted students from the dorm and I told them Macri's, an Italian sandwich place east of the campus. On the day before I was scheduled to go there with five students, the producers called up the restaurant and asked if they could film. The on-site manager thought it was a hoax, but when they called back and were able to verify their authenticity, the owner readily agreed and even drove back from Bloomington, where he was exploring business opportunities in another college town. When we arrived at the restaurant, the owner and manager were quite welcoming and solicitous. They asked the students with me to hold their menus in such a way that the Macri's logo

could be clearly seen by the camera. Despite the bright lights, our dinner turned out to be a lot of fun and the students, at least for a few moments, felt like celebrities.

The one part of the *60 Minutes* presence that was most stressful for me was a two-hour, one-on-one interview with Morley Safer on the second floor of the Hesburgh Library. I knew going in that he would spend most of the two hours establishing rapport and asking relatively innocuous questions, leaving the zingers until the end. And so it turned out. In the last ten or fifteen minutes, he asked me about birth control, abortion, homosexuality, married and women priests, and other controversial subjects which sometimes seem to preoccupy the secular media. My intention was not to get trapped in an ambiguous sound bite. When the cameras were turned off at last, Morley Safer paid me the compliment of saying that he was impressed with how well prepared I was. One lesson from the whole experience is that, if *60 Minutes* comes a-calling, it is better that it be before one becomes a CEO than after years in office. Most the latter have scars to show for the encounter.

Throughout the spring semester, I made it a point to meet with all of the major academic and non-academic units on campus; Bill Beauchamp frequently accompanied me. These were valuable opportunities to allow issues to surface and to hear multiple points of view. We always started by alerting the participants that we were not there to promise anything or to hand out goodies; we simply wanted to maximize our learning curve as we prepared for our new responsibilities. Most of the units abided by these terms, although a few of the academic departments used them as opportunities for lobbying.

In the middle of February I attended the trustee meeting in Naples, Florida. The relaxed context there was ideal for me to interact with a cross section of those who had elected me. No one expected me to make a speech about my top ten priorities or anything like that, but everyone (including spouses) was eager for

some face time. While the board was not as large as it would later become, the total number present in Florida was still rather daunting as I tried to make myself available to as many people as possible. Meanwhile, Ted was still responsible for the running of the University for four more months so I could not assume center stage.

In addition to my outreach to faculty, staff, and administrators, I also began a regular schedule of open forums in student dormitories. Sometimes I did two in one night. Separate from the forums, I usually had two hall masses on Sundays, and I kept up my schedule of masses at Sacred Heart. While I could have avoided some events, I was happy to respond positively if my presence seemed to be an asset.

In those two months, I also interacted with people who would later be connected to issues that were challenging ones during my presidency. Gene Corrigan, Bill Beauchamp, and I began to discuss Gene's intention to step down as athletic director, and his recommendation that Dick Rosenthal be considered to replace him. I had meetings with Dan Harshman and Dick Rosenthal to review plans for the International Special Olympic Games which were scheduled on campus for August 1987 and would turn out to be a spectacular success.

I had lunch several times with Father Dick McCormick, Father Drew Christiansen, and Leslie Griffin to explore the future of Catholic ethics at Notre Dame. I met with the president of a local minority construction firm as he tried to push for more Notre Dame business. This related to the broader issues of our diversity as an institution and our role in the local community, upon which I would place a lot of emphasis.

I also attended the main events of Junior Parent Weekend as Ted was appropriately feted during his last year as president. For the next eighteen years, I would be a faithful participant in JPW, from the Friday night dance to the Sunday morning brunch, and I would be the celebrant of the Saturday evening mass and

the main speaker at the Saturday evening dinner. With each passing year, this great Notre Dame tradition became even more central in the life of the undergraduate student body.

My plan for the spring semester was to sneak away from campus when I could to observe what was going on at other campuses and to solicit the advice of some of the leaders in American higher education. In mid-March I visited the Pew Trust in Philadelphia, then flew to Charlottesville where I had accepted an invitation to come to the White Burkett Miller Center of Public Affairs at the University of Virginia and speak in the dome of the Rotunda building designed by Thomas Jefferson. From Virginia I flew to Boston and spent a full day exploring the grounds of Harvard University and having a memorable meeting with Henry Rosovsky, an economist who served for many years as dean of the arts and sciences faculty and who was a great raconteur. Next I flew to Nashville to visit with the leadership at Vanderbilt University. I finished as the speaker at a fund-raiser at Saint Edward's High School, a Holy Cross Brothers' institution in Lakewood, Ohio. In April, after Holy Week, I took a similar trip, starting in New York City and ending in Portland, Oregon, for a meeting of the University of Portland board of regents.

Close to commencement in May, I had my first one-on-one lunch with Bishop John D'Arcy, beginning what would become a mutually respectful relationship and friendship. When I could, I enjoyed keeping my teaching cap on. I participated for two days in a medical ethics conference for the Alumni Association, not only because I was interested in the topic but also because I wanted to signal that I felt that such outreach activity should be a big part of the programming offered by the alumni group. In fact, under the title Hesburgh Lectures, such initiatives would soon become characteristic at both the national and local level.

The spring semester appropriately included a number of special events to honor the extraordinary contributions of Ted Hesburgh and Ned Joyce. They reached a climax on May 9 when Ned emceed a Universal Notre Dame Night telecast from Wash-

ington Hall. This was the first time that local alumni clubs all gathered on the same evening to celebrate their relationship with their alma mater and receive the uplink portion of the main event from campus. Notre Dame grad and TV producer Don Ohlmeyer oversaw the preparation for the event and the telecast, which opened with photographs of Ted in his various roles during his years as president.

After fitting and moving tributes, I was introduced. My main theme was that I wanted to be a peripatetic president, a leader who would meet regularly with faculty, students, rectors, alumni. I highlighted the Catholic nature of Notre Dame, saying it needs to be a place where the Church could do its thinking and where the great issues of the day could be grappled with. We also need to cultivate the relationship between worship and social service, I said, to foster the development of the mind, heart, and spirit of our students, and to become more diverse. I concluded by thanking Ted for encouraging me to be myself and for providing wise counsel.

Don Keough announced the opening of the new fund-raising campaign, *Notre Dame: A Strategic Moment,* with a target of $300 million. That was one reason for focusing so much energy on one night: in a time of transition Ted had been responsible for the quiet phase of the new campaign, but now I would be responsible for its public phase. The event concluded with "Notre Dame Our Mother" and the "Victory March." By the time the evening ended, I felt upbeat about the future. There was manifest enthusiasm in Washington Hall (including among the trustees present) and I was hopeful that the response in the local clubs had been comparable.

In ceremonies connected to their spring meeting, the trustees of the University gave Ted and Ned a recreational vehicle and two scooters which were intended for transportation on a trip through the West and far Northwest. (As far as I know, the scooters were never used except as a photo op after the ceremony.) A second gift included two trips on the *QE2,* one for several weeks on a

Caribbean Christmas cruise and the second on an around-the-world cruise. Both Ted and Ned had been inveterate travelers during their leadership years, so these gifts seemed ideally suited in a time of transition in their lives. In their year-plus away from the campus during my first year in office, Ted and Ned traveled in the United States, through several Latin American countries, twice on the *QE2,* and to Antarctica. It was a well-deserved break for each of them, and for me it provided an opportunity in the transition to be my own person, to establish my own style and rhythm of administration, and to relish the newness of it all. I will be eternally grateful for this gift of absence, so to speak. When I stepped down as president eighteen years later, I tried to do the same for my successor, John Jenkins.

I continued to be active in Sorin Hall that spring, liturgically and otherwise. The men of the hall seemed to relish having the president-elect living in their midst, and they were amazingly cooperative in giving me my private time. I played Monk Hoops as regularly as I could (a great stress reliever) and I had a team in Bookstore Basketball. I even participated as a faculty reader in a former student's doctoral dissertation defense. On two occasions I had dinner with Sorin seniors that I was particularly close to.

The events of commencement weekend were not only major moments in the lives of the graduates and their families, but also the end of a Notre Dame era. On Friday of that weekend, I attended the reception for grad students and their families. On Saturday morning, I spoke on the topic of liberal education at the Phi Beta Kappa recognition ceremony. In the middle of the afternoon, I joined Ted, Ned, Tim O'Meara, and Bill Beauchamp for a couple of hours in the Center for Continuing Education where we made ourselves available to greet graduates and their families. After mass in the basketball arena of the ACC at which Ted preached, I joined the festivities on the fourteenth floor of the library for the honorary degree recipients, the commencement speaker, the Laetare medalist, and their families. Ted had estab-

lished the tradition of ending this meal with a discussion of some major issue on which he sought the opinions of the honored guests. Depending on the topic, these sessions could go a bit long. However, the group of honorees that night was so distinguished that everyone present was interested in what they had to say.

At the commencement itself on Sunday, every attempt was made to recognize individuals and/or works with which Ted Hesburgh had been associated. He himself, by a separate vote, had been chosen as the Laetare medalist. The commencement speaker was Derek Bok, the president of Harvard University. (Ted was on the Harvard Board of Overseers for many years.) Honorary degree recipients included Norman Borlaug, who won a Nobel Peace Prize for his development of high-yield, disease-resistant wheat varieties; Rosalyn Smith Carter, former First Lady; Coretta Scott King, widow of Martin Luther King, Jr.; Joan Kroc, widow of the founder of McDonalds; Tim O'Meara; Yevgeny Velikhov, a Russian scientist involved in discussions on nuclear disarmament; Dick Warner, C.S.C., provincial for the Holy Cross Indiana Province; and Archbishop Rembert Weakland of Milwaukee.

Later that day I went to a reception at the Provincial House celebrating Dick Warner's honorary degree, after which I joined a group of Sorin seniors and their families at Tippecanoe Restaurant. On Monday, we threw a surprise-party lunch in the Snite Museum for Ted and Ned. Later that day, in a symbolic passing of the mantle, I recorded the closing prayer for the broadcast day for WNDU-TV, which Ted had been doing for years.

On the Tuesday after graduation we had a luncheon honoring Helen Hosinski and Pat Roth, Ted and Ned's long-time secretaries and personal assistants. That evening we had the event which, for everyone present, served as the closing of the academic year, the annual Faculty Recognition dinner. Ted gave his final address to those assembled and received long, heartfelt applause. With that, he implicitly began the process of disengaging from the presidency, both physically and otherwise. He had to move out of

his office so that some renovation work could be done before I moved in. Although it would be couple of weeks before I would officially take over, the real changing of the guard had begun.

In the course of my spring travels, I received a fund of valuable advice from sitting or previous presidents. Here is a list of some of the more useful things I heard.

(1) *Do not renovate the president's house the first year.* At face value this did not apply to me since I lived in Sorin Hall. Many of my counselors mentioned this topic because so many incoming CEOs had been burned by the issue. I saw this advice in metaphorical terms. My rephrased version would go something like this: "Do not expend any large sums of money in the first year that would seem connected to your personal pleasure or perquisites." In other words, keep a low profile in matters peripheral to institutional priorities.

(2) *Only you can decide what level of staffing you need in the president's office to get the job done most effectively.* Different people proposed different models for how the president's office should be organized. For example, Tim Healy, S.J., the president of Georgetown, developed a system where he invited bright and talented recent undergraduate degree holders to work with him for two years on a rotating basis, after which they would move on to professional or graduate schools or into the work force with strong letters of recommendation. Some presidents had a staff of speech writers (which I never wanted). Others had multiple assistants who concentrated on different areas of responsibility as the eyes and ears (and sometimes the voice) of the president. In my first year, Carl Ebey was my only assistant along with my secretary, Annette Ortenstein. By the time I stepped down, I had three assistants— Chandra Johnson, Matt Cullinan, and Pete Jarret, C.S.C., along with Joan Bradley, my secretary-assistant. I had learned through experience to delegate different parts of my responsibilities to maximize my impact as a leader.

(3) *Get enough sleep.* I already knew that I grew testier and less resilient when I was sleep deprived. This advice was only

partially about a healthy lifestyle; it was also about public perception. As one president explained to me, trustees and faculty and staff (not to speak of students, alumni, and others) were always looking for clues about how things were going in the institution, and one seemingly reliable sign was how the president appeared—in body posture, level of alertness, and attention span. One yawn might be acceptable but not two or three. And for someone like me who had a reputation as being composed and relatively undemonstrative, it would have been hard to fake gregariousness or simulate a perky mien. Concretely, that meant that I adjusted my routine and tried to get to bed by midnight. The big remaining problem was jet lag connected to my many international trips, but even then, I was able to find a routine that worked for me.

(4) *Take an annual vacation.* Some chief executives in the business world and in government service become well known for their 24/7 habits. They are always on call and they eschew time away from the office. Some higher education leaders followed their examples, particularly at struggling institutions that were understaffed. I, on the other hand, had always made room for an annual vacation (usually up to two weeks in duration) and enjoyed the opportunities available within the academic calendar for holidays and semester breaks. I also knew that when I traveled to new places I usually returned renewed. I pledged to make every effort to keep a sense of balance in my weekly, monthly, and yearly schedule, and more often than not I succeeded. I do not believe that I would have been able to survive eighteen years as president if I had not taken seriously this important consideration.

(5) *With the media, always be prepared.* In some ways, I had a dangerous background for becoming the public face of Notre Dame. I was an ethicist who tried to see the multiple sides of issues, liked to foster debate, and had confidence that the pursuit of the truth has a value in itself. But in the age of sound bites, it is dangerous to engage in speculation or seem nonplussed or, even worse, appear devious or unreliable. One of the most valuable

things I did as vice president was to take a one-day television training course along with Dave Tyson and Bill Beauchamp. The three of us did on-camera interviews in a variety of formats and then critiqued each other's presentations. We were instructed how to lock eyes with the interviewer, how to sit erect, how to turn negative questions into positive answers, how to get our message across no matter what we were asked.

In the course of my presidency, I found radio interviews to be the easiest, primarily because I did not have to worry about how I looked. The challenge of newspaper and magazine interviews depends on whether the topic is known in advance and how much emotional resonance it has. Matters related to religion and athletics are usually the most volatile. My biggest mistakes usually occurred in circumstances where I agreed to be interviewed on the phone without prior warning. I found that once such conversations started, there was no going back. As for television, most of my experiences were positive. My most distressing media day took place after we received our first major NCAA penalty for violations connected to the football program. I did three hours of interviews (press, radio, and television) in fifteen-minute increments, with the fundamental message being that I wanted to apologize for what had gone wrong and to assure our constituencies that we would do everything we could to prevent a recurrence.

(6) *Be involved in presidential associations.* The greatest temptation of the new president is to become so preoccupied with internal concerns that he or she loses a sense of higher education as a whole. Ted Hesburgh had been active in all the major higher education associations at one time or another, and I was determined to follow his example.

(7) *Teach if you can, whether in a classroom context or not.* Those presidents who had been faculty members before they became administrators seemed to be torn between their previous and present lives. Some spoke nostalgically about how much student contact time they had before and how much they missed it, but few

if any of them had ever lived in a student dormitory as a staff member. One president bragged to me about how much he and his wife prized their relationship with the undergraduate students who cut the grass at the president's house. I managed to teach my seminar course to approximately eighteen students each semester for the last seventeen years of my presidency.

China and Tibet

After the events of the post-commencement week, Tim and Jean O'Meara and I flew to China where we were to be guests of the Chinese Academy of Sciences. The three of us were also part of a group that included dean of science Frank Castellino, his wife Mary, and their future son-in-law Rick Metzger. We were met at the Beijing airport by Professor Gu YiJian, secretary-general of the Academy of Sciences, who had earned a master's degree from Notre Dame in 1950 and was awarded an honorary degree in 1985. One interesting effect of the recent appearance I had made on *60 Minutes* was that I was stopped three times in O'Hare Airport, once in Seattle, and once in Tokyo by people who had watched the show.

In our travels through Beijing we were impressed by the expansive scale of the main tourist sites like the Forbidden City, Tiananmen Square, and the National History Museum. The people, especially the young, were beginning to diverge in dress from the uniformity imposed by the Cultural Revolution. On Sunday, we attended mass at the Southern Cathedral, where the liturgy was in Latin, with Chinese hymns, and the church was packed with worshipers. That evening we hosted a banquet at the Bamboo Garden Restaurant for a contingent of eighteen people with Notre Dame connections. It was a cordial, relaxed meal.

A day or so later we joined Bishop Fu, Bishop Tu, and two local priests for a lunch that had been set up after Bishop Fu

ran into us after Sunday mass (which our Chinese interpreters/ watchers had not been too eager for us to attend). The bishops fed us an eighteen-course meal while we discussed the relationship between the so-called "above ground" and "underground" Catholic churches in China. I was taken, on this first trip to China, by the persistence of Catholic and Christian churches there despite so many years of suppression and persecution.

One evening we had a twenty-course banquet in the Great Hall of the People—the place where all major state banquets are held and dignitaries entertained—as guests of one of the members of the Central Committee of the government whose son was a graduate student at Notre Dame. During the course of the banquet, our host and I engaged in a conversation that ranged over topics from higher education to technological development and the mutual desire for peace.

The next day, Tim, Frank, and I took the train to Tianjin to visit Nankai University. The president and a group of his administrators hosted us for lunch and a meeting, the main topic of which was about an agreement for some of their doctoral students to come to Notre Dame to complete their degrees in the sciences. After our return to Beijing, we had a twenty-course meal at the home of our host Professor Gu. Both of his children had attended Notre Dame and he was a major promoter of American higher education opportunities for Chinese students.

Next day we journeyed to the Summer Palace, one of the great historical and cultural sites in China, and then took a late evening flight to Chengdu, the capital of Szechwan Province and the jumping off spot to Tibet. Like Beijing, Chengdu was full of construction activity. In a wise travel decision, we decided to leave one bag apiece in Chengdu and take only a carry-on to Tibet.

Our flight to Lhasa took two hours, with our route taking us across the Himalayas, the highest mountain chain in the world. The plane was full. The airport serving Lhasa turned out to be a major air base for the Chinese air force, with three helicopters, twelve fighter jets, and armed soldiers keeping sentry all around

the perimeter. After going through security, it took us about an hour and a half to get to Lhasa.

Our hotel was a brand new Holiday Inn. In the lobby, two American tourists recognized me from *60 Minutes*—who would have ever thought? After a bit of twenty-four hour altitude sickness, our group visited the Potala, the traditional headquarters of the Dalai Lama and the central symbol of Lhasa. Built on the side of a cliff, it is considered one of the great architectural wonders of the world. The building is an endless maze of altars, small rooms, ladders, passageways, and courtyards. Within are Buddhas in all shapes and configurations, usually attended by a monk and sometimes his young son. There were numerous small stands set up with yak butter and candles burning in otherwise dim rooms. The smell was pungent, pervasive, and rather unpleasant to our Western noses. Devotees were chanting prayers or making offerings. Personally, I found this one of the most amazing sites I had ever had the privilege to visit.

On Sunday morning we toured the Dreping Monastery, once the largest concentration of Buddhist monks in the world, although the numbers were down to 200 by the time of our visit. Two large Buddhas painted on boulders frame the monastery, and inside are several thousand more, in all shapes and sizes. Photographs of the present Dalai Lama were commonplace. There were hundreds of Tibetan adherents present during our visit. Most were families, with everyone from little infants to older grandparents. The monks were simply robed with shaved heads. In the afternoon we went to Sera Monastery, which is identified with the burial traditions of Tibetans. In the past, the custom was to cut the corpse into little pieces that are placed on a mountain peak for the hawks and other birds of prey to consume. Later, the bones would be buried.

On Monday morning we left early for our flight to Chengdu. The date was June 1, which happened to be the day I officially took over as president of Notre Dame. Interestingly, I spent the first part of the day in Tibet and the second part in China, symbolizing

my interests in international education and what would later be called globalization. I really had no idea who was officially in charge back on campus, but I had no anxieties in that regard.

In Chengdu we visited the Dujiangyan Irrigation System, which allowed me to see the rich agricultural areas of Szechwan Province, especially the rice paddies. The irrigation system had been begun in 250 B.C. The river was divided into two channels: a canal and the main river. The water from the canal flowed through a vast region and filled a network of irrigation canals. On Wednesday we toured the Institute for Biochemistry, where a friend of Frank Castellino's was our host. Frank gave a lecture to a class of about thirty-five, focusing on his research on blood coagulation. We then had lunch with representatives of Shanghai No. 2 Medical University. An old friend, Father Larry Murphy, M.M., was traveling in China with a group and joined us.

On Thursday morning Tim and I joined Larry and three other members of his party for a trip to Shanghai Seminary. The grounds were adjacent to the site of the only European-style basilica in China, which was finished around 1935. I was the main celebrant for a mass in the basilica for the Americans and fifteen Chinese; Larry and another priest concelebrated. During my homily I spoke of the suffering the Chinese have so often endured, and of the unity we Americans felt with them in our baptism, our faith, and our Lord. The whole mass was very moving and a fitting way to conclude my last day in China.

AFTERWORD

In being elected by the board of trustees as Notre Dame's sixteenth president, I knew that I was succeeding an iconic, legendary figure in Ted Hesburgh. But I was buoyed by the confidence that others had shown in me and by what I had discovered about myself during my years on the theology department faculty, in the central administration, and in a variety of pastoral roles on and off campus.

I had discovered, for example, how much I enjoyed being involved in the processes of fundamental decision making at the University. I believed deeply in the mission of the institution and in its potential to become one of the great universities of the world, while remaining faithful to its Catholic identity. All of my experiences had reinforced the sense that we needed to become more diverse, more international, more involved in our local community, and more committed to excellence in professional and graduate education while at the same time preserving our traditional strength in undergraduate teaching and residential life.

Fortunately, through my years on the faculty and in administration, I had come to know a broad cross section of Notre Dame people, including trustees, advisory council members, and alumni representatives. I had also visited other campuses and sought the advice of sitting presidents and experts in higher education. My involvement in professional associations and my domestic and international travel had broadened my understanding of the challenges facing the academy as well as its opportunities for service.

Finally, my identity as a Holy Cross priest and as a theologian and my long involvement in the ongoing discussion about the nature of a Catholic university had set the stage for what

would become the heart of my responsibility—remaining faithful to our distinctiveness as a Catholic university while being open to the inevitable changes in how we realized that goal over time.

When I assumed the presidency, I was forty-six years old, in good health, and full of enthusiasm. As I would discover in subsequent years, just about everything I had been engaged in during my time of preparation would turn out to be an asset in one sense or another, even my developed capacity to deal with conflict, disagreement, and disappointment.

When I returned from China in June 1987, I offered mass and said a prayer for guidance from the Holy Spirit and plunged right in. Eighteen years later, I would hand over the mantle of leadership to Father John Jenkins. My report on what took place in between will be the subject of my third and final volume.

INDEX

Bruno's Pizza, 98
Burke, Father Eugene, 51
Burke, Jim, 184, 192
Burns, Arnie, 201
Burrell, Father David, C.S.C., 4, 213,
 214, 257–58
Burtchaell, Father James, C.S.C., 214,
 257, 281
Bush, Barbara, 176
Bush, George H. W., 175, 176, 177, 178,
 183–85, 186, 187, 188
Business/Higher Education Forum
 (BHEF), 168–70
Byrne, Father Peter, 138
Byron, Father Bill, 235, 239

Cahill, Lisa Sowle, 234
Califano, Joseph, Jr., 192–94, 197, 199
Camp David, 176
Campus Compact (CC), 172–73, 178
Canepa, Father Jorge, 140
Carney, Tom, 279
Carter, Jimmy, 177, 192
Carter, Rosalyn Smith, 291
Casper, Dave, 54
Castellino, Frank, 295–98
Castellino, Mary, 295
Catholic Theological Society of
 America (CTSA), 156, 157–58,
 251
Cavadini, John, 120
Cavanaugh, Father John, C.S.C., 51, 280
Center for Addiction and Substance
 Abuse (CASA), 192–99
Center for Continuing Education, 280,
 290
Center for Social Concerns, 173, 263
Center for the International Lay
 Apostles, 138
Chambers, Ray, 176
Chapin Street Health Clinic, 263
Chapman, Alvah, 184, 185–86
Charles, Isabel, 260

China, 295–98, 300
Christiansen, Father Drew, 287
Cisneros, Henry, 164
Clinton, Bill, 164, 171, 178
Code of Canon Law, 98, 211–12
Cole, Johnetta, 176
Colegio Andacollo, 141, 143
Coleman-Morse Hall, 65
College Advisory Councils, 270
College of Arts and Letters, 107, 263
College of Commerce, 54
College of the Holy Cross, 192
Collegiate Hall, 46
Collins, Austin, 34, 39–40
Collins, Marva, 176
commencement weekend, 54, 80–81,
 290–91
Commission for a Drug-Free Indiana,
 186–88
Community Anti-Drug Coalitions of
 America (CADCA), 178, 185–86
Congregation for Catholic Education,
 210–12, 215, 224–26, 232, 234,
 239, 242, 244, 250
Congregation of Bishops, 250
Congregation of Divine Providence,
 164
Congregation of Holy Cross, 149
Conlin, Mike, 69
Conlin, Tom, 69
Copple, Jim, 185
Corby, Father William, C.S.C., 21
Corby Hall, 21–29, 45, 65–66, 99, 101,
 264, 277
Corporation for National and
 Community Service, 178
Corrigan, Gene, 287
Cortazar, Rene, 142
Creevy House, 25–26
Cullinan, Matt, 69, 292
Cullinan, Sean, 69
Cullinan, Shannon, 69
Cunningham, Bubba, 64

Dantley, Adrian, 68
D'Arcy, Bishop John, 231, 241, 243, 245, 247–48, 253–54, 288
Dease, Father Dennis, 162–63
Deep Creek Lake, 6–7
Deer Park, 7
Demerle, Pete, 54
Dewey Ballantine, 192
Doe Memorial Library, 31
Doherty, Father Joe, 142
Donodeo, Fred, 190
Dorais, Gus, 54
Doran, Bishop, 251
Dreisell, Lefty, 28
Drug Advisory Council, 183–85, 187, 188
Dulles, Avery, S.J., 215, 234

Ebey, Father Carl, 140, 141
Egan, Jack, 214
Eisner, Michael, 176
Eldred, Marilou, 165
England, 145–49
Ex Corde Ecclesiae
　beginnings, 212–24
　EAM reflections on, 253–55
　final vote, 247–53
　IFCU leadership, 166
　implementation debates, 232–47
　Plenarium, 224–29

Faculty Glade, 31
Faculty Recognition dinner, 291
Faculty Senate, 276–77
Farley, John 'Pop,' C.S.C., 51
Fenlon, Paul, 47–49, 55, 92, 101
Figueres, Don Pepe, 145
Fiorenza, Bishop Joseph, 250
Fischer Graduate Housing, 47
Fitz, Brother Ray, 239
Flanigan, Father Jim, 70
Flanner Hall, 104
Flutie, Doug, 272

Fly-In Weekends, 284–85
football team, 55, 79, 98, 272, 294
football weekends, 72, 78–81, 270
Ford, Betty, 192
Ford, Gerald, 177, 178
Foxley, Alejandro, 142
France, 145–49
Fraser, Douglas, 192
Fremantle, Australia, 161, 162
Frosh-O team, 74, 78
Fu, Bishop, 295
Furay, Sister Sally, R.C.J., 222, 225, 229

Gabriel, Canon Astrik, 271–72
Gallin, Sister Alice, O.S.U., 212, 240
Garrone, Cardinal Gabriel-Marie, 210
Gee, Gordon, 164
Georgetown University, 169, 172, 292
Gildea, William, 283
Glide Memorial Church, 36
Goizueta, Roberto, 176
Golden Dome, 2, 16
Golden Dome Productions, 185
Goldman, Mark, 190
Gordis, Enoch, 188, 189
Graduate School basketball league, 69
Graduate Theological Union, 14–15, 16, 29–30
Greece, 136–37, 145–49
Griffey, Ken, Jr., 201
Griffin, Bishop, 236
Griffin, Leslie, 287
Gross, Kim, 176
Grotto, 56, 78
Grou, Father Claude, C.S.C., 238
Guest House, 26
Guttley, Brother Cosmos, 24
Gu YiJian, 295, 296

Hanzlik, Bill, 68
Hatch, Nathan, 166
Hauerwas, Stanley, 4, 105, 116

EDWARD A. "MONK" MALLOY, C.S.C.

is president emeritus of the University of Notre Dame, where
he served from 1987 to 2005 as the sixteenth president and where
he is currently professor of theology. He serves on the board
of directors of a number of universities and national
organizations and is the recipient of numerous honorary degrees.
Monk's Tale: The Pilgrimage Begins, 1941-1975, the first installment
of Father Malloy's memoir, was published by the
University of Notre Dame Press in 2009.